Learning Together

Learning Together

Organizing Schools for Teacher and Student Learning

ELHAM KAZEMI

JESSICA CALABRESE

TERESA LIND

BECCA LEWIS

ALISON FOX RESNICK

LYNSEY K. GIBBONS

HARVARD EDUCATION PRESS

CAMBRIDGE, MASSACHUSETTS

Paperback ISBN 9781682539194

Library of Congress Cataloging-in-Publication Data is on file.

Published by Harvard Education Press,
an imprint of the Harvard Education Publishing Group

Harvard Education Press
8 Story Street
Cambridge, MA 02138

Cover design: Patrick Ciano
Cover image: SDI Productions via iStock

The typefaces in this book are Minion Pro and ITC Stone Sans.

This book is dedicated to the teachers, coaches, and leaders we have learned alongside.

Your work continues to inspire change.

And to the brilliant students who never stop surprising us.

Contents

1 Doing Better for Children Requires Doing Better
   for Teachers   1

2 How We Learn Together Matters   19

3 Spaces and Practices to Support Learning and
   Collaboration   47

4 Teachers and Principals in Partnership   81

5 Teachers and Coaches in Partnership   119

6 Leading Teacher Learning and Collaboration   161

7 Shared Intentions Means Sharing Challenges   209

8 Working Together to Make Schools Work Better   235

Notes   251
Acknowledgments   257
About the Authors   261
Index   265

1

Doing Better for Children Requires Doing Better for Teachers

Imagine a time when you felt seen and heard, when you felt capable and supported to take a risk, when you respected, trusted, and valued the people with whom you were working or learning. This is what we want for every child in elementary school, and we believe that collectively creating this same experience for every teacher is the key to creating the schools children deserve.[1] Children thrive when teachers thrive. Teachers thrive when children thrive.

Like you, we want schools in which children's capabilities, curiosities, and identities are nurtured. We want their classrooms to be boisterous and intellectually vibrant, and we want academic outcomes to be racially equitable. And, critically, we want teachers to have the capacity to create these learning environments so children experience each other's brilliance in classrooms every day. We also want coaches and principals to continually develop and use their expertise and authority to create the conditions that grow teachers' capacity. We are writing this book for teachers, coaches, principals, and district leaders; this book is for everyone who makes decisions for students or teachers.

We want classrooms to be very different for the many children for whom school doesn't work. We want school experiences to enrich and support the development of children from marginalized communities. We want children to develop agency and voice and to have economic access to develop their own ambitions as adults. We want equitable outcomes for Black, Brown, Indigenous, and Asian American children whom our schools have not served well. This is the future we have been working toward. This vision has been the focus of the many amazing teachers, coaches, and principals whom we've worked with and learned from, and we believe that what we've learned together can inform the work you are doing.

> **"** For me, there's something about the element of joy that's felt when creating authentic spaces for learning for adults and students. I think that the spaces in which we are allowed to experiment, investigate, revise our thinking, be curious, and unapologetically bring our whole selves ultimately re-creates a sense of joy that many of us haven't been able to tap into since our early childhood, especially in formal education settings. It's what keeps me excited about the work.[2]
>
> *Principal*

We believe that how schools are currently organized, what we prioritize, and how we work together are major barriers to realizing our vision of student and teacher learning and development.[3] The organizational structures, routines, and priorities that currently exist are doing exactly what they are designed to do, resulting in too many schools being places where neither students nor teachers love to learn or work. We feel lucky because our experience has shown us a different way of working and learning. We've been able to create the supportive, trusting, collaborative learning spaces that we all need in order to take the risks necessary to shift our practices, and we have seen the results.

Our research-practice partnership (RPP), still active today, began in 2011 in the context of a federally mandated school transformation grant focused on a racially diverse, predominantly low-income elementary school that was performing in the bottom 5 percent of all schools in the state as measured by standardized test scores. As an authorship team, we played various roles in the school where the partnership began: the principal, the math coach, a teacher, and university teacher educators and researchers. Through our partnership, we worked to create a school learning culture that supported teachers to meaningfully shift their practices from teacher-centered, proceduralized learning of content to student-centered, discussion-intensive learning. We initially focused on mathematics teaching and learning as a means of re-envisioning how teachers could learn from and with their students. Teachers created inquiry-based, dialogue-rich communities that positioned students as powerful sensemakers who grow ideas together and develop independence. Within two years, there were transformational changes in student learning, a schoolwide ethos that valued students' sensemaking, a schoolwide intentional design for teacher learning, and widespread teacher reports of a strong professional community. By the end of the third year, the school was named a School of Distinction by the state and recognized federally by the Department of Education.[4]

As our collaboration continued, and with district sponsorship, the principal was named a principal supervisor in the RPP's sixth year and now leads a network of six schools to build responsive, coherent, and sustainable learning experiences for adults and students. Importantly, although the work began in mathematics, it expanded to literacy (beginning in year two), social emotional learning (beginning in year three), and science (beginning in year seven) in all schools in the network. In dialogue boxes throughout this book, you'll hear directly from teachers, coaches, and principals involved in this work across the network. We do not identify participants by name because their perspectives were shared in the context of interviews and observations conducted through our research activities, requiring us to maintain their confidentiality. We wish we could credit each teacher, coach, and school leader with whom we have had the privilege to work. Our hope is that their words, actions, and commitments will inspire many more teams to create schools where children and teachers engage in joyful and equitable learning.

Through our partnership, we've learned that it takes more than a book study, some tweaks to your school improvement plan, better curriculum, or evidence-based practices to change schools in meaningful ways. Our big idea is that we must intentionally and explicitly organize our schools to nurture teacher learning in service of creating flourishing learning environments for each student. In essence, form must follow function; if we truly want to support all teachers in routinely designing learning experiences that result in students developing agency, the skills to be independent learners, and the confidence to use their voices, we must significantly reorganize our schools.[5] We all have to embrace that if we want something different for our students, then we are the ones who will have to do things differently—all of us. We must revise how we enact every role within the school and how we use the time and resources available in public schools. Further, we must support principals and coaches to understand how teachers grow in their skill and practice and legitimize principals making that the priority of their leadership.

STICK WITH US FOR A MINUTE

Writing about doing something every reader does every day is tricky! We're all educators, and we all have the same basic set of tools and resources available. Like you, we've tried to use all the same strategies and ideas everyone else has used over the last couple of decades of "school improvement" to make schools better. Every term or strategy you're about to read, you've heard before. This is why writing about getting better at what we do is tricky. Terms like *professional learning, instructional coaching, grade-level meetings, coplanning,* and *equity* are ubiquitous. We're going to ask you to resist the urge to say you've heard it all before (even though you have!). Stick with us through this chapter. That frustration of having heard it all before, tried it all before—that's why we're writing this book. That is exactly what we felt and what led us to try making different choices about *how* to engage in the work of inspired teaching and learning that our children deserve. We wanted different experiences for our students, and doing the same things with the same resources wasn't working.

It wasn't enough for our brilliant, diverse, curious, in-the-process-of-being-marginalized-by-our-society students.

Let's take the term *professional development (PD)*, a term used all the time in education. We've all spent many hours either engaged in or planning PD. It's central to the work we want to share with you. We started by recognizing that traditional PD was not impacting the experiences teachers were designing for students; it wasn't even designed to. *Open secret among teachers: time spent in PD is time not spent doing your real work.* Teachers, this is why you're always looking for more time to do your "real work," designing the actual student learning experiences. And you're doing it alone. Principals, this is why teachers are often frustrated with the PD that you thought they'd love, because at the end of that PD, they're going to have to spend two extra hours planning the actual lessons the PD didn't help them plan.

The truth is that PD is often experienced by teachers as something that delays them from getting to their real work. We reconceived the way we use the resource of professional development. Assuming that we all agree that teachers are the most valuable resource that we provide to students, we should be asking: How can we all work together to support the real work of teachers designing and facilitating student learning experiences?

> I think what's super powerful just in terms of my own instruction but also in terms of staff culture and the culture around learning at our school is just the fact that everyone's in there learning together, including the principal. And then we all come into a classroom and try something out and usually fail, and we'll stop halfway through and try to figure out something else to do. What I think those Learning Labs have created, which is something completely different from what I had at my old school, is this culture of, we're all learning how to be better teachers all the time. No one's perfected it, and no one is going to be perfect. Everyone's going to make mistakes, and we can be a support to each other in that. I think it creates a culture that makes all of our instruction across all subjects more effective.
>
> *Fifth-grade teacher*

Teachers, coaches, and principals learning and planning together is what we are working toward when we use the term *professional development*. How we use the term professional development is just one example. We're asking that you stick with us to get an idea of how we're using very familiar terms to mean different enactments than you've likely experienced.

THIS BOOK IS FOR EVERYONE

Every author of this book believes that teachers are the most valuable resource our system offers to students. It starts and ends with teachers. Coaches and principals, you create the contexts, the possibilities, the constraints, and the expectations that foster the vision. This book is just as much for you. None of us alone can change the system that frustrates all of us. As authors, we represent each of these roles, and this book is for all of us. What we are offering is a framework of how the school can be organized and how roles can be enacted that aligns with our vision of student engagement. We must accept that students are not served well by leaving teachers to do this alone. That is why we organize the schools around teacher learning and collaboration.

THE TEACHER EXPERIENCE IS CENTRAL TO THE WORK

Let's talk about being a teacher. What's it like to go to work every day? Teachers, our guess is that you like your colleagues, you like your principal, and you like your students. You like teaching second grade. It's a good fit for you. Your team works together, but mostly on logistics. The truth is, your *real* work—when you're planning how to engage your kids in learning—is done alone. You rarely talk deeply to anyone about your instructional decisions. Planning instruction is just you in your classroom, thinking about the curriculum, the standards, and your students' needs and abilities. You're the only one working on it. That's the real work. You know you want to get better. You try things on your own. But what if that changed?

What if you believed that your coach, your principal, and your teammates all wanted to grow their practice, and to help you grow, by learning together? What if the coach and principal were participating in order to identify the additional learning or time or resources that would support your continued growth?

What if you and your teammates really were planning together to teach the same thing to your students, and you actually had a larger team around you to help you? What if you were able to puzzle through the very hard job of figuring out how to meaningfully support your students *together*? What if you were really working together on how and what *you felt* you needed to teach your students, and it wasn't in addition to your own planning?

What if there was time every week to work together on this? What if your principal were scheduling and budgeting and planning for you to have this time during the school day so it didn't have to be before or after school or at the cost of something else?

❝I don't think I would have been able to figure out . . . like how do I teach children if I'm not checking in with people? If I didn't feel comfortable being like, "I have no idea what we're doing, I don't understand this." I've always felt that was the norm. People come into our Grade-Level Team Meetings and they're like, "OK, this did not go well; what did you do in your class?" And that's normal. Versus putting on your game face, "I've got this." So I think those things with professional development or how we do team meetings, I feel like that is super helpful because we're constantly challenged to grow as teachers.

Third-grade teacher

So there's part of you that wants to prove yourself as a coach. But then there's the other part that knows that you have to learn it deeply, and to learn it deeply, you have to wade in and get just as messy as everybody else. I made the decision that I was going to put learning before looking good—as our principal says, "You can't look good and get better at the same time." I was going to have to trust that over time I'd earn teachers' respect. When I approached coaching in this way, that was when some really interesting things happened.

Math coach

Because how you model and what you model as a principal, that's what teachers are going to be watching—although not con-sciously—but they're going to be watching how you're receiving this new professional learning. If you're receiving professional learn-ing as an administrator who's going to be evaluating teachers on it, then teachers will do this as compliance. If you jump in and you learn new ideas as a learner. If you say, "This is fascinating, I want to learn this too." And you make some mistakes and you get messy, then they'll go, "Ah, OK. This is how we learn together." Everything a principal does is going to set the tone for how teachers engage.

Principal

CREATING THE SCHOOLS WE WANT

We care deeply about creating schools that racially diverse children and families love and where they thrive. The typical school boxes us in like an egg crate, with an allure of autonomy that prevents us from actually devel-oping and getting better together.[6] We know that schools can be different. We've been doing the collaborative work to support the student and teacher learning that we describe in this book for more than ten years. And we want to help you think about how it can be different at your school.

We don't believe in the common narratives that teachers are better off if they are left alone to do what they think is right for their students, that coaches work only with teachers who are struggling, and that principals make teachers better through evaluation. Like most of you, we work in public schools, where the traditional school organization lays everything at the teachers' feet. We recognize the barrage of demands that educators regularly face:

> *Teachers, here are all the standards you need to meet this year. And while you're trying to do that, please use this new curriculum, even though we only have two half days this year for you to make sense of it. But remember, teachers, it's vital to be aware of everything that's happening in the world outside of school, so you'll need to be very thoughtful and intentional in helping students make sense of the racial reckoning that we are facing, the mass shootings that just won't stop, and the continual racism, homophobia, and xenophobia that our communities endure. While you're navigating these significant issues—after a pandemic, no less—be sure to put aside some time to address students' socioemotional needs. Just don't forget about those academic standards, please. . . .*

It's daunting what schools are asked to do every day for every child because nothing ever comes off the list. And of course, the list just keeps growing.

We recognize that all these expectations are true. Despite the ongoing criticism that schools face, we actually put enormous faith in teachers and schools. So it's contradictory and unfathomable that we provide so little time and space where teachers consistently and predictably get to explore their own practice. Little space where teachers reflect with others. Little space where teachers can move past the logistics of what to teach when and actually learn together about how to engage their students. Little space where teachers work on problems of practice with a team.

If we are to consistently and reliably create the schools we all wish we worked in, we need shared spaces where we can get better together. The problems of practice teachers face are hard. And we all need to be working on them. On a daily basis, teachers tackle the problems of why some children are not engaging in particular content and which prerequisite skills need to be developed. They continually wrestle with how classrooms are racialized, gendered, and classed spaces. Some students are included and feel safe, while others feel isolated. They think hard about how to help children develop skills to learn independently. They see the larger racial inequities in their own data and try by themselves to address them in the nine months they have with their students. When they work with small groups to focus on skill development, they have to figure out how to engage the others in the room without giving them busy work. They have to reshape curriculum to meet the needs of their students without skipping any standards or unintentionally overscaffolding. And they have to create classroom communities that are safe and loving enough to support the high expectations they must hold for all children. These are all vital to how teachers create learning communities where their students thrive.

Most of the PD teachers experience is largely disconnected from all the actual work that they do when planning, teaching, and adjusting their instruction to better meet their students' needs. After most PD, teachers still go and plan for two hours for their own specific students. As a coach, a principal, and teacher educators, we have tried to support teachers within this existing model. As teachers, we have tried to grow within this model. Then we started working together to change the standard set of practices because it wasn't working for anyone, especially not the teachers and leaders trying to change outcomes for students of color and students living in poverty.

So we began to ask: What if we worked together with teachers on what they are actually going to teach their own students? What if we reorganize time to create spaces in which teachers experience the opportunity to learn things that leave them eager to actually go try what we all just learned? What if all the teachers felt that way, and you could go and see the teacher next door trying what you're trying? What if we could work together to compare and adjust what we're all doing? And what if the principal is going to come into classrooms and try this too because she just learned it with you? Teachers, what if your evaluation would no longer be a surprise because the principal is documenting *your* work in this shared learning space designed to grow *your* practice? Principals, what if you rarely had to schedule time to observe teachers because you spent most of your time with them, learning and experimenting with how to design learning children will love to engage in? Principals and coaches, what if you had the team and the time to facilitate the conversations, experiments, and planning that actually support teachers in developing the practices and strategies that change student experiences?

We know everyone has heard about organizational change and school improvement processes. We are not talking about those. We are talking about fundamentally reorganizing schools. Specifically, we are talking about how schools are run, how time is spent, and how roles are enacted. We don't mean what usually happens when schools create a vision; typically, a "vision" is a document, not an organizing principle. What we are describing is not a tweak. We're talking about changing everything. And for over a decade, we have seen how it can transform public schools serving low-income communities, with the sponsorship of the district and in partnership with the teachers' union. This effort has made schools better places for both students and teachers.

> Actually the last time we had a Learning Lab, a student left me a note that was like, "I hope you have a great learning day and you learn a lot." Because we just set it up as this . . . your kids and your learning. But we're adults and we're your teachers, and we went to college, and we have degrees, but we're still figuring it out. We don't have everything figured out. We're not masters of everything. We think it's a great model for our kids. These people that you look up to—that you think know all the answers in the world—really don't. I just love that the professional development is so embedded. We learn the thing and then we go and do it. Then there's other people there to support you.
>
> *Fourth-grade teacher*

I approach coaching as a learner. Because I think if you approach all of this work as a grand adventure that you get to do together, if you can get excited about the adventure and joining teachers on this exploration together, it captivates everybody. You know? It's not something I do to you. It's like, look, we get to puzzle through this

> together. This is really cool. What are we going to see together? What problems are we going to encounter that I didn't have the answers to, you don't have the answers to? Let's see if we can figure it out together.
>
> *Math coach*

CHANGING SCHOOLS REQUIRES CHANGING EVERY ROLE

Significantly changing how a school functions is predicated on coordinated change in coach, principal, and teacher practice. Coach, principal, and teacher practices must shift to align with the common goal of creating the learning experiences and equitable outcomes that we want for children. Teachers, you know that nothing substantive changes without the principal backing it. Principals, you know that you alone can't change instruction. Teachers must be deeply invested in the vision and the strategies in order to engage in the risks of professional collaboration and growth.[7] Coaches, you know that everything you do is in the context of the culture and vision of the school. And everyone knows that without district sponsorship, no lasting change will result.

Coaching for Professional Learning

Coaching exists in all kinds of forms. You're probably most familiar with the idea of coaching that takes place through one-on-one coaching cycles with some, but not all, teachers in the school. Sometimes coaches must wait for teachers to invite their participation. We've come to call this "coaching by invitation." Other times, coaches are assigned to work with particular teachers who are deemed as struggling or are new to the profession. The coach is perceived as the one who is supposed to "show me how to do it better." Occasionally, the coach serves as another administrator, checking to make sure teachers are on pace with the curriculum, coordinating testing, keeping track of data, or supporting interventions.

We think of coaching quite differently.[8] We envision a person who works with all the teachers in a school, spending most of their time planning, teaching, and debriefing with teams of teachers. The coach isn't there as an expert who judges teachers and teaching. Instead, working alongside teachers, a coach tries out new ideas that are purposefully related to transparent goals for student learning and teacher learning. A coach also works on continually developing her own knowledge of subject matter and teachers' learning trajectories and has a close working relationship with the principal.

Coaching is not an optional bonus

You may be reading this and thinking, "We don't have a coach. How does this apply to me?" But if you agree with and feel compelled by what you've read so far, we encourage you to continue reading with the goal of interrogating your beliefs about what it will really take to make schools the places you believe they should be. Then, if you find yourself connecting with the principles in chapter 2, perhaps your next step is to begin examining your beliefs about supporting teachers and your school's/system's commitment to teacher learning. In every system, priorities are set and budgets are aligned with those priorities. Choices are made and can be changed. If you're a district leader, you are very likely someone who makes choices that impact children, teachers, and schools. We're betting that if you come to share our belief that teacher learning is foundational to student experiences and outcomes, you too will find a means to support them with coaches. If you're a school-level leader, how can you advocate for teacher learning to be elevated as a priority? If you are a coach or teacher, what opportunities are there to engage your union in elevating coaching in their current bargaining priorities?

Principal Leadership for Professional Learning

Typically, principals' interactions with teachers and students are very limited. They occasionally get into classrooms when there is a problem or they are formally observing a teacher, or they schedule and attend PD because there is a new initiative. They are often limited to looking in a pacing guide to see what a teacher should be teaching. In terms of knowing student learning experiences and outcomes, they must primarily rely on summative data to identify problems that can be addressed in the next year. They are managing the school's resources and processes with a problem-oriented approach.

Instead, we offer that the principal is a learner and a leader and keeper of the instructional vision. This version of instructional leadership results in the principal spending 60 percent of her time with teachers, participating as a learner who will practice new instructional strategies right alongside teachers in front of children. This includes the principal giving and getting real-time feedback during instruction, spending time with teams looking at formative data that they will use that day to make decisions about the next week of instruction. A principal like this deeply understands where each teacher is on a learning trajectory and works with the coaches to support that growth; they know each teacher as a learner because they are participating in instructional decisions alongside that teacher. The principal's time is spent primarily on instructional collaboration.[9]

Teaching for Student Learning

While we assume that pretty much everyone who reads this book is or has been a teacher, we don't assume that we all mean the same thing when we talk about "teaching." So we want to elaborate what's in our minds when we think of teaching. We mean teaching that is always about learning, about being a student of your students, coming to understand them as people, and continually building relationships with students and their families. Teaching is built on a foundation of valuing students' perspectives and attending to their thinking, curiosities, and capabilities (see figure 1.1). Students have to care about each other as both learners and people. Teaching, then, is about building community in the classroom where students are invested in each other's learning and are oriented to one another and the disciplinary content. Teaching is about helping students own the ideas they're developing so they can use them with

Figure 1.1   Kindergarten students joyfully engage in finding patterns in numbers

Source: Matt Hagen

confidence, with the ability to be critical thinkers who question what is and imagine what can be. We mean teachers and students working together to enact instructional and social goals that decenter the teacher as the source of knowledge and that make inquiry into making sense of our world as an important driving goal for being educated. Teaching is about building children's agency and independence right alongside their knowledge.[10]

EVERY SCHOOL HAS A STARTING POINT

If, like us, you feel powerfully excited about working in a school like we have described; if you too believe that schools can and should be reorganized to intentionally prioritize teachers' learning and collaboration aimed at designing classroom learning communities that are joyful, inquiry-oriented spaces where students' thinking and identities are cultivated; and if you can imagine yourself working in a school where every teacher actively participates in a team that is supported by instructional coaches and administrators who prioritize their teamwork as the core of their professional efforts; then we encourage you to take a few moments to consider your current context. How does your current school or system position teachers, coaches, and principals to work together in service of student learning? How does the culture in your school or district support or constrain the realization of a better vision of teacher and student learning?

We've offered some questions here to help you start thinking about what is happening in your school. (You may find yourself pausing at some of them to wonder what the questions mean. We hope that they will become clearer as you read!) See how they strike you and take this moment to be honest with yourself. Answer the questions for yourself and then think about how your colleagues in similar and different roles would answer them.

Teachers

- When was the last time you engaged in professional learning or collaboration that changed your instructional practice and impacted all the students in your grade level?
- What is the relationship between autonomy and collaboration? Do you value their potential to improve your practice differently?
- How do you think teachers develop and deepen their instructional practices?
- In what ways, if at all, do you work with an instructional coach that impacts your instructional decision-making and your capacities as a teacher?
- When you get feedback from your principal, to what extent do you think that she understands your practice, your students, and your efforts to grow?
- What shared beliefs or principles drive teaching and learning at your school?

Coaches

- How do you think teachers develop and deepen their instructional practices?
- How would you describe your goals as a coach?

- How much impact has your work had on the learning experiences of teachers? Of students?
- Does your collaboration with your principal include clear and shared goals for teacher learning?
- How would teachers describe your role in and impact on their learning?

Principals

- How do you determine what PD your teachers need?
- How do you think teachers develop and deepen their instructional practices? What is your role in their development?
- When was the last time that you participated alongside teachers learning something that you didn't know yourself? How did this inform your next leadership decisions?
- What PD have you planned for teachers that you believe and could observe changed their teaching or collaboration practices? How do you know that?
- How much do you think your work, including evaluative feedback, has impacted the experiences students have?
- If your school has an instructional coach, what is your role in supporting the coach's impact on teacher and student learning?

Do you have a school where you can authentically share your reflections and responses to these questions? If not, figuring out ways to start conversations is important, and we'll help you think about how to do that. The principles and practices underlying these questions are critical drivers for creating schools in which teacher and student learning results in equitable experiences for children. These principles and practices can be developed and nurtured, but only as a result of teachers, coaches, and principals working together.

In chapter 2, we offer the foundational principles that drive our design for teacher and student learning. We include principles for teaching, learning to teach, and creating the adult learning context. These principles undergird all the collaborative learning spaces and practices that we introduce in chapter 3. We help you think about how the spaces work together and how they must be facilitated to create a coherent professional learning system that nurtures teacher agency and the shared responsibility for enacting our vision for teaching and learning.

Chapters 4 through 6 dive deeply into the partnerships among teachers, coaches, and principals that are necessary to enact the principles. In chapter 4, we elaborate how principals must shift their relationships with teachers to partnering with them to learn and grow professionally. We provide specific practices and dispositions to guide both principals and teachers in shifting how they work together to better serve students. Chapter 5 examines the relationship between coaches and teachers. Through an illustrative case study, we bring to life our approach to coaching grade-level teams. In chapters 3 and 6, you'll read about the Instructional Leadership Team (ILT) and how coaches and principals work in partnership as they respond to teachers' learning needs across the professional learning system and in classrooms. A detailed case study will help you envision the way that leaders work together to create and sustain rich, purposeful, and coherent teacher learning.

In chapter 7, we take on several problems of practice that schools may face when they try to organize the workplace to keep students at the center of collaborative adult learning. Finally, in chapter 8, we address how everyone throughout the system must engage in the work of reimagining how to use time, money, and operational flexibility to support the work of changing teacher and student learning experiences.

At the end of each chapter, we offer concrete and manageable questions or exercises to help you in your own journey to build the schools that you want for adults and students. We understand that different schools have different assets and entry points, and you may be reading this as a team, a coach, a principal, or a teacher. Wherever you are able to start, we hope you'll keep reviewing and reflecting on the foundational principles in chapter 2 because how we position each other will lay the foundation for how we position our students. If we want students to experience each other's brilliance in vibrant learning environments, we must create those learning environments for our teachers and school leaders.

2

How We Learn
Together Matters

To us, teaching is about building children's agency and independence right alongside their knowledge. Students' curiosity is nurtured, and learning happens in classroom communities where children are oriented to each other, growing ideas together through discourse and developing both academic and emotional skills. We know that teachers alone cannot build these classrooms and routinely design this kind of instruction. To design the learning experiences and the learning community that accomplishes this vision of teaching and learning, we argue that every system and all decisions should be driven by deep knowledge about how and under what conditions teachers learn.

A note about "vision"

Like many ubiquitous educational terms, we use the term "vision" and think it's important to clarify our meaning. We recognize the importance of having a shared vision as a frame of reference that serves to ground the work, and we certainly use our vision to foster a shared focus. We also make a conscious effort to examine and

---

grow our vision as we learn more and gain deeper and broader perspectives on the work. So while the values behind our vision remain consistent and serve as our north star, we see the process of learning together much more than the product, as a powerful driver of our collaboration in support of ever better methods of supporting learning for both children and adults. A vision grounds you, but as you journey (and hopefully gain deeper insights), it should evolve and continually help to reveal the next steps.

DECISIONS MUST BE DRIVEN BY DEEP AND WELL-EXAMINED BELIEFS ABOUT TEACHER LEARNING

Over the course of our partnership, we have worked to support many school teams to design teacher and leader learning with the goal of creating classrooms and schools where student experiences and outcomes are equitable. We've learned with and from every one of these endeavors. And we know with certainty that skipping the step of learning and leading based on a set of beliefs about teacher learning will not work. As we cautioned in chapter 1, many of the terms we use are familiar; it's the effort to enact them in alignment with what we know about how teachers learn that results in powerful change in teacher practice.

We hold firmly to the belief that *how* we position and engage teachers as learners will fundamentally affect how they position and engage students. As a result, it is important that we examine the principles that drive our decisions as leaders of both student and teacher learning. How we believe people learn must drive how we position and engage them in learning. This chapter unpacks the principles that guide us and anchors them in service of our vision of student and teacher learning. In this chapter, we also elaborate the elements of the school context that are essential to supporting the ongoing shared learning that we owe our teachers and students. This foundational understanding of how teachers learn has been essential to every effort we have designed or supported others to design. *How* we work truly matters in supporting teachers and students.

Our work is informed by three sets of principles:[1]

The *Principles for Teaching* guide the way we design student learning experiences.

The *Principles for Learning to Teach* guide the way we design teacher learning experiences.

The *Principles for the Adult Learning Context* can support (or constrain) both.

THE PRINCIPLES FOR TEACHING GUIDE THE WAY WE DESIGN STUDENT LEARNING EXPERIENCES

Our working vision of really good teaching is that teachers love and care about the subject matter they are teaching. They love figuring out how their students make sense of those disciplinary ideas. This view necessitates that teachers are actively involved in thinking about what is worth learning, what funds of knowledge their students have, and how to invite critical thinking and engagement in their immediate classroom community, leading to greater possibilities for social engagement and power. When educators in schools are motivated by shared principles, they are excited by the possibilities and challenges of putting the principles into practice. A shared set of Principles for Teaching brings focus to teachers' collective experimentation so that students' learning experiences across the whole school are coherent. That's why grounding principles matter— our work is based on them because they represent the commitments or values we hold true.

It's important to note that when learning together is based on shared principles, the principles themselves are also continually elaborated and revised, and educators keep learning and developing what they thought was possible. Simply put, you learn more about what the principles mean as you work together toward your goals.

Principles for Teaching

1. *Children are sensemakers.*

Children are capable beings, continually trying to make sense of the world around them. Children actively construct meaning by having multiple entry points, taking the time to process, and making connections among new ideas. Their educational experiences should be additive, not subtractive.[2] Our schooling system has perpetuated and constructed a racial, class, and gender hierarchy of intelligence and achievement that does not exist. Race, class, and gender are not related to intelligence. Our work to dismantle inequitable structures of schooling involves recognizing and revising our actions that treat children explicitly or implicitly through a deficit lens. Because we believe that children are sensemakers, teaching isn't about getting students to do things or filling in gaps in knowledge. It's about positioning students as competent and putting them in dialogue with one another, actively making sense of new ideas.

2. *Teaching includes becoming a student of your students.*

Teachers must know their students as individuals and as learners.[3] This involves noticing children; building relationships with them, their families, and their communities; valuing their perspectives; and attending to their thinking, curiosities, and capabilities. Teachers must be continually examining and expanding their racial and cultural literacy with respect to the particular students they teach. Teachers must have detailed knowledge of their students' evolving ideas in relation to the disciplinary work they are doing.

> ### A note about attending to our own development and impact on teaching for equity
>
> As we consider these Principles for Teaching, it's important to consider the lenses through which we understand ourselves and the communities we serve. We all bring our own racialized, gendered, and classed experiences forward, and they shape our beliefs and practices as educators and leaders. When Gloria Ladson-Billings

wrote about culturally relevant pedagogy, she explained that it required developing students' academic learning and success, cultural competence, and critical consciousness.[4] To develop these capacities in our students, as educators and leaders we must be critically reflective about our own histories, our own cultural and racial identities, and how they shape the way we think about teaching and learning. Following Ladson-Billings, we must also continually seek to develop cultural competence beyond our own multifaceted identities. Our own limitations will form barriers to understanding the cultural and racial experiences of our students and their families.

Decoteau Irby writes that it is vital to have "Black and Brown people's influential presence" in any efforts to create schools that Black and Brown students, families, and educators rightfully deserve.[5] We underscore Irby's view that to achieve the transformation we seek, school leaders and teachers must continually broaden the racial perspectives and representations they engage with to be able to understand and address problems in "race-visible ways." This work is different for white teachers and leaders than teachers and leaders of color, but we are all limited, in that our knowledge of racialized, gendered, and classed experiences is necessarily partial. We have to work continually to learn more about the particular students we serve. This intentional and reflective work matters because we have to be able to recognize when schooling practices and policies dehumanize children and their families and communities. While this book is not specifically about culturally competent instruction, we are committed to the fundamental responsibility to continually learn from and with our students and their families. We must learn to value diversity in our communities as a resource rather than a deficit as we endeavor to teach each child.

3. *To design equitable instruction for each child, teachers must leverage the social knowledge, community and cultural capital, and linguistic resources students bring to the classroom.*

We want children to experience school as a place where they are known, seen, and heard and where they come to know themselves and others through ongoing, reciprocated relationships. Children's full humanity—their racial, cultural, linguistic, classed, and gendered experiences—bring richness, nuance, and complexity to the school community. When teachers are "open-eyed and present" as they learn alongside their students, then they can continually seek ways of making the classroom a space where children's many funds of knowledge are drawn upon to meet instructional goals.[6] Rather than impose content on students, teachers must help students build bridges between new content they are learning and the constellation of their current understandings and identities.

4. *Equitable instruction requires clear instructional goals.*

Clear instructional goals provide the compass as teachers choose instructional tasks and navigate instructional interactions, helping guide what to listen for and which ideas to pursue.[7] Teachers have to be able to articulate what they are teaching and why. Clear and well-understood instructional goals anchor the instructional decisions teachers make about the learning opportunities they design with the intent to support children in becoming critical thinkers and engaged contributors to their learning communities.[8]

5. *Teachers must be responsive to the requirements of the school environment. At the same time, they must wrestle with why schools function as they do and how schools might need to improve as institutions in a democracy.*

Schools play a critical role in what Mike Rose has called "possible lives."[9] Schools as institutions can be sites of both oppression and liberation. Curriculum, standards, assessment systems, attendance boundaries, and teacher assignments are all necessary for schools to function, but they are often tangled up with how our schooling structures limit marginalized students' capabilities rather than enable them to flourish. As teachers and leaders, we are expected to abide by the policies set by our districts and states. In pursuing more equitable experiences for children, we are also obligated to interrogate policies and practices and make changes when they produce inequities or cause harm.

A note about instructional decisions

We want to be clear that we are not suggesting that everyone teach in exactly the same way or there's some uniform ideal we desire. We are not saying that any teacher, given the same content, should design the same experience for their students. We strongly assert that teaching is both intellectual work and a craft with important contextual considerations, the goal of which is to nurture the learner, not simply teach the content or strategy.

Teachers need a combination of knowledge, skills, and resources to make instructional decisions while planning instruction and while teaching to best equip them to improvise in response to student learning. Instructional decisions are an intersection of a complex combination of knowledge, skills, and resources.[10]

Figure 2.1 Knowledge, skills, and resources inform instructional decisions

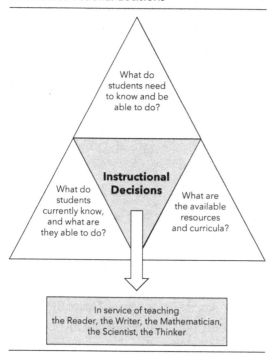

The graphic in figure 2.1 has been helpful to some principals and coaches as they strive to design timely and responsive teacher learning experiences. It is not meant to diminish teachers' judgment or portray teaching in a reductive way. Ultimately, teachers are the ones who bring all the dimensions of their craft together in the moment and then continually adjust based on student responses. As we design adult learning, we have to be careful not to overemphasize any one dimension, such as "unpacking standards," "getting to know the curriculum," or "implementing best assessment practices." We must not lose sight of the responsibility to teach the teacher, not the strategy, curriculum, or any specific "best practice." This graphic represents a commitment to continually formatively assess each teacher's and team's knowledge and skills so we can balance the support in all the dimensions of practice that they are called upon to enact. A deep understanding of these three areas of practice are foundational elements of both effective planning and instructional improvisation during instruction.

THE PRINCIPLES FOR LEARNING TO TEACH GUIDE THE WAY WE DESIGN TEACHER LEARNING EXPERIENCES

We believe that teachers must be trusted and engaged as competent sensemakers in messy and experimental learning. For teachers to take risks, they need to also see their colleagues and school leaders take risks and both succeed and fail. A favorite mantra of ours is, "You can't look good and get better at the same time" because trying out new instructional practices will be a messy process.[11] The Principles for Learning to Teach reflect how we view teachers as learners, the goals and processes for learning, and what supports learning to occur.

Principles for Learning to Teach

1. *Teaching is something that can be learned.*

   Teaching is intellectual work that requires specialized knowledge and skills. Teachers must be positioned as active, capable contributors to developing insight into the complex practice of teaching. Deborah Ball writes that we are not born teachers. Teaching requires development of the specialized ability to unpack big ideas, to design experiences that provide multiple entry points and invite learners to make sense of these new ideas, to assess ideas and skills from other people's perspectives, and to manage a productive learning environment for a broad range of learners.[12]

2. *Students' ideas and experiences should be central to teacher learning.*

We often hear in schools that teachers are expected to teach a certain text or a particular curriculum. But the goal of teaching is not to implement a curriculum with fidelity. Learning to teach well means developing clear goals, understanding the big ideas students will be grappling with, and then investigating how our students make sense of those ideas. Teaching is everything the teacher does to intentionally put children in conversation with one another and orient them to the content ideas they are exploring. What needs to be at the heart of teacher learning is understanding the development of student ideas and their life experiences in relation to meaningful disciplinary content.[13]

3. *Learning to teach is a continual process of knowledge, skill, and identity development.*

Learning unfolds along a complex trajectory of knowledge, practice, and identity development, and it is always situated in particular contexts.[14] This learning entails processes of knowing more, doing more, and becoming new kinds of professionals. As teachers gain knowledge for teaching and learn to use that knowledge in practice, their identities as teachers also develop. They come to see themselves as certain kinds of teachers. So learning is never just about accumulating knowledge. Developing knowledge and skills requires repeated opportunities to practice, to experiment with ideas, come to own them, and integrate them into one's developing identity as a teacher.

4. *There is value in making teaching public.*

Teacher learning is supported by ongoing, collective opportunities to experiment with new knowledge and instructional practice. These ongoing opportunities require both teaching and learning to be public. If we only talk and reflect about our teaching without seeing how each of us puts the ideas into practice, we can assure you that we'll interpret the same ideas in very different ways. Because we know that achieving the vision for equitable instruction across classrooms is complex, teachers need opportunities to plan together so they can make their instructional decisions transparent. Then, during and after putting those plans into practice, they must collectively grapple with how they are being responsive to their own students. How do our particular students respond to our instructional decision-making, and how do we make adjustments based on what we see? When teachers have opportunities to learn together before, during, and after instruction, they grow collectively as instructional decision-makers.

5. *Teacher learning experiences must be sustained, connected, and coherent over time.*

Because learning unfolds across a complex trajectory and involves developing knowledge, skills, and identities, the spaces in which teachers have opportunities to learn have to be connected and coherent. What happens inside a Grade-Level Team Meeting, a professional development session, or a coteaching experience needs to fit together. The continuity of teachers' learning over time across these learning spaces supports teachers to enact new learning and commitments in their classroom instruction.

A note on teacher autonomy

Teacher autonomy versus collectivity is a false dichotomy that undermines equitable learning. Ensuring equitable learning environments for students doesn't mean that every classroom has to look the same. At the same time, students' success shouldn't depend on which teacher they have. The principles in this chapter are offered to foster the collective learning that supports teachers in exercising their agency. Teachers spend most of their days alone with their students. What we want is to support all teachers to make effective instructional decisions as they improvise to meet the needs of their students. This contributes to the equity of student experiences across classrooms by ensuring teachers develop common repertoires and capacities from which they make decisions that meet the needs of their specific students. Our children need and deserve teachers who can hold their vision as their north star in their planning and then improvise mid-instruction to figure out what works. We strive to create the conditions in which we can support and count on teachers to make such decisions *and then share their learning about what worked with their team.* Each student benefits when each teacher contributes her individual learning to support collective growth in practice. We believe in collectivity in service of autonomy in instructional decision-making.

Understanding Teacher Learning Trajectories

In our work, we have tried to identify the shifts that we have observed as teachers develop their knowledge, skills, and identities in their efforts to move from teacher-centered classrooms to student-centered ones. Teachers, this may feel as though we're talking *about* you rather than *to* you, but this transparency is critical. You are the ones making a thousand decisions each day that, threaded together, create the experience of "school" for students. You are the most valuable resource we can provide to children. Understanding and supporting your growth are paramount duties. If we are sincere in our commitment to creating schools where all children thrive and inequities are examined and disrupted, then we must ensure that no matter which teacher a child gets, they will benefit from the collective learning of all teachers and leaders working to enact this vision of learning and teaching. This means that we must meet each teacher where they are, and it will necessarily include unlearning some traditional practices, such as the teacher in front of the room, holding center stage and modeling what children later practice. A classroom where students are engaged in robust discussion and are oriented to each other's ideas, and where students' capabilities and identities are nurtured is not commonplace or easy to accomplish. It's important to acknowledge that growth in teaching follows a complex trajectory that has many starts and stops, setbacks, challenges, and leaps forward. We're sharing these ideas now to fuel your imagination of what can unfold and to lay the foundation for how the school context must foster teachers' growth trajectory.

> "It raises the bar if the person who is the head of your school is willing to step up and admit that she doesn't know everything and admit that she's still learning. That sets the bar for the rest of us. "OK, it really is OK." And then, the more comfortable she becomes, the more comfortable we become admitting to our kids, "Hey, I don't know everything, or I made a mistake, or that lesson was awful." The more we do it with our kids, I've noticed the more willing our kids are to say, "Oops, I made a mistake, or I guess I really didn't know the answer." So it's this kind of ripple effect that I don't even think our principal realized has happened. Her willingness to admit that she doesn't know everything and that she's still a learner makes us as teachers willing to admit we don't know everything either. We're still learners, which influences how our kids see themselves. Because now our kids see learning as an ongoing process. It's not like a thing to achieve. It's something that will stick with you all through your life, and you're constantly going to be learning.
>
> *Fourth-grade teacher*
>
> I remember the first time someone said we would spend a whole day talking about math in professional development [PD]. I was like, I don't want to go to this thing. I don't know what this is. This is so foreign to me. That sounds terrible, you know. I don't want to go into someone else's class and watch them teach. I don't want to go into someone else's class to teach the lesson to kids that I don't know. I remember that being such an awkward thing. And now, if a PD gets canceled for whatever reason, I'm sad. That's not how I would have felt four years ago.
>
> *First-grade teacher*

We sketched out the trajectory in figure 2.2 in collaboration with principals and coaches by identifying what happens as teachers begin to fundamentally change their relationship with students and with teaching disciplinary content.[15] It is not linear and appears messy on purpose

Figure 2.2 A possible trajectory for learning as teachers learn to facilitate student sensemaking

Concerns
- Focusing on challenges
- Thinking that curriculum won't work for students

"My kids can't subtract."

"I can't move on until they..."

"There were some good ideas but most of them just aren't getting it."

Understands Teaching as Getting Students to Do Things

Delivering Content
- Modeling content leaves little time for conferring with students
- Questioning is not used during instruction
- Focused on step-by-step formulas
- Planning is primarily preparing slides

"I need to assess ___ before we can ___"

"They need to ___ before they can ___"

"We need to spend more time on routines before we start with content."

Started but Stuck
- Repeating student ideas but unsure where to take the discussion
- Feeling the need to spend all conferring time with struggling students
- Differentiating only to meet needs of groups of learners (e.g., ELL)

"I have a lot of students who are still ___ can I just teach them to ___?"

"But what about the students who are so far behind, do we have a system for that?"

Teacher focused on own actions

"Should I use these talk moves in literacy too?"

Going Through the Motions
- Following the activities in the curriculum word for word
- Needs guidance for what to teach next and why
- When conferring asking same questions over and over
- Not sure what students will do
- Students not listening to each other

"I get why we teach this way but I still think kids need to know certain things before they can go to next grade…"

"This all feels so disjointed."

"How are they going to learn if we only do two problems?"

"When will they practice?"

Little Celebrations

"OMG – you won't believe what so and so did in my class today!"

"I'm going to change my carpet area because kids can't access the board when they're sharing their thinking."

"I can't wait to try this."

"What is something else I can try?"

Getting Started, Trying

Talk moves effectively used in some lessons but not all

Willing to try something at least once

"I've been over scaffolding, I need to focus on saying 'what do you think?'"

Purposeful Talk and Student Ownership
- Planning clear questions to support student talk
- Students using signals and talk moves without prompting

Collaboration Valued
- Coming prepared to team meetings, talks and reflects
- Planning, implementing, reflecting on lessons
- Wants to be aligned and on the same page with teammates

"I don't understand this concept…can you help me?"

Internalized Belief in Principles for Teaching

Instruction Based on Student Thinking
- Teacher intentionally calling on students with specific strategies to build connections among students' ideas
- Monitoring all students during practice/explore and responsively planning for summary of lesson

"I saw kids using some unique strategies I want to highlight."

"We had a closing discussion where we compared and connected two strategies."

"This assessment only shows me if they got it correct or incorrect. How do we collect info/data about their reasoning and strategies?"

Embrace Messiness
- Has internalized the purpose of every lesson
- Sees student struggle as learning
- Ok with students making own choices for particular tasks

"Let's just see what they do."

"They surprise me."

Differentiating for Diverse Learners
- Attending to where students are and where to go next
- Has developed long view for how student learning develops
- Asking students a variety of questions
- Confident about adapting/adjusting for students
- Noticing what students can do, monitor students in more nuanced ways
- Nurtures students' identities as readers, writers, mathematicians…

"How can I provide access to ___ during the discussion?"

because that's how learning happens. In the graphic, the headers capture the progression forward, while the quotations illustrate what teachers notice or worry about as they develop their knowledge, practice, and identities as teachers who facilitate student sensemaking. Please do not take it as an absolute truth or the only path. It represents the bumpy, curvy path we have witnessed dedicated and talented teachers take in creating engaging, joyful, student-centered classrooms. Teachers, we think you'll recognize the forward movement that happens if you've worked within contexts that support you to keep experimenting with student-centered instruction.

We want to take you through the journey depicted in figure 2.2. When we say that learning is a sensemaking process, think about what teachers are trying to understand as they share concerns like, "My kids just aren't getting it" or worry about how quickly they are moving from lesson to lesson, insisting that "we need to spend more time on this content before we move on to the next." Teachers are responsible for student learning and typically feel a lot of pressure to make sure students learn. Seeing students at very different places in their skills is alarming, so it's natural for teachers to identify what's missing in students' skills and try to fix those. And in fact, the pressure and expectation to examine data in schools typically orient teachers to identify where students are not succeeding. Discussion-based teaching practices and the use of open-ended tasks can make teachers feel like students are awash in loose instructional conditions where their learning is uncertain. So it makes sense that teachers feel compelled to direct and model what good work looks like as a way to ensure student learning. But when we are at the beginning of the journey of shifting our classroom norms to be less teacher-directed and more focused on growing and making sense of ideas together, it takes time and experimentation for a teacher to realize how intentional goal setting and facilitation within more open-ended, complex tasks enable student learning and in fact better support sensemaking and conceptual understanding.

Teachers, you'll start down a path but then you'll get stuck and worry again about how to meet the full range of students' needs. Working on these thorny problems together will generate more nuanced practices, and you'll find yourself excited by how students surprise you: "You won't believe what Jackson did today when I asked him to model his idea with a diagram." You'll find yourself drawing on your own creative imagination to start addressing the inequities you notice in your classroom: "I'm going to change how much time students have to think through their ideas in partner talk before we come back to share in the whole group. I want them to listen to each other better, so I'll ask them to share who they were talking with and what the other person helped them think about." You'll start asking, "What else can I try?" You'll start to reflect critically when you notice that you are leading students to a solution or end product too quickly. You'll think, "I've been overscaffolding. I need to focus on saying, 'What do *you* think?'" The trial and error and the back-and-forth between your planning, teaching, and reflection will start to open up more space for you to listen to and with your students. They too will change through the process of your own learning. As you change the tasks and questions you pose, students learn to share more of their thinking with you and with peers. They become less concerned with sharing the correct answer they think you are looking for and more focused on sharing what they think, being heard, and participating in growing ideas together.

As more space opens up for you to gain more detailed knowledge of your students' sensemaking and experiences as learners in your classroom, you'll notice that how you assess their learning will change. In addition to keeping track of the right answers, you'll find ways to note how they are approaching their tasks and what strategies and arguments they are constructing. Understanding what puzzles students will help you design and modify the next instructional conversations to provoke them to troubleshoot and revise their thinking. Your students will no longer look to you to validate each of their responses. They will see value in hearing their peers, adding on to ideas, making conjectures, and taking risks. Your classroom will become a different kind of learning community. Your students will own the power of their ideas. And in the process, you'll come to see yourself as a teacher who elicits and builds on students' ideas to advance their learning rather than directly giving students new ideas.

Like all the tools and resources that we share in this book, you should regard this sketch of a learning trajectory as a dynamic, working resource. Does it help you have conversations with colleagues and leaders in your school and district about what learning is and how to recognize progress? Does it help you think about what you or your colleagues are grappling with and what you might be aiming for next? Does it help you appreciate that teachers don't learn from brief exposure to new models that they then try to implement with fidelity? If you tried building a trajectory for teacher learning with your colleagues, what would it look like?

Teachers' learning and growth over time does not happen without leadership and community among colleagues in a school that creates the conditions for both individual and collective growth. Next, we consider how the school context supports or constrains teacher growth.

THE PRINCIPLES FOR THE ADULT LEARNING CONTEXT IMPACT BOTH TEACHING AND LEARNING TO TEACH

The school context in which adults work (and hopefully learn) is a result of decisions made by school and district leaders. How time is allocated and who participates are leadership decisions. This section elaborates the beliefs and commitments we have developed in parallel with the preceding principles. Everyone can agree that "leadership matters," but we need to know more about what leaders do that directly impacts growth in effective instructional practice. This next set of principles is our effort to make transparent the dispositions we have seen accelerate the development of strong adult learning communities where collective responsibility for student learning develops and risks are taken in service of growth. Our experience has repeatedly underscored that how leaders attend to the school as a learning context for teachers directly impacts what teachers can accomplish.

Creating the schools we want for our students means creating schools where teacher learning is at the center of what we do and how we do it. Teacher learning is paramount. This means applying the Principles for Teaching to teaching teachers. It means committing to continually figuring out how to support and position teachers to make the skilled, nuanced planning and instructional decisions driven by our vision for student learning. Leadership that creates a school context in which teachers will continually learn and collaborate is fundamental to better serving students.

Parallel to student learning, teacher learning is fostered in an intentional, responsive context. Our experience has led to the unequivocal conclusion that commitment to the Principles for Teaching and Learning to Teach requires a commensurate commitment to creating the workplace in which teachers and leaders, together as learners, have the necessary contextual supports and spaces to learn to enact them.

Principles for the Adult Learning Context

1. Learning must be connected and coherent.

In the Principles for Learning to Teach section, we concluded with the assertion that teachers' learning experiences have to be coherent and connected as they move from one space to another. This must extend across the whole school context. What teachers are learning and expected to do across content areas in relation to building classroom community, and even our expectations about how to engage families, must all align with each other and be grounded in the same vision. The individual conversations happening between teachers and coaches and principals must intentionally and explicitly connect to each other and the shared vision. To develop increasingly nuanced instructional practices, the relationship between the parts and the whole has to be clear. As new ideas, practices, or questions are introduced, school leaders must be intentional when working with teachers to ensure that new ideas are connected to the larger vision and build upon teachers' current effective practices. Learning is supported by opportunities to integrate new concepts with existing understandings.

2. As we learn together, our vision for equitable teaching and learning must evolve.

Equitable, dialogue-rich, identity-affirming education is a complex and nuanced vision that we strive to achieve. It requires ongoing learning and a willingness to adjust goals based on what we learn. As we collectively engage in cycles of inquiry into practice and consciously attend to diverse racial, linguistic, and cultural perspectives, we must embrace that the vision will necessarily grow and be refined.

3. *Learning is messy, not linear.*

Learning to teach is a continual process of knowing, doing, and becoming.[16] It unfolds along a complex trajectory of knowledge, practice, and identity development. Such growth is not linear, and learning, doing, and becoming in one subject area may not immediately transfer to others. Because learning requires repeated opportunities to practice, we must disrupt the "teacher training" mentality and design integrated, thoughtfully paced opportunities to practice together. Finally, learners' intersectional identities will shape their trajectory and must be honored and leveraged, requiring us to attend to the personal aspects of adult learning.

4. *Everyone has to take a learner stance.*

We have to value vulnerability, risk taking, and effort; experimentation and curiosity are essential. In schools, this requires shifting professional relationships to mitigate the impact of positionality to instead foster collective, collaborative, and shared responsibility. This cannot be expected solely of teachers; the school context must flatten the power structure to support all adults to engage as learners with and from each other. If all collaboration between teachers and principals is set in the context of evaluation and supervision, this will never happen. We must shift from avoiding individual risk or vulnerability to seeking collective solutions.

5. *Learning happens when there's time and space in the day and week.*

The work of learning to get better must be embedded in the work. Not only must it be during the school day, it must be frequent enough for teachers and building leaders to gather the momentum to keep evolving toward the equitable, joyful, and rich learning environments we are after. Further, these times and spaces must be facilitated as learning spaces where we get better at instructional decision-making. The professional context must provide the spaces for both learning and practicing in various configurations of people so learning together in ways that make us better instructional decision-makers becomes just part of the routine. Embedded and frequent time must be worked into the schedule in which everyone—teachers, coaches, and principal—engage in learning, hypothesizing, trying ideas out *with* students, reflecting, and coming to collective commitments about how to shift practice. This requires us to normalize spending time together puzzling over what is and isn't working in terms of positioning students as sensemakers.

Together, these three sets of principles inform every aspect of how we do the work of enacting the practices and engaging in the spaces we share in the chapters that follow. We led with the principles because, like you, we have seen so many schools and districts implement the latest model, practice, or strategy, and three years later, all they remember is "that initiative." We are acutely and humbly aware that there is no magic strategy or practice. What we want to emphasize is that committing to continually figuring out how to support and position teachers to make these important planning and instructional decisions based on shared beliefs about what we want for students can powerfully impact teachers' capacity and ability to improve their practice. Therefore, leaders must recognize that taking this stance means accepting that it will never be done. Building leaders—coaches and principals—must continually engage in principled planning for teacher learning and consistently keep the balance and hold the tension necessary to create the context even within systems that are not designed to support such leadership.

THESE PRINCIPLES REQUIRE NEW WAYS OF WORKING TOGETHER

If you read the principles and thought . . .

- "My school doesn't look like this."
- "We can't . . ."

- "My principal doesn't get teaching."
- "Teachers want autonomy too much to . . ."
- "Our students are so behind."
- "We don't have coaches."
- "We're under too much pressure to raise test scores."
- "This is just one more thing to do."
- "We don't have the time or resources."
- "Our students can't . . ."

. . . then you're in the majority. We understand what you are facing. We know from personal experience that you can enjoy your school environment and like your colleagues but still not work in a setting that is characterized by deep collaboration. Public schools are simply not designed to foster the set of conditions that support the productive, messy, and experimental adult learning that we need as educators. If we want to work together as adults in different ways in service of student learning, we need new norms for our collective work.

But what exists right now is affecting you, your students, and your hopes and beliefs about your professional impact. So what's true right now? What are the spoken and unspoken norms for working together? These questions are worth explicitly interrogating because how we engage in the work, what unspoken assumptions we bring, and how we perceive the possibilities and constraints of how we choose to work together are huge factors in what we can accomplish in service of students. It will be helpful to attend to this dimension of your setting if you decide to dig more deeply into the ideas we share in the ensuing chapters.

To establish a different set of norms, intention is not enough. You have to start to interact differently to build new norms. Beliefs change as you practice differently. And that cycle reinforces itself. Then the insights that you gain as you practice differently shape and shift your beliefs.

Whether you are part of a teaching team, a coach working with a single grade level, or a principal eager to explore new ways to support teachers, there are ways to get started!

CONCLUSION

These principles, as well as the norms that have supported enacting them, have evolved over time and continue to evolve. Fueled by a vision of what we want for students and the joys of working with so many dedicated, talented, and skilled teachers, coaches, and principals, our work is translating these principles to a new way of thinking about teacher learning. To us, this means never being done with learning, committing to not becoming overly focused on one aspect of teacher practice or a single new initiative, and accepting that every person we hire will need support to engage in the ways we have imagined here. It motivates our work to develop the spaces and practices introduced in chapter 3 in service of reorganizing schools around teacher learning and collaboration. Same staff, same funding, same students—but we offer ideas for putting the pieces together differently. And depending on your context, you can start in different places, but we urge you to base your efforts on shared principles and a codeveloped intention. The power is in the process of working and learning together to build practices and systems that better serve our children.

IDEAS FOR GETTING STARTED

Here are some ideas to get you started thinking together about the future you'd prefer for yourself, your school, and your students. Whatever your circumstance, perhaps you're a coach looking for ways to strengthen collaboration, a teaching team exploring new practices, or a principals' group learning together about leadership that strengthens instructional practice, these ideas will assist you in examining your individual practice or beginning to develop a shared intention. These are small steps you can take now or as you explore the ideas in the coming chapters.

Looks Like/Sounds Like

After reading this chapter together, make three T-charts. What would it look and sound like for teachers, coaches, and principals to be engaged in this type of adult learning together? Think about time, roles, interactions, students, authority, curiosity, and system requirements. What's possible?

A Small Experiment

Make space to have some fun and experiment with teaching. Take some time to observe your students in a specific content or context, compare notes, and then choose something your team is curious to know more about. Perhaps you're wondering how to support more students in sharing developing ideas or you'd like to increase student-to-student discussions. The goal is to try and play with a teaching idea rather than be overly focused on implementing an idea correctly. You're not trying to model perfect teaching; rather, you're opening up space to think about teaching.

Watch and Reflect on a Video of Instruction

Watch a video clip of instruction where teachers and learners are engaged in discussion. Although no teaching is perfect, we are imagining you would select a video in which good teaching is on display. Notice what ideas are shared by the students and how those ideas are taken up in the discussion by the teacher and students. How does the teacher navigate the discussion? What's complex about the decisions that she is continually making? What questions might the teacher have about student learning when the discussion is over, and what might she consider doing next? What questions do you have about the racialized, gendered, and classed experience of the students in this class? How are students' community and cultural funds of knowledge invited, affirmed, and expanded through the interactions?

After you've had a chance to think about what's valuable about the way the teachers and students are interacting, using the trajectory as a tool for reflection, consider the learning pathway that the teacher might have traversed to get to this point in her practice.

Self-Reflect Using the Principles and the Learning Trajectory

Teacher:

- *Using the Trajectory*: Pick something in your teaching that you are really good at. Work backward and try to think of some major shifts you had to make along the way to get there. What helped you along?
- *Using the Principles for Teaching*: Print the Principles for Teaching and keep them on a clipboard for a day. After each chunk of instruction, take a moment to reflect on how aligned your teaching was to the principles. Did your students engage as sensemakers? What opportunities did you provide them to do that? Did you take notes about their thinking? Were you curious at times, and in ways that created new questions about your learners?
- *Using Past Growth Experiences*: Think about the content you least enjoy teaching as opposed to the content you love to teach. Be sure that you have a specific content area topic firmly in mind. Observe yourself and how you plan and engage students with that content. What's different about who you are and where you might place yourself on the trajectory? If you are farther along the trajectory in one content area, how did you get to that place?

Principal:

- *Using the Principles for Learning to Teach*: Reflect on the PD teachers engaged in last year. Using the Principles for Learning to Teach as the lens, reflect on how teachers were positioned and how they had opportunities to make sense of new ideas, to practice, and to learn together. Or examine decisions made in the spring or summer (like yearlong PD calendars) that may be limiting your responsiveness and/or are based on assumptions about either student or adult learners.

Coach:
- *Using the Principles for Teaching*: Think back on the last professional learning that you planned for teachers. Using the Principles for Teaching, and framing the teachers as your learners, how did you engage your learners as sensemakers? What opportunities did you provide them to do that? Did you take notes about their thinking? Were you curious at times, and in ways that created new questions about your learners?
- *Using the Principles for Learning to Teach*: How could you use the Principles for Learning to Teach to support the planning of your next professional learning? How can you integrate teaching together? How could spreading the learning over time and in multiple contexts (e.g., Grade-Level Team Meetings, Classroom Visits, and group planning) support sensemaking?

Identify Experiences That Support Adult Learning

In small groups, examine personal experiences with learning outside of school.

- Think of a time, outside of school, when you learned something new or difficult or you observed someone close to you learning. Tell a story about it.

As you share these stories, notice themes that relate to getting better at something. How was new knowledge gained? How were new practices developed? How were identities shaped? Who helped the learner, and how? Notice how the themes come together into a broader, more expansive view of learning that involve processes of knowing, doing, and becoming.

Identify What Professional Learning Norms Can Be Leveraged and What Can Be Strengthened

Learning to work collectively in ways that make our learning and teaching public requires intentionally changing the typical ways we interact around our teaching. What are your school's or team's norms? Does everyone agree? Did you think both about norms that support the work and those that constrain it? Use table 2.1 at the end of this chapter as fodder for this conversation about the predictable interactions or beliefs that are true in your context, and then try to figure out the assumptions that lie underneath them. For example, do teachers feel tense, worried, or judged when a principal or coach walks into their classrooms? If this is true, is it because teachers feel that they are continually being evaluated and feedback from these visits doesn't seem to actually support improvement? Is it because the visits are too infrequent or there isn't space to have conversations about what teachers are trying to do for the feedback to feel authentic? Perhaps teachers don't have faith that the principal or coach understands the instructional challenges they face.

It's valuable to examine what's happening in the school environment that perpetuates these feelings so you can explore what it would take to start shifting these dynamics so Classroom Visits are welcome and contribute to named goals for teacher learning. For example, it could help if, during a Classroom Visit, the principal or coach confers with students alongside the teacher so that they can debrief what each person learned from students.

Think about what's true in your own context and push each other to figure out why these interactions happen. These conversations may cause defensiveness. Try to guard against pointing fingers, knowing that the point of the conversation is to begin to imagine new ways of interacting with new intentions.

Next are two more norms we have observed in school contexts that tend to constrain good collaborative learning. See if they resonate with you and your context. If they don't, generate the ones that do authentically fit with your context:

- Sharing teaching practices is uncomfortable and infrequent.
- Trying new things is impossible in an already demanding and overwhelming job, so teachers publicly respond: "Are you asking me to do one more thing? I can't do one more thing."

Once you have a few points that ring true for you, write them in the table and then talk through them:

- What's underneath the reaction, feeling, or assumption?
- What are things that adults do or don't do that contribute to or perpetuate this?
- What might be an explicit way to work on shifting this?

We also know that most schools have valuable assets that foster collaboration. For example, teachers might be very willing to share materials they create. Many schools have schedules that allow teams to spend considerable time together. Teachers may work in teams that have a lot of fun together. Take the time to identify the ways of interacting that are positive and support collaborative learning in your building. Think about what enables those ways of interacting. How might you be able to use those strengths in service of changing the types of interactions that are constraining collaborations around making teaching and learning public?

Table 2.1 Assets and constraints in collaborating to make teaching and learning public

Assets			
Interactions, beliefs, or reactions at your school or on your team	What's underneath the reaction, feeling, or assumption?	What are things that adults do or don't do that contributes or perpetuates this?	What might be an explicit way to use this strength?
EXAMPLE: We trust our coach and are comfortable teaching in front of her.	She is in our rooms a lot and understands our kids and the challenges.	She offers to teach with us and asks our opinion in the moment while she's teaching. She doesn't assume that she could do it better.	If our principal/evaluator were in our rooms more and could teach with us sometimes, we'd feel more like she understands what it takes.
Constraints			
Interactions, beliefs, or reactions at your school or on your team	What's underneath the reaction, feeling, or assumption?	What are things that adults do or don't do that contributes or perpetuates this?	What might be an explicit way to use this strength?
EXAMPLE: When the principal or coach walks into a classroom, the teacher may feel tense, worried, or judged.	The principal is always evaluating me and does not actually give feedback to support me in getting better. The visits are too infrequent, so the feedback doesn't seem authentic. If the coach or principal doesn't really understand what the teacher is trying to accomplish, feedback is "off."	There is little time to talk about instructional intent and goals. Visits are tied to evaluation cycles that seem high stakes.	Begin to talk more about instructional goals. During a visit, confer together while students are at work and then debrief what you learned from the students.

3

Spaces and Practices to Support Learning and Collaboration

What kinds of professional learning spaces and practices allow teachers, coaches, and principals to work together in service of student learning? How do we create a workplace for teachers and school leaders to be in continual conversation with one another so they can successfully create the joyful and meaningful learning experiences they want for students? As we explained in chapter 2, an effective adult learning context requires time and space for everyone to be engaged together, learning alongside each other and students. In this chapter, we share the professional learning spaces and practices, which we refer to as a *professional learning system*, that allow teachers, coaches, and principals to work together in bold, invigorating new ways. Yes, we are talking about professional development, and as we said in chapter 1, we draw on many of the same tools and resources that most schools have. What is different is how we collaborate to facilitate team learning in and across these spaces. We continually work on connecting the work that happens in one space to other spaces to advance teacher, coach, and principal learning in service of our vision for student learning. The spaces you will read about in this chapter bring people together with enough frequency so teachers don't just learn new ideas and then become solely responsible for implementing them. Through this collaboration, everyone shares the responsibility for codeveloping the questions, ideas, and strategies that are tried and refined over time.

AN EXAMPLE OF A PROFESSIONAL LEARNING SYSTEM

The professional learning system across the schools in our research-practice partnership involves five learning and collaboration spaces with interdependent purposes and practices:

- *Learning Labs* are embedded professional learning experiences for grade-level teams led by instructional coaches that take place about four times a year, during the school day, and at the teachers' school. The principal participates actively in this space. Learning Labs can be half day or full day.
- *Grade-Level Team Meetings* are weekly meetings, forty-five minutes long, led by coaches for a grade-level team to carry forward new learning from the Learning Labs, as well as plan for and analyze student learning as units unfold over the course of the year. Based on priorities set in the Instructional Leadership Team meetings and experiences in the Learning Labs, the principal participates actively in select meetings. In our schools, we call these meetings "professional learning communities (PLCs)." Because PLCs are often associated with locally agreed upon protocols, we have opted to use a more general term in this book, *Grade-Level Team Meetings*.
- *Individual Classroom Visits* are brief visits to classrooms across the school where teachers engage in one-on-one collaborations with either an instructional coach or the principal.
- *Informal Hallway Conversations* and quick check-ins are more spontaneous spaces that help teachers, coaches, and principals to remain connected as ideas and practices evolve.

Instructional Leadership Team (ILT) Meetings are weekly meetings during which school leaders (principal, assistant principal, and all instructional coaches) meet to set teacher learning goals, assess and reflect on plans for meeting those goals, make necessary adjustments, and coordinate responsibilities and actions for supporting teacher learning across the learning and collaboration spaces in the school.

This professional learning system has iteratively developed over time based on our specific context. We know that context matters. These spaces work for us, but it's just one possible configuration of a learning system. There are other possibilities. You'll need to carefully examine what's possible in the contexts in which you work and identify a feasible starting point. In the elementary schools we work with:

- Each school serves approximately three hundred fifty to five hundred students and has two to four teachers per grade level.
- Each school has a principal and an assistant principal.
- Each school has two to three content-specific coaches that work with all eighteen to twenty-five classroom teachers in one subject area.
- Teachers have daily planning periods of forty-five minutes and have collectively agreed to use two of them per week as a collaborative Grade-Level Team Meeting time facilitated by a coach. In addition, the principal participates in at least one meeting with each grade-level team per week.
- With district sponsorship and union collaboration, the work, which began in one school, has grown to a network of six schools. All six schools are guided by the same set of principles and make decisions about how to enact the resources of the professional learning system to meet the unique needs of their own school communities.

TEACHERS' VIEWS OF A STRONG PROFESSIONAL LEARNING SYSTEM

As we describe the professional learning system more fully and how the spaces are facilitated by coaches and principals, you may find yourself thinking that it is a top-down system where teachers are "made" to teach in particular ways. Remember that we do not believe that teaching is something that is done to students. Nor do we believe that professional learning is something that is done to teachers. We believe that leadership matters because the point of having coaches and principals attending to teacher learning is that they are continually considering how the Principles for Teaching, Learning to Teach, and the Adult Learning Context are helping teachers to create thriving learning environments for students. Here's how two teachers explained what mattered to them:

> I like to know that I'm not just in my classroom teaching and doing my thing, and everyone thinks it's fine and dandy and lets me go about doing my own thing. Because I'd like to know that I'm part of a bigger picture and that I'm connected to what everyone else is doing. So if the principal is not in here seeing what we're doing or in any other classrooms seeing what they're doing, then I feel like, how do you know that this is all being connected? Are our students going to be held to the same standards when they leave my room and go to first grade? But because she's in here and she's working with us and she's working with first grade and she's working with all of the grade levels, I know that she knows what we're holding the students accountable to and what they're capable of. And she's going to make sure that those same standards are held through all of the grade levels. That's important because you don't want to come in and feel like you're just one isolated little classroom. Or at least I don't.
>
> *Kindergarten teacher*

> When we first were labeled a failing school, we had a conversation about what we needed to help our kids be successful. There were a lot of material things that we were asking for, like more teachers, more whatever. And then now, the flip side, seeing the things we have in place that are helping us be successful have nothing to do with things that we have. It's the practices that are in place, the practices that are almost sacred to us now, that we really don't want people to touch. Like the fact that we have a literacy Grade-Level Team Meeting and a math one every week, that we have Learning Labs where we get to go into classes and do some research surrounding kids' thinking.
>
> *Second-grade teacher*

What these teachers are saying is how much they value being part of something bigger in their school and understanding that school leaders—the principal, the assistant principal, and the instructional coaches—are paying attention to what is happening for students and teachers across the whole school. Because school leaders are with teachers and students in both formal and informal spaces across the school, they better understand what teachers are doing, what challenges they are facing, and what insights they are gaining.

Teachers also have access to each other's classrooms and come to rely on collaborating as a way of making progress in meeting goals for their students. These ways of working together reflect an important principle for learning to teach which we call "making practice public." The teachers we have worked with continually emphasize the importance of this principle in improving their practice, as well as changing what it feels like to work with one another. A third-grade teacher put it this way: "It's amazing how making teaching public has changed my practice but also the culture of the school, how teachers view themselves. As opposed to just being focused on leading our own classrooms, it's like we are intellectual members of our community. It's changed everything."

THE PURPOSE, STRUCTURE, AND RESPONSIBILITIES IN EACH PROFESSIONAL LEARNING SPACE

As you read the detailed explanations of each space, please bear in mind that our goal is to help you understand the intention, design, and goals for each; we do not want you to conclude that our design is the right or only way to create a good professional learning system. What matters is creating the conditions in the school for teachers, coaches, and principals to learn well together and alongside their students. As you read through our more detailed descriptions of each space, try to not get caught up in thinking, "Well, that could never happen in our school." Rather, focus on these questions:

- How do the different learning spaces serve different purposes?

- How do the different learning spaces work together to create a coherent learning experience for all adults?
- How are the principled ideas about instruction, learning to teach, and leadership from chapter 2 intentionally enacted across the system?

Learning Labs

The Purpose of Learning Labs In our research practice partnership work, we have created a space for professional learning that we call "Learning Labs."[1] Learning Labs are anchors for introducing and making sense of the big ideas related to instruction and student learning. They are concentrated, immersive learning experiences during which teachers, usually in their grade-level teams, along with a coach, a principal, and specialists, delve deeply into honing their instructional decision-making skills and practices. Each team has four to six Labs during the year, and they take place during the school day, ranging from three hours to a full day. Each Learning Lab also includes teaching a lesson together in one of the teacher's classrooms. Learning Labs create the grounding experience for the commitments that teachers, specialists, coaches, and the principal will follow through on in Grade-Level Team Meetings, informal conversations, and Classroom Visits. In our schools, everyone looks forward to being part of a Learning Lab; the atmosphere is both serious and light-hearted. The time is treasured, and the opportunity to spend time with students is always inspiring and invigorating.

The Learning Lab is a place to experiment with new ideas to build specialized capacities for teaching that are an essential part of the craft and intellectual work of teaching. Learning Labs consist of cycles of investigating new ideas, crafting and teaching lessons based on those new ideas, and experimenting and reflecting on those ideas together. In the Labs, guided by our Principles for Learning to Teach, students' ideas and experiences are always a central part of investigating and reflecting on practice. Teachers develop shared understandings and goals for the classroom learning communities they are trying to foster. By making their questions and insights public to one another, Learning Labs help teachers cultivate practices that match their shared beliefs. For example, teachers may agree about the importance of orienting students to one another during a discussion. But what that means to each may actually be different. During a Learning Lab, they can work together to develop the specific moves to make in particular situations so that students listen to and respond to each other rather than always directing their comments to the teacher. Thus, Learning Labs are a time to learn alongside each other and students, leveraging the collective knowledge of the team.

Coaches plan and lead Learning Labs with particular teacher learning goals in mind. These goals are identified through conversations with teachers, the principal, and other coaches, and in relation to the disciplinary standards and student learning goals at each grade level. Clearly identifying teacher learning goals supports teachers to engage in intentional learning about students' sensemaking and social relationships both during the Lab and once back in their classrooms.

Here are some examples of teacher learning goals:

- Learn how to facilitate discussions to foster equitable participation—both talking and listening—in the context of text-based discussions in literacy.
- Learn how to create a public class record that students can use as their sensemaking about a particular scientific concept develops.
- Learn how to invite and draw on children's community and family funds of knowledge in the context of particular content, such as mathematical modeling situations.
- Learn the progression of students' approximations as they practice and gain proficiency as writers in different genres.

The learning goals are substantial enough to be worked on across a unit, or even the year, and merit continued engagement across other teacher learning spaces, and yet they are specific enough for teachers to deepen their subject matter knowledge. Because we are committed to the principle that teaching is both intellectual work and a craft, we recognize that teaching requires specialized knowledge and skills. Teachers need ongoing opportunities to deepen their knowledge and practices about subject matter, how children's ideas develop, and how to build equitable learning environments. They also need opportunities to share and examine their instructional decision-making; this includes opportunities to analyze their stance toward schooling and its impact on children who belong to many different racial, cultural, and linguistic communities. Each Learning Lab drives the need to continue the work in Grade-Level Team Meetings and individual classrooms following the Lab as teachers pursue subject matter goals and try on new practices.

> " In Labs, I get to really deeply understand what the standards are, what we want kids to understand, know, and be able to do. We practice that; we do the tasks or activities ourselves. It also helps me when we plan a lesson and go in and teach a class that experimental lesson. It's more detailed planning than I would do myself for a lesson. But it really helps me think about exactly how I want to say something and what I do not want to give away. It really helps me identify what part of the load is mine and what part of the load is going to be the kids'.
>
> *Fifth-grade teacher*

Learning Labs have been a foundational means for extending time for teachers' collaborative learning in our work, but there are other similar structures for collective learning, such as Lesson Study, Lesson Studios, and Video Clubs.[2] Depending on the context, resources, and personnel, these and other collective learning structures can serve a similar purpose.

The Structure of Learning Labs   In this chapter, we want to give you an overview of Learning Labs. Other chapters will help you think about how Learning Labs are a key element of supporting teacher learning. In chapter 4, we share a case that illustrates how the focus of a Learning Lab helps teachers with an emergent instructional challenge. In chapter 6, you'll gain insight into how a coach plans and facilitates the Learning Lab and then threads ideas from the Learning Labs to Grade-Level Team Meetings and Classroom Visits. We also offer a set of resources that provide additional guidance about how to use Learning Labs in your own setting.[3]

Whether three hours long or six, Learning Labs have four phases. They begin with new learning. Based on the learning goals for the Lab, the coach selects a reading, a video clip, artifacts of practice, a subject matter task like a mathematics problem, a literacy practice, or a science concept that allows everyone to dig into material that deepens and pushes on their current understandings (see figure 3.1). The subject matter focus is always relevant to what teachers are teaching or are about to teach. This collective exploration phase of the Learning Lab generates the impetus for experimenting with some aspect of the teaching and learning process.

Once the teacher learning for the day has been introduced and explored, the second phase begins. In this phase, the group identifies a related student learning goal, and everyone works together to plan a lesson that they will enact together in one of the teacher's classrooms. The planning process usually takes thirty to forty minutes. Again, the coach has done some work toward considering what the possible starting point or focus of the lesson might be and whose classroom will be visited.

Figure 3.1   Planning together involves teachers, coaches, and principals making sense of the subject matter content

Source: Matt Hagen

Learning Lab participants create a plan for the lesson together. The plan is loose enough that there's room to shift things during the enactment, but it is clear enough that everyone understands what they as teachers are hoping to learn about students' experiences and develop understanding as they enact the lesson. The goal is not to teach the perfect lesson or to make sure that students learn something very specific by the end. Rather, it is to learn from and with students so that when teachers return to their classrooms, they feel better prepared to make instructional decisions (see figure 3.2).

In the third phase of the Learning Lab, participants lead the lesson in one teacher's classroom. The teacher who hosts the lesson usually does not teach it to avoid getting distracted by the need to prove something about their own or their students' abilities. Host teachers report that it is a welcome opportunity to see their students in action without having to worry about being the person leading the lesson. One or two other participants in the Lab, including the coach or principal, take the lead in facilitating the lesson. By regularly volunteering to be one of the lead teachers, coaches and principals convey and model how important it is to take some risks during the lesson and let go of the need to be perfect. It takes some time to build these norms of experimentation when first starting Learning Labs.

> " Being really flexible is a huge part of a Learning Lab. Being open to your colleagues' thoughts and opinions about what they think you should try next or what you should do to make it better. Not being afraid to make mistakes is something that we teach the kids is totally OK and that it's the only way that you're going to learn, and I think that is represented in a Lab as well. Taking risks and trying things out is the biggest way that we're going to learn and see what works well and what doesn't. And then going back in and reflecting is something that's also a big part of the Lab. How can we adjust for our own classrooms?
>
> *Fourth-grade teacher*

Figure 3.2   During Classroom Visits, everyone listens carefully to learn from and with students

Source: Matt Hagen

> ❝ In the beginning, it felt like the Classroom Visit of Labs was more focused on me as a teacher, and now it seems like it's more focused on this new practice that's going to help students. How can we make it make sense for students? It's like we're all building this new thing together and we don't know how to do it necessarily, but

> we're all helping each other get there. I didn't realize that, but I think that probably the biggest shift for me is, it seemed like it was less about me as a teacher and it's more about the students as learners.
>
> *Fifth-grade teacher*

During the lesson, we typically pause several times to confer with each other or with students to calibrate and make adjustments if necessary. These pauses have come to be expected as a norm in the school, and the students know that adults are learning as well. We affectionately call these pauses "Teacher Time Outs."[4] During these brief pauses—sometimes lasting just a few seconds, sometimes fifteen to thirty seconds—Learning Lab participants can ask each other a question, confirm a shift in an instructional decision, or pose a new idea that has emerged from talking with or listening to students. Everyone participates: the coach, the principal, and the teachers. And anyone can initiate. Examples of how Teacher Time Outs get initiated include:

- "How about we ask students to turn and talk now?"
- "I think it might be helpful if we ask this question next."
- "Ooh, I'd love to see what students might do if we asked them to draw this idea out."
- "Should we do this next or that?"
- "Before we move on, can we hear what students meant when they said ____."
- "I'm not sure what to do next."

Because we are all taking new risks, the lesson plan has to be adjusted, or sometimes it really goes sideways, or the students say something that we completely did not expect. Just like any teaching, we have to think on our feet, and this provides the rare opportunity to look to each other for ideas.

The reason why teachers say Teacher Time Outs are a practice that has come to be sacred and welcome, rather than one that undermines their authority with students, is that we always frame working together as experimenting with all the ideas that occur to us during lessons because often they can be pursued only in the moment. By giving each other permission to pause the lesson, we do not have to wait until after the lesson to reflect and say, "I wish we had asked this." The Classroom Visits during Learning Labs are always invigorating and generate new surprises and puzzles that require ongoing reflection. We often get asked how the children feel about Teacher Time Outs. Is it a waste of their time? Are we treating them as guinea pigs? We always tell the children at the beginning of each Classroom Visit that this is one of those special days when they get to be our teachers. They giggle and laugh, but because we treat their ideas as gifts to us, they come to understand that their teachers have to find ways to learn and make mistakes just as they do. It's not unusual for students to also weigh in on a Teacher Time Out and give the teachers suggestions for what to try next: "I think we should be in a circle." "Yes, we need a turn and talk now." "Let's talk about the second question." "Can we draw that?"

The fourth phase of the Learning Lab is collectively processing the visit to think more deeply about what the group learned (see figure 3.3). The

Figure 3.3 Teachers, principals, and coaches collectively reflect on instructional decision-making

Source: Matt Hagen

collective reflection is an important step in establishing a shared vision and agreements about practices that support students. If the Learning Lab is a full day rather than a half day, there is usually time to reflect on what happened in the first Classroom Visit, make revisions, and try the revised lesson in a second classroom. Building on their shared learning, the Learning Lab ends by establishing commitments about what the team will try in their own classrooms to integrate the new insights that have emerged from the Learning Lab into their own instructional practice.

Finally, the next date when teachers will specifically follow up on the ideas in the Learning Lab is usually confirmed so the coach and/or principal can be sure to swing by the teachers' classrooms to continue to participate and support as each teacher puts these new ideas, learning, and strategies into practice.

Teacher, Coach, and Principal Responsibilities in Learning Labs   The Learning Lab in some ways is a playground, an incubator, a launching point for what a grade-level team is specifically working on with respect to instruction. Successful Learning Labs have important implications for how everyone is prepared to participate in it and to keep the commitments that emerge from it. Students, of course, are also essential partners in teachers' development, so students must be positioned competently and their contributions during lessons have to drive everything.

Coaches, teachers, and principals work together to identify the focus. Coaches prepare the learning activities, the discussion prompts and any readings, and materials for the Lab, including arranging ahead of time which classrooms will be visited and when. Principals help to shape the learning goals ahead of time and then come ready to learn alongside teachers, especially attentive to any implications the new learnings will have for the support teachers may need in between Labs.

Here's how one coach explained the impact of a principal's active participation:

> By embracing Learning Labs as a learner, by jumping into it saying, "I'm going to learn this," the principal was modeling exactly what she wanted the teachers to do. If you jump in as a learner, if you say, "This is

fascinating, I want to learn this too." And you make some mistakes and you get messy, then teachers go, "Ah, OK. This is how we learn together." By jumping up to try out our lessons, even the ones that kind of went sideways, she modeled that it's OK to try and fail. In fact, it's even a good thing. She modeled, "This is so important to me that I will set everything aside"—which for a principal is next to impossible. She was learning exactly what it is that teachers are supposed to be doing so that when she walks into their classrooms they don't ever have to explain to her, "This is what I'm doing." She just knows.

Math coach

In this description, we see a range of purposes in the principal's active participation: modeling engagement as a learner, fostering risk taking, conveying importance, and digging deeply into what teachers are learning. They participate in rather than just observe all the activities of the Labs. Reciprocally, teachers have to embrace the opportunity to engage in shared inquiry with their colleagues and principals and coaches, not expecting them to have the answers or tell them what to do. Chapters 5 and 6 delve more deeply and specifically into how teachers, principals, and coaches must partner across these spaces.

We know that spaces like Learning Labs are not common in schools. In our experience, they are vital for building trust and continuing to flatten status differences between more and less experienced teachers and between school leaders and teachers. Coaches and principals have to plan and participate in these spaces intentionally to provide teachers the opportunity to uncover their feelings of nervousness or fear and develop a willingness to be vulnerable and experiment with teaching with one another. Acknowledging these feelings and uncertainties is vital to making practice public. Intentionally taking the time to discuss why Teacher Time Outs might be helpful, what they communicate about thinking together, and how they are not meant to be used to correct each other is important.

Grade-Level Team Meetings

The Purpose of Grade-Level Team Meetings   Grade-Level Team Meetings can serve several purposes, each one requiring that teachers and coaches come ready to collaborate to meet the intended goal for the day. One purpose is to engage and act on the commitments about student learning and instructional practices initiated in the Learning Labs. A second purpose is to work continually on the content and instruction of each unit, responding to what teachers and students are experiencing as the unit unfolds, carefully following students' progress. Based on the composition of the particular grade-level team, whether there are new teachers to the grade level or the school, the purposes can shift. New teachers may need a different kind of content support, for example, and may also bring new practices that the team will want to experiment with.

The Structure of Grade-Level Team Meetings The schools in our research practice partnership hold two Grade-Level Team Meetings facilitated by an instructional coach each week. Each meeting is roughly forty-five minutes long. Because the meeting content is shaped by how it falls in relation to a Learning Lab and in relation to the particular unit of instruction, the flow of conversation and tasks change to reflect the purpose. While the particular focus of the conversation will change from meeting to meeting, what is common in all of them is that teachers are continually sharing the instructional decisions they are making and what is happening in their classrooms as a result. Because teachers always make the decisions that make the most sense to them, hearing each other's ideas helps them reflect on the relationship between their decisions and student learning. Teachers outside our network are often surprised about the regularity with which teachers meet as a team and with their coaches. A third-grade teacher explained what makes this kind of meeting so important to her:

> I never feel like "I'm good, I got it." And I think friends that work at other schools are like, "I can't believe you would agree to give up two planning periods a week." Well, if I didn't, I would be spending way more time trying to figure out "How do I do this?" And it's fun for me to think about teaching, and think about how to make it better, and "Why is this not working for this particular crew when I felt like it worked well last year?" "Now hold on, all of this adding and subtracting is really, really hard for the majority of my kids and then really, really easy for these two and I'm like super stressed, and my

colleagues are like 'Me too!'" And now we are doing different math lessons for the next four days because we're meeting the needs of our kids.

As this third-grade teacher explained, Grade-Level Team Meetings involve a lot of troubleshooting, conjecturing, and designing the kinds of lessons that will help students access and be successful in meeting subject matter goals. The Grade-Level Team Meetings immediately following a Learning Lab are focused on extending the ideas that emerged in the Learning Lab and the commitments that teachers made. Typically, the coach and principal have been in classrooms with teachers for these follow-ups, and during the Grade-Level Team Meeting, the agenda is focused on instructional decisions and examining student responses. Grade-Level Team Meetings also are a place to make sense of the flow of ideas across new units of instruction. Early in a unit, the grade-level team checks in about how students in each classroom are making sense of the important ideas. Coaches facilitate the conversation by inviting teachers to discuss in detail the emerging understandings that students are showing, and they help surface for teachers the different decisions that they are making.

> " We try hard to have the bulk of the meeting time focused on making sense of upcoming instructional units, understanding students' approaches and ideas about subject matter learning, and making sense of student data instead of calendaring, dividing up tasks, or discussing concerns about what students can't do.
>
> *Math coach*

> The Grade-Level Team Meetings are not about fidelity of implementation—they are about making our instructional decision-making visible to each other. As a coach, I can raise questions around experiences that should be coherent for students but might not yet be. And I can help bring teachers' good ideas to each other.
>
> *Math coach*

Teacher, Coach, and Principal Responsibilities in Grade-Level Team Meetings   Coaches and teachers both have important responsibilities to make the Grade-Level Team Meetings productive. Because the coach is responsible for facilitating the conversations, she spends a lot of time in classrooms and considers what she is observing in order to decide what to prioritize during the forty-five-minute discussion. Considerations might include problems of practice that teachers are encountering, student sensemaking, and the need to revise lessons from existing curricular resources. The coach draws on her weekly visits to classrooms, her experience in the Learning Labs, the perspectives shared at ILTs, her familiarity with the current unit materials, her deep knowledge of standards, and input from teachers. Typically, the day before the grade-level team meets, the coach sends an email with the agenda for the meeting. The coaches with whom we work maintain a running document with past agendas, notes, and commitments that support the work moving forward.

Teachers' preparation for and responsibility in the Grade-Level Team Meeting are just as important as the coach's. Teachers often teach particular lessons around the same time so they can bring their observations, reflections, and student work to the meeting. Samples of student work or notes from a classroom discussion are often examined during Grade-Level Team Meetings. Active participation during the meeting is essential for everyone's learning. Teachers bring their own questions about their instructional decisions and their students' learning and come prepared to discuss the commitments made in prior Grade-Level Team Meetings, listen carefully, and ask each other questions as the conversation unfolds.

> " You have to be really accountable when you come to Grade-Level Team Meetings. My coach will help us know what we need to bring and what we are going to be talking about. So you go in and there's an agenda, and you're going to be expected to discuss these certain things and show this kind of work. That's been one of the coolest things when we get to share the work that our students have been doing and then talk about our instruction. It's really cool, and we

get to see and get our coach's feedback too on what we see my class doing and what my colleague's class is doing and how it's similar and how it's different.

Fourth-grade teacher

Principals participate in Grade-Level Team Meetings across the school and support the coach in identifying priorities and pacing the work for teams. They must know each team's current practices well enough to contribute to the developing thinking during the meeting, but also across the professional learning system. Typically, principals attend one of the weekly Grade-Level Team Meetings for each team, often strategically choosing which to attend in response to new ideas that are being learned in Learning Labs and emergent needs that are discussed in ILTs. The principal's participation is an important opportunity for her to support teacher collaboration practices and the team's efforts to enact the developing practices that support the current goals.

The same principles that guide teacher learning in Learning Labs underpin Grade-Level Team Meetings. Teachers are open to sharing their practice, building trust with one another as they embrace the ideas that the whole team is getting better together and the students at the grade level are all their students. When teachers share student work or exit tickets, it's done in the spirit of being responsive to student sensemaking, not competing with one another. Whether instructional obstacles are common across the grade level or unique to particular classrooms, the Grade-Level Team Meeting is an important space that enables teachers and coaches to be responsive to student sensemaking and learning experiences on a weekly basis.

Individual Classroom Visits

The Purpose of Individual Classroom Visits Another setting for professional learning that emerged in our research practice partnership work is individual Classroom Visits. They have an important purpose—namely, supporting teachers and instructional leaders to engage in instructional decision-making together *in the moment* and *with students*. It is a space where ideas from the Learning Labs and Grade-Level Team Meetings continue to be worked on.

If you are a teacher, we invite you to pause and think about the last time an instructional leader was in your classroom: *What was the purpose of the visit? How did you feel leading up to the visit and during the visit? Did you do any additional planning or preparation? What was the role of the instructional leader during the visit? How did students react? How did you feel after the visit?*

If you are a coach or a principal, we invite you to pause and think about the last time you were in a classroom: *What was the purpose of the visit? What kinds of interactions did you have with the teacher before, during, or after the visit? How did students react to you being in the classroom?*

Often, the idea of coaches or principals visiting classrooms can feel stressful for teachers and students. Teachers might feel pressure to do additional planning to make the lesson stand out in some way. And students might feel pressure to perform. And both teachers and students worry that each move they make is being watched and evaluated by the visitors to the classroom.

We aim for a different kind of experience for teachers and students in the schools where we work. Classroom Visits are not about providing corrective feedback or modeling a perfect lesson. Nor are they about providing an "extra set of hands" to help the teacher succeed. Instead, Classroom Visits have developed into an opportunity for coaches or principals to join teachers and students in whatever is happening in the moment. It might be collaborative problem solving or taking a pause to think together about the next instructional decision. If the students are sitting on the rug in the middle of an interactive read-aloud or number talk, the coach or principal sits on the carpet right alongside them. If students are writing independently or exploring a mathematical task and the teacher is conferring with them, the coach or principal might jump right in—either conferring with students and comparing notes with the teacher or even joining the teacher in her conferring. When coaches and principals enter a classroom, they position themselves as a student of the students and a thought partner with the teacher. The teachers we work with have described how

Classroom Visits are a space that supports their learning and continued growth:

> Mid-teaching, we'll do a Teacher Time Out, just off the cuff. It's really cool to have that relationship where she's not coming in to judge me. She's coming in to try to help me figure out how to best get the kids to where they need to be, and if that means jumping in and having a conversation with me or asking the kids a question that I haven't thought of or coming up to me as the kids are working and suggesting something or asking a question, it's really helpful.
>
> *Fifth-grade teacher*

> When my principal or coach jumps into a lesson and asks, "I wonder what would happen if we ask them this, or what would happen if we tried to do it this way?" Then we'd have a little conversation and kids see that happening. We're learning too. The kids don't even notice anymore when people walk into the classroom. Because it's not a big deal. You can have a genuine learning conversation in front of the kids with a colleague, and then go back into the lesson. And it's a normal thing. I think of it as open-source teaching.
>
> *Fourth-grade teacher*

Classroom Visits also help teachers, principals, and coaches be in sync with each other. For teachers, there are opportunities to continue the work and conversations started in other professional learning spaces. For principals and coaches, there are opportunities to see and experience how strategies and ideas from Learning Labs and Grade-Level Team Meetings are taken up—celebrating when exciting things unfold, sharing ideas across classrooms, and engaging in new problems of practice that emerge. And all three roles can draw on their experiences in classrooms as they consider future goals for both teacher and student learning.

The Structure of Classroom Visits Learning Labs and Grade-Level Team Meetings tend to be formalized through schoolwide master schedules and calendars, whereas Classroom Visits tend to be more flexibly scheduled in response to the learning that is happening in the other professional learning spaces.

We have found that it is essential for both the coach and the principal to each visit all classrooms on a regular basis (although not necessarily together), with the goal of continuing to learn and work on instructional practice together. We are often asked, "How often should I visit classrooms?" or "How often should my coach or principal visit my classroom?" The answer is more complex than a number. Classroom Visits should be frequent enough that they feel like business-as-usual to everyone: students, teachers, coach(es), and the principal. To participate in ongoing conversations about instructional decisions, they have to know firsthand what students and teachers are experiencing.

Classroom Visits should also be ongoing. In other schools, coaches often work with just a few teachers for a short cycle (e.g., six weeks) and frequent Classroom Visits occur only as part of that cycle. In the schools we work in, the coaches and principals visit all classrooms regularly across the whole school year.

And yes, this can feel overwhelming at first. For teachers who are used to principals visiting one to two times a year to evaluate them, you might feel anxious when you imagine coaches and principals visiting on a regular basis. For coaches who are used to working with just a few teachers at a time or principals who visit classrooms around evaluation cycles, you might wonder how you can possibly get into every teacher's classroom on a regular basis. We have learned a lot through our research practice partnership about structuring Classroom Visits in ways that are intentional and connected to the learning happening in Learning Labs and Grade-Level Team Meetings. Teachers predictably develop an appreciation for these visits and even integrated them into their planning process, and coaches and principals share their enthusiasm about their value and impact:

- "In my old school, you always knew ahead of time if a coach or principal would be coming. It was always scheduled. So it was a shift when I came to this school. But learning about Teacher Time Outs in my first Learning Lab and then seeing that my coaches and principals really were willing to jump in to a lesson with me ended up being a real game changer." —Second-grade teacher

- "One thing I've started doing as part of my planning process is emailing my coaches and asking them to join me for something I'm not sure about or something I'm working on. Last week, I asked my literacy coach to join me for a mini-lesson because my pacing is off. They are taking way too long. My kids aren't getting enough writing time, and I'm not sure how to adjust it. Next week, the math coach is going to come in during a subtraction number talk because I want another person listening to kids' strategies and thinking with me about how to represent their ideas." —*Fourth-grade teacher*
- "At the end of each week, I add Classroom Visits for the next week to my calendar as appointments. This holds me accountable to actually getting in classrooms." —*Math coach*
- "It's not physically possible to be in every classroom every week so I have to prioritize. Each week, my two highest priorities are the grade-level team that just had a Learning Lab and the grade-level team that has the next Learning Lab. This way, I can be sure to support the learning from the previous week, as well as check in with how things are going for the team who I'll work with in the coming week." —*Literacy coach*
- "I tried to visit classes for an entire math block and it was pretty much impossible to get to every classroom in a timely manner. After talking with other math coaches, I tried shorter visits. For example, I might visit all of the third-grade classes for fifteen-ish minutes on the same day. Or try and see a number talk in each of the fifth-grade classrooms in the same week. I still do some longer visits, but it has been really surprising how much learning we can do together in just ten- or twenty-minute visits!" —*Math coach*
- "We started a routine at the end of Learning Labs where we make concrete plans for what we're going to try next and schedule either the coach or myself to be with each teacher so we can try it out together." —*Principal*

Teacher, Coach, and Principal Responsibilities in Classroom Visits For Classroom Visits to become a space where teachers, coaches, and principals learn together, each person has important responsibilities. Coaches and principals are responsible for making Classroom Visits a priority in their schedules, visiting often enough that teachers and students are not surprised when they walk in the door. Coaches and principals are also responsible for entering the classroom and positioning themselves as a student of the students and a thought partner with the teacher. If leaders want teachers to value vulnerability, risk taking, and effort, leaders are responsible for engaging in these ways themselves. This might mean that the coach or principal finds herself standing alongside the teacher with a marker in hand ready to record a student's idea mid-lesson or responding to a question posed by the teacher during a Teacher Time Out.

Teachers have equally important responsibilities during Classroom Visits. An important part of learning to teach is making teaching public. Teachers are responsible for being open to transparently sharing their instructional decisions, as well as their questions or problems of practice. If teachers aim to "perform" their best teaching when coaches and principals are in their classrooms, there will be fewer opportunities to be thought partners who focus on students' ideas and experiences. By raising questions about instructional moves, students' ideas, and content, teachers can invite coaches and principals to grapple with the complexities of teaching that feel relevant in that moment.

The Classroom Visits that serve the purpose we describe here require thoughtful planning when building a schoolwide instructional schedule. For many reasons, the schools we work in have a master schedule that establishes when different content blocks are taught at each grade level. This ensures that, for example, math instruction is spread across the day. If mathematics were taught only in the mornings, it would make it very difficult for the math coach to visit classrooms on a regular basis.

Informal Hallway Conversations

The Purpose of Informal Hallway Conversations Outside of the formal scheduled times that teachers, coaches, and principals have to work with one another, the informal touch points are timely and critical opportunities to continue conversations and connect ideas across spaces and people.

The Structure of Informal Hallway Conversations Inspiration and unexpected realizations foster the momentum and joy of learning together. They literally can't be scheduled! Informal and brief conversations spontaneously emerge as educators bump into each other in the hallway or the office and take the opportunity to share their exciting or puzzling insights or realizations. Updating each other in real time keeps us connected and engaged between scheduled meetings and ensures that that quick story or really important question is heard and woven into the group's developing thinking and will be included in the follow-up conversations.

Instructional Leadership Team Meetings

The Purpose of Instructional Leadership Team Meetings ILT Meetings are weekly meetings where school leaders (principal, assistant principal, and all instructional coaches) have dedicated time to operationalizing their commitment to the guiding principles. It is the time where they step out of the fray to ask: Are we working on the right work consistent with all our principles? Are we doing what we committed to doing?

- Are the *Principles for Teaching* guiding the way we design student learning experiences?
- Are the *Principles for Learning to Teach* guiding the way we design teacher learning experiences?
- Are our plans and decisions in alignment with the *Principles for the Adult Learning Context*?

It is the space where leaders engage in their commitment to principled leadership by assessing and reflecting on how instructional and collaborative practices are developing, making adjustments, and coordinating messaging and support. They share what they are observing and work together to make sense of what they are seeing and hearing from teachers across the school to make decisions about what's next for teacher learning.

The Structure of Instructional Leadership Team Meetings ILT Meetings happen weekly for sixty to ninety minutes and include the principal, assistant principal, and two to three content-specific instructional coaches. These meetings are held each week at the same time and take into careful consideration coordinating schedules to mitigate the impact on the school. For some schools, this means ILT Meetings are held an hour before school starts; in other schools, ILT Meetings happen during the day.

ILT Meetings are facilitated by the principal, but the agendas change in relation to what's been happening in different learning spaces, as well as what opportunities are coming up. The meetings involve rich discussions, with everyone in the group asking questions, sharing ideas and perspectives, and positioning teachers as both sensemakers and decision-makers.

Coach and Principal Responsibilities in Instructional Leadership Team Meetings   Each ILT member is responsible for making ILT Meetings a productive space for developing, attending to, and adjusting plans to support teacher and student learning. As the leader of the school, the principal is responsible for holding the vision and learning priorities for the school, leading decisions about what will be focused on within and across school years.

Coaches are responsible for helping the principal develop the vision and learning priorities, often asking questions and offering feedback based on their content expertise and experiences working with teachers across learning spaces.

The principal, assistant principal, and coaches have some shared responsibilities. All are responsible for visiting classrooms on a regular basis so they have firsthand experience as the group makes decisions. All are responsible for positioning students as sensemakers, teachers as decision-makers, and holding the group accountable for staying aligned to the principles. Everyone in the group is responsible for participating in discussions: asking questions, sharing ideas, pressing one other. And everyone is responsible for following through on commitments and decisions the group makes collectively.

Sometimes we get asked how teachers feel about principals and coaches having a meeting space about teacher learning that doesn't involve teachers. In our experience, teachers both appreciate and understand the need for leaders to plan together and coordinate professional learning across spaces.

> ❝We're totally aware that they're meeting all the time, and we could all infer that they're talking about how the kids are doing or what they're seeing in our classrooms. Like if I was really struggling with something and the coach was coming into my classroom every day and I was having a really hard time, I wouldn't be surprised if the principal knew. Because for both of them, their role is to support us, helping our kids understand whatever it is that we're teaching them. I don't ever think it comes from a place of trying to get anyone in trouble. It's how can we support the teacher or how can we support the kids? And I think that's because the kids are at the center of everything we do.
>
> *First-grade teacher*
>
> Basically, if you're a teacher at this school and you're committed to the work, then everything you do is transparent. How students do and what you do is readily available for your colleagues to see, for the coaches to see, for the principal to see at any time and to receive helpful feedback.
>
> *Fourth-grade teacher*

ILT Meetings are not a secret space hidden from teachers. And while teachers may not know exactly what happens in the meetings, teachers understand how transparency and open communication across roles results in centering students and supporting teachers. Because they see the results of leaders' decisions across the learning spaces in the school, teachers see that the school leaders position them as competent and trustworthy sensemakers and decision-makers. Chapter 6 delves more completely into the ILT roles and process.

CRAFTING A COHERENT PROFESSIONAL LEARNING SYSTEM

When we have described the various professional learning spaces to others, sometimes people respond, "Oh, we should do Learning Labs at our school." However, while Learning Labs are powerful, they alone do not constitute a full and rich professional learning system in the school. What matters for teacher learning is the shared and ongoing effort leaders and teachers exert to make the learning coherent and the work uplifting, joyful, and focused at the same time! In most schools, this means that the fundamental structure of a teacher's day, a coach's day, or a principal's day needs to change. In most schools, this means that the structure of a week, month, and school year must also change. A few days of in-service professional development scattered throughout the year are not enough for the kind of transformational learning we are talking about in this book. The principles we ascribe to indicate some fundamental instructional practices, such as eliciting and responding to students' thinking and experiences, orienting students to each other's ideas and the content, and setting and maintaining expectations for equitable student participation. Developing and honing such practices that align to the principles is what the learning system is designed to put at the center of *everyone's* work.

Based on how we have set up the various professional learning spaces, we've sketched out a typical week or month in the life of a principal, coach, and teacher (see figures 3.4, 3.5, and 3.6). You can see that the principal has protected time to facilitate ILTs, participate in Learning Labs and Grade-Level Team Meetings, and flexibly follow up on priorities identified in any space (e.g., Classroom Visits, individual work with teachers, or district collaboration). The coach distributes her time across planning for teacher collaboration, facilitating Learning Labs and Grade-Level Team Meetings, and visiting classrooms, with time each week to contribute to the Instructional Leadership Team. In a typical month, teachers may participate in one Learning Lab and engage in twice-weekly Grade-Level Team Meetings. In our partnership, these meetings have primarily focused on mathematics or literacy and evolved to include socioemotional learning in some schools and science in one. What gets focused on is connected to what is needed for teacher learning.

Let's zoom out now and think about how the opportunity to grow ideas together across the different spaces creates coherent learning experiences for teachers. First, notice how the learning and collaboration spaces we described each serve different but interdependent purposes. Learning

Figure 3.4   Example of a teacher's monthly collaboration and professional learning time

October 2022

Monday	Tuesday	Wednesday	Thursday	Friday
3	4 **Grade-Level Team Meeting** (ELA)	5 **Staff Meeting**	6 **Grade-Level Team Meeting** (Math)	7 90 min Late Start: **Whole Staff PD**
10	11	12 **Learning Lab** (Math in morning; ELA in afternoon)	13	14 90 min Late Start
17	18 **Grade-Level Team Meeting** (ELA)	19 **Staff Meeting**	20 **Grade-Level Team Meeting** (Math)	21 90 min Late Start
24	25 **Grade-Level Team Meeting** (ELA)	26	27 **Grade-Level Team Meeting** (Math)	28 90 min Late Start: **Whole Staff PD**
31				

Note: Individual planning time is not reflected in this calendar.

Labs provide a space for teachers and leaders to collaboratively make sense of something new and begin to experiment with it together, in a classroom with students. Grade-Level Team Meetings provide a regular space in which teachers and leaders can carry forward new ideas from the Learning Lab space and puzzle through what they are experiencing in classrooms as they try out new instructional practices with students. Classroom Visits provide a way for leaders and teachers to continue to think together and develop instructional practice in response to students. These visits also support leaders to ground themselves in how teachers and students are making sense of instructional practice and content. All the interactions across the spaces inform the leaders' thinking and responses as they engage in the weekly ILTs. Meanwhile, other practices like Teacher Time Outs and examining student work appear in multiple spaces

Figure 3.5   A coach's typical weekly schedule

	Monday	Tuesday	Wednesday	Thursday	Friday
7:30	Participate in **Instructional Leadership Team (ILT) Meeting**				Support Professional Learning during Late Start
8:00					
8:30					
9:00		Facilitate **Grade-Level Team Meetings**	Facilitate **Learning Lab**	**Classroom Visits** and **Planning** for Learning Lab and Grade Level Team Meetings	
9:30					
10:00					
10:30					
11:00	**Classroom Visits** and **Planning** for Learning Lab and Grade-Level Team Meetings				**Classroom Visits** and **Planning** for Next Week
11:30					
12:00		**Classroom Visits** and **Planning** for Learning Lab and Grade-Level Team Meetings	**Classroom Visits** and **Planning** for Learning Lab and Grade-Level Team Meetings	Facilitate **Grade-Level Team Meetings**	
12:30					
1:00					
1:30					
2:00				Participate in PLC with other Math Coaches	
2:30					
3:00					

as repeated, predictable ways that teachers and leaders can experiment with practice and engage in instructional decision-making together. Continually working together across the spaces in the learning system creates an ongoing learning conversation in the school, where all involved can continually experiment with, and make sense of, new instructional practices over time.

Second, notice how across the system, the Principles for Teaching and Learning to Teach are reflected in how leaders and teachers work together. In each space, there is a foundational focus on student learning and sense-making; student thinking is held up as brilliant and as the core of what educators need to learn to support and respond to. In each space, there is a clear vision of the role of the teacher as a facilitator of student

Figure 3.6 A principal's typical weekly schedule for participation in teacher learning and collaboration

	Monday	Tuesday	Wednesday	Thursday	Friday
7:30	Lead **Instructional Leadership Team (ILT) Meeting**				Facilitate/Participate in **Professional Learning** during Late Start
8:00					
8:30					
9:00		Participate in **Grade-Level Team Meetings** (Math, Grades 3-5)		Follow up on Priorities identified in ILT (e.g., classrooms visits, individual work with teachers, or district collaboration)	
9:30					
10:00					
10:30					Follow up on Priorities identified in ILT (e.g., classrooms visits, individual work with teachers, or district collaboration)
11:00			Participate in **Learning Lab**		
11:30					
12:00	Follow up on Priorities identified in ILT (e.g., classrooms visits, individual work with teachers, or district collaboration)				
12:30				Participate in **Grade-Level Team Meetings** (ELA, Grades K-2)	
1:00					
1:30					
2:00		Participate in **District Principals' Meeting**			
2:30					
3:00					

sensemaking rather than a deliverer of knowledge. In each space, there is a clear belief that teacher learning requires public experimentation with practices, by everyone. Leaders participate as curious learners alongside teachers. In each space, leaders pay close attention to how teachers are making sense of new learning, collaborating with others, and moving along the messy learning trajectory of developing knowledge, skills, and identities. Each space is grounded in a belief that learning to teach is a long, complex process that must be supported over time. Educator learning goals cannot be achieved in one session; rather, learning goals are stretched across multiple learning spaces as teachers and leaders make sense of new knowledge, skills, and ways of being over time.

Designing for coherence also means carefully attending to the adult learning context. If a professional learning session is encouraging teachers to take risks and experiment with new instructional practices but the broader culture of the school is not yet encouraging such experimentation, then the culture is likely to prevent full engagement in the professional learning session. Attending to this broader learning context includes attending to informal teacher conversations in the staff lounge, the brief interactions in the hallway when the principal mentions something to a teacher, or the framing of student reading data at a staff meeting. All these interactions come together to form a culture that will either foster or inhibit further learning and experimentation; teachers carry these interactions with them as they consider how to participate in a professional learning system or whether to try something new they learned when they go back to their classroom.

IDEAS FOR GETTING STARTED

Here are some ideas to get you started thinking about what spaces and practices could be a part of the professional learning system of your school. Depending on your role and context, some of these spaces and practices may already exist, and others may be new or different from how things are currently done. We want to help you begin to think about how you can grow a professional learning system that positions teachers and leaders as learners alongside students, strengthens collaboration, and builds a joyful learning culture in your school.

Examine Your Current Professional Learning System

Spend some time thinking about the different professional learning opportunities or sessions experienced by teachers. If you are a teacher, make a list of all the professional learning experiences you've had over the last year. If you are a coach or a principal, consider this task from the perspective of a particular teacher, or do this in partnership with a teacher or a grade level. Create a visual sketch of the different learning opportunities or sessions, noting any connections between them. Here are some questions you might consider as you reflect:

- Where does each of the learning opportunities take place?
- Who else participated?
- What were the goal and the content?
- Who identified the goals?
- What connections are there between learning opportunities or sessions?
- Would the sketch you created be similar or different for each teacher in your school? Why?

Consider:

- Are there pieces that seem to be missing or infrequent (e.g., they happen only in August) in your current professional learning system?
- Where are opportunities to create a new space or repurpose an existing space? Who would need to be involved in making changes?

Create a Sketch of Your Weekly Schedule

If you are a principal or coach, create a sketch of how you spend time across a week. Here are some questions you might consider as you reflect:

- How would you categorize the various activities in your schedule? What percentage of your time is connected to teacher learning?
- If you could make one change to your schedule to support teachers better, what would it be? What would it take to make that happen?

Make More Time for Focused Teacher Collaboration

An important part of the learning spaces we have experienced with teachers is time to plan, teach, and reflect together. We recognize this is not the norm. So if you are in a setting where you only have one to two days of professional development, here are some ways to experiment with creating more time for two or more teachers with their instructional coaches and principals to puzzle through something together. Begin any of these steps by identifying a learning goal for teaching. Try to select a goal that is fresh and intriguing to everyone involved. For example, could a book study or an article inspire experimentation?

- Consider starting with one grade level. Identify budget capacity for substitutes or other available adults to release the grade-level team to discuss the ideas related to their learning goal, plan a lesson, and try it out with one of the classes.
- If there is no time during the school day, consider opportunities for teachers to collaboratively engage with students during an after-school program.
- Identify times when there are already two adults in a classroom (e.g., when there are paras, a dual-language specialist, or a special educator). How can the pair, along with an instructional coach, plan and teach together, focusing on something new they want to learn?
- Consider bringing multiple teachers together by combining two classrooms into a larger space in the school.
- Think about how you could stretch collaborative learning across existing spaces. Begin a conversation in a Grade-Level Team Meeting during the day, before or after school. Come together the following day for the Classroom Visit portion, requiring a shorter amount of time that one or two teachers' classrooms might need coverage for. Then debrief the Classroom Visit in another Grade-Level Team Meeting, over lunch, or before or after school.

4

Teachers and Principals in Partnership

WE WORK TOGETHER VERSUS WORKING TOGETHER

Teachers and principals. No public school exists without them. Yet in most schools, they spend very little time together, and almost no time actually working together on the work at the heart of schools: student learning experiences. There are lots of reasons for this, but none of them justify the fact that this reality does not serve anyone well, especially students. Teachers and principals both work hard, want better outcomes for students, and spend all day in the same building, but they are working on very different things. Principals and teachers are not learning with or from each other; they are not getting to know each other better in ways that reveal opportunities to support growth. This robs them, professionally and personally, of the benefits of sharing the responsibility, privilege, and opportunity to build practices and systems that help them to provide the learning experiences they want their students to experience every day, in every classroom. But this can change. Intentional efforts to work together on learning to teach can shift what and how teachers and principals work on, even in public schools. The change in the teacher-principal relationship is the cornerstone of efforts to change schools.

"Our Work" Means Sharing the Work

This book is premised on the belief that if we really want different experiences and outcomes for our students, then we must recognize that we are the ones who must do something different. It starts with changing how we relate to each other and the work. In almost all schools, the principal has the opportunity and authority to change the dynamic between teachers and principals, to initiate the shift in roles necessary to reposition teachers and principals as partners in designing better practices. The change we're describing is not a tweak; it's not something either teachers or principals add into their current practice. When a principal aligns her practices to the principles we've described, the work of refocusing the school itself on learning to teach becomes her work and student learning becomes our work. This is what changes the fabric of the relationship between a teacher and her principal; when the principal directly centers student learning as the purpose of her leadership, teachers and principals have the same goal.[1]

What do principals say?

Principals who have made this shift in the focus and execution of their role as instructional leaders have reflected that "learning can be a distant piece of your day and life if you allow it to happen. You can become a firefighter, constantly tending to the management needs in the school." Making this shift was "really just focusing and making that commitment as the principal that learning is important." Another principal described the shift in her relationships with teachers as follows: "When you're managing a building, you surface-level know people," explaining that now she has "more personal relationships with teachers, I know them as people." Implicit in both reflections is the recognition that the shift in their identity as an instructional leader changed their perspective and their relationship with teachers and student learning.

Yet this shift in leadership will only impact students if teachers step into the space it creates to collaborate. So, while the principal has to intentionally shift her practice to create and sustain the collaborative learning and planning spaces, the teacher has to be open to the collective learning, planning, and adjusting cycle that brings principals and coaches into that space that teachers have traditionally occupied alone. It's important to acknowledge that teachers have often been held publicly responsible for student outcomes without much control over the process that yields them and are subjected to rating systems that compare schools. There is seldom public recognition of what teachers *did* accomplish in the 180 days they had with their students, despite the fact that it's so often amazing, reaching far beyond the scores children "earn" on a single day in May.

What do teachers say?

I think the principal participates equally in our professional learning, just the same as anyone else on the team. They are asking questions. They're reading the articles. They're trying it out. They're teaching with us. They have to teach with us because that's how you build trust. I think admin can be really intimidating for people, and if they're not getting messy and trying it with us, then we're not all doing it. Then I'm just doing the work and she's just watching. And I also think it's important because then they're aware of how hard it is and how impactful it is. I think they have to be part of it. We have different conversations now. You know, when we have evaluation meetings or even just when I'm talking to the principal about a student. She knows what we're doing in the classroom and what content we're covering. So when I say "Oh, this is so hard for a student," the principal has a context of what that means. Which is different than it's ever been before.

Principals and coaches, working in partnership with teachers, engage in complex, relational work that pushes on status and positionality dynamics. Teachers might understandably enter collaboration with their principal with a bit of reserve or skepticism since the principal is also their evaluator, and coaching can often be viewed by teachers as a way to help "struggling teachers." Reciprocally, principals and coaches have to learn to trust that teachers do not expect them to have all the answers or to be experts ready to "train" them or to provide a set of steps they can simply comply with to ensure a favorable evaluation. Instead, working through these traditional dynamics opens up the possibility of a whole new context for us as adults who want to both do better for students and have more productive, professionally satisfying, and authentic working relationships. We have repeatedly seen it happen—teams of adults embracing that if they want different experiences and outcomes for children, they are the ones who will have to do something differently. It powerfully and fundamentally changes the work they are able to do together in service of children.

HOW DOES IT BECOME *OUR* WORK?

In chapter 3, we described the spaces that we assert are necessary to foster deep, ongoing professional learning for all adults. But those spaces are only a means to do the work differently; they provide the opportunity. How we all show up in them is what will drive the development of shared practices that are created in service of better experiences for students.

Principals and teachers, for each of you, we elaborate three dispositions that we have seen impact how successfully (or not) schools grow as places that support teacher learning (table 4.1). These dispositions reveal themselves in a variety of situations: in the way we position ourselves in relation to the opportunities and challenges created by being in all the spaces together, in how we navigate differences in positionality, and in how

Table 4.1 Overarching principal and teacher dispositions

Principal	Teacher
Be a learner and a leader	Make your practice public
Keep connecting decisions back to the *why*	Take risks through a lens of inquiry
Balance the pressure and the support	Engage as a decision-maker

authentically we make space for each other to learn and lead. Supporting each other to act with agency and in partnership in the workplace learning environments is the whole point of the professional learning system.

Principal Dispositions

Be a Learner and a Leader   Learning can powerfully inform leadership if the principal sees leadership as a practice that can grow and deepen with experience and effort. Only by learning more does leadership become more intentional and responsive. What's hard is that this disposition compels a principal to offer and lead toward a vision *and* demonstrate the humility to learn with and from others to inform her evolving vision and plans. It's admitting right from the start that "the vision" is the collective best thinking of the team about where to start, and recognizing that "the plan" will be adjusted as our learning unfolds.

This leadership disposition dispenses with the illusion that there is some magic that only leaders possess, which qualifies them to draft a plan in June that will work for whoever the students and teachers are *next* September through June. Nope. This disposition drives a leader to prioritize strategies that continually create opportunities to bring teams together to learn, plan, try, and adjust. It assumes partial success and opportunities to learn from what didn't work. And it requires the leader to participate in the execution of the planned work so that she can learn alongside the practitioners and contribute to and facilitate the adjustments that become the next iteration. Learning with practitioners in order to drive the work forward iteratively is the essence of this disposition. It's staying intimately engaged in the work of moving in the direction of your vision by making a conscious effort to keep doing better as you gain deeper and broader perspectives on the work.

One kindergarten teacher describes her principal's impact on the culture of learning in their school as follows:

> She's a principal that's fully aware that she doesn't know everything. Having a principal that's so open, that's willing to say, "Hey, I don't know what the answer is," or "Well, let me try this. This could be a train wreck, but

let's see what happens." It sets the standard for the rest of us. It raises the bar a little bit if the person that is the head of your school is willing to step up and admit that she doesn't know everything and admit that she's still learning. The more comfortable she becomes, the more comfortable we become admitting to our kids, "I made a mistake," or to admit that the lesson was awful. The more we do it with our kids, I've noticed the more willing our kids are to say, "I made a mistake," or "I guess I really didn't know the answer." So it's this kind of shuffle effect. Because now our kids see learning is an ongoing process. It's not like a thing to achieve. It's something that will stick with you all through your life, and you're constantly, constantly going to be learning.

Supporting people's capacity to evolve together is not usually included in principal preparation programs. It is one of the most nuanced and challenging parts of leadership, which is necessary if we want to disrupt the system and outcomes of public schools. We need leaders who will place their faith in their team's efforts to grow together and dive in with them, requiring leaders to admit when they don't know something, share their thinking while it's still developing, and *still* make some decisions about next steps when necessary. This means leaders must lean into the mantra that "you can't look good and get better at the same time" because no learner can.

Keep Connecting Decisions Back to the *Why* One of the essential functions of leadership is giving people something to say yes to. This is probably true in all leadership contexts, but it's especially important in the context of leading within a system that has been producing the same results for generations. Supporting practitioners to engage in planning and executing ambitious instruction each day *and* participate in developing those strategies requires us to challenge past practices and the expectations of the current system we all work in. And that requires an extra measure of leadership. It calls on principals to consistently assist practitioners in seeing the direct relationship between the greatest goals we have for our school and our students, the specific problem we are engaged in addressing, the principles that guide us, and the options and constraints that currently exist.[2]

The threat of becoming either overwhelmed or paralyzed is always present. The easiest option is often the one that involves expecting compliance rather than engagement from learners, but we know that this leads to the same outcomes we aim to disrupt. Railing against the reality that there is not enough time, funding, or support won't change anything because no one is coming to do the "right thing" for us or our students.

Principals supporting the teachers who are doing this work *can* foster teachers' motivation and determination to partner in this effort by naming and narrating when they make the moves that align with the shared vision despite these barriers. Recognizing when we do hard things helps us get better at doing hard things, so underscoring a team's identity as a group who does hard things can sustain the team in those efforts. Knowing your leader sees it and makes the time to honor it reinforces the importance of the intention and the effort. Reminding people that if it were easy, everyone would do it reminds those doing the work that not knowing exactly what to do doesn't mean we're not capable or we're not going to eventually get better. We're the ones who set our sights on the really hard and important goals for our students and our community. Hard means we're chipping away at the barriers that stopped others before us. Leaders must take every opportunity to message the ways that following our *why* is working.

When principals are fully engaged in the hard work with teachers, they share the frustrations and fatigue, which gives them the credibility and opportunity in those moments to remind practitioners of the *why* behind the big and little decisions we have to hold ourselves accountable for making in service of our vision for students. By leaning in to listen to and engage in the questions, fears, concerns, and challenges, you are also there when remembering their *why* is most powerful and to celebrate when the *why* is achieved.

Balance the Pressure and the Support Schools function within the context of our larger society, and prevailing societal influences systematically pressure schools to continue to do what they have always done. Attempting to change schools as organizations requires an opposing pressure, a force that drives toward something different. But pressure can result in resistance if the people who comprise "the system" don't also feel supported to make the changes that directly impact them. This means constantly balancing what we expect from teachers with how we support them along the way, and it requires a specific leadership mindset related to how teachers experience the work. Teacher experience is seldom a topic of training or a problem of practice at district principals' meetings, but it is a huge determinant of teacher engagement and the sustainability of that engagement. The absence of the intentional effort to balance what you expect of teachers over time with how you support them in approximating the necessary growth creates a dissonance for teachers. It contradicts the ethos that we are working together by learning together when teachers commit to ambitious practice goals but don't have adequate support in terms of time, learning, feedback, resources, or recognition of effort. To be fair, even *with* all those supports, the work is hard! Leaders who embrace this role carefully attend to making it possible.

We have come to refer to this dimension of leadership as "balancing the pressure and support," in part based on Michael Fullan's thinking about positive pressure.[3] How teachers perceive the balance often determines how they gauge their chances of succeeding, whether they feel "set up," to what degree they will take risks, and ultimately if they feel seen and valued. Principals attend to this balance by recognizing that growth is fostered when there is a balanced combination of pressure and support. This means thoughtful, intentional efforts to balance expectations and accountability with commensurate support such as professional learning, differentiated support, and necessary materials and resources. Leadership is necessary to ensure the pace of the work is responsive to student needs but also achievable for teachers.[4]

Leaders who embrace that balancing pressure and support makes an important contribution to the work in their schools demonstrate it by knowing teachers as people and as practitioners; by listening to what is planned, then observing firsthand to see how close it came to the goal for students; by giving honest and timely feedback; and by being fully present in these interactions. They actively seek to understand if teachers are experiencing the work as motivating, viable, achievable, and effective in its impact on student experiences and engagement. They do not avoid the signals that teacher participation is shifting from active engagement to compliance or that one teacher disagrees with a course of action. This disposition reveals itself in how the principal prioritizes her proximity to the actual teaching in her school. To know where one teacher is in her mathematical instructional practice versus her writing instructional practice on the trajectory we have shared requires close and frequent contact with teachers and their students. Equally important is the principal's willingness and ability to engage teachers in conversations about their practice. Principals lean into the tensions and transparently name that learning and collaborating in service of developing better practices necessarily means puzzling through the hard parts together. They are transparent about their desire to know these things in service of maintaining the balance so that teachers can engage as sensemakers, authentically growing their own practice.

Balancing the pressure and support also requires leaders to stand in the discomfort and vulnerability of examining the discrepancy between collective beliefs and current practices. The leader is not exempt; she too must participate even knowing that the discrepancies inherent in her practice and her role will also be revealed. Principals, this means facing the fact that *you* will never fully succeed, and you will never be able to give people everything they need, and yet you hold yourself and others accountable for not letting what we can't do stop us from doing what we can do. The limitations, barriers, frustrations, and resources we lack do not exempt us from the fight. Leaders who balance the pressure and support recognize this tension and support others to hold it as well.

Teacher Dispositions

Changing the relationship between teachers and principals also requires teachers to engage differently. The changes in the principal role outlined in this chapter will be insufficient if left unmatched by shifts in teacher practice. This partnership can develop only if teachers are open to the collective learning, planning, and adjusting cycle that brings principals and coaches into the space that they have traditionally occupied alone. This looks like a willingness to take risks, experiment, and openly discuss the challenges that teachers typically tackled alone. The learning system we describe is only as good as the ideas and intentions we bring into these spaces. Teachers, you are the most valuable resource we give to students. You know the most about your students, their ideas, and the community in your classroom. We cannot know what is possible without your willingness to let us learn with you as you navigate into new areas of practice in search of better strategies. Your willingness to lead in many aspects of the work is critical.

Make Your Practice Public To learn together, we have to be together. We don't mean teachers sharing the surface-level aspects of practice like the math lesson they're on, the worksheet they used, or the book they're reading aloud. We mean sharing the messy, challenging, and exciting realities of teaching. Teachers, this means sharing the moment when you had no idea what to do next, the story of how you thought you had a *great* plan and it totally didn't work, and the time when you made a sudden, improvised shift that supported your students to come up with some fascinating ideas.

Let's be clear. For many teachers and in many schools, this is a huge change. In 1975, Dan Lortie described schools in the US as "egg crates": teachers isolated in their own classrooms behind closed doors.[5] In most schools, that hasn't changed. Our school schedules are organized to keep us mostly separated from our colleagues throughout the day. Our principal only comes in to evaluate. Teachers often plan and teach in a different way when the principal does come in. Teachers avoid coaching support because that would mean they are struggling. While teachers talk about what is happening in their classroom in the staff room at lunch, they're usually not talking about the real, messy work of teaching and learning.

Engaging in real learning about the complex work of teaching in ways that are fundamentally different from what most of us experienced as children is learning that teachers can do only with others. It requires the team to share collective access to the messiness of real teaching practices with real children. For the principal, coach, and teaching colleagues to be able to meaningfully learn with and from each teacher, each teacher will have to let the team see the messy highs and lows of their teaching practice. The principal, for example, will be able to learn more about the complexities of transforming teaching practice only if teachers let them in to see that process. A coach will know what additional supports teachers might need only if teachers make their planning, teaching, and reflection practices transparent. Colleagues will engage in reciprocal and collaborative sharing and experimentation with practice only if their whole team does. Teachers making space for leaders and colleagues to learn with and from them requires both opening up the reality of their teaching practice and tuning into, and then expressing, their individual needs, questions, and concerns.

Take Risks Through a Lens of Inquiry   Teachers, have you ever not tried something new in your classroom because you weren't quite sure how to do it or didn't think it would work? We all have been there. But learning a new way of teaching requires that we try out new things, and it's going to be messy. Letting go of the need to have answers, and instead leaning into sharing our questions is the heart of developing a willingness to take risks. Engaging together from a position of curiosity and inquiry affects how we see opportunities and challenges. It's the difference between "I guess I can give it a try" and "I'm so curious what will happen when I try ___."

For teachers, taking a stance of curiosity and inquiry means embracing that they are also a learner. And just like their students, they will learn from being messy with their own ideas, trying out things, seeing what happens, discussing with others, and trying again. Notice how this stance requires embracing the Principles for Learning to Teach from chapter 2, that teaching is something that can be learned, and that your learning is a continuous process along a messy trajectory of developing knowledge and skills. With the shared goal of designing better experiences for students, this also drives us back to the value of being students of our students. Through a lens of inquiry, teachers embrace that students' ideas and experiences are the greatest drivers of and resources for their own learning. Their most powerful learning will come from trying things out *with their students* and seeing what happens, not by sitting in a presentation or having a leader tell them what they should have done.

Engage as a Decision-Maker Teachers may fear that a significant increase in collaboration between principals, coaches, and teachers will represent a loss of agency and independence. This may come from the typical ways in which interactions between teachers and leaders unfold—often, such interactions are about delivering "the decision" or explaining "the way things are to be done," with little room for teacher voice. Often, teachers pay attention just enough to know what it is they will have to do to make it look like they are "in compliance." For a true and powerful partnership to come to life, teachers *cannot* show up waiting to be told what to do or looking for compliance indicators. On the contrary, teachers must be actively involved in thinking about what is worth learning; what funds of knowledge their students have; and how to invite critical thinking and engagement in their immediate classroom community, leading to greater possibilities for social engagement and power. We all have to share responsibility for coinquiry into instructional practice and student learning. We sink or swim together now.

This disposition really has two parts. First, teachers have to trust the process *and* expect that there will be lack of certainty. If everyone is part of a collaborative, iterative inquiry process, then leaders can't know exactly what teachers will be working on in future collaborative learning spaces—leaders and teachers both need to see what happens first. As we described throughout, the principal needs to use what they learn to inform the plan, which relies on teachers to give them the space and flexibility to do so. Simply put, learning together about how to powerfully transform classroom instruction involves uncertainty, and teams are not going to have all the answers right away. Learning Labs and Grade-Level Team Meetings won't always end with clear answers and a concrete plan. The goal is to collectively identify next steps to try.

Second, teachers have to trust the value of their own wisdom and experience, while also allowing both to evolve. This means believing that they have something important to contribute to group conversations and what they're experiencing matters and has value, while also being willing to refine their thinking as the group develops new theories and practices together. So there is immense value in teachers sharing what they are noticing about their students' experience with a new instructional activity or their thoughts about the draft of a future professional learning agenda. Teachers should trust that their wisdom and knowledge are valuable assets to the group's learning, regardless of their level of seniority or knowledge of any specific content area. Decisions have to be made. Teachers' willingness to revise their thinking as they engage in deeply listening, learning, and experimenting with colleagues can powerfully drive better decisions on behalf of students.

HOW DO TEACHERS AND PRINCIPALS ENGAGE IN PARTNERSHIP ACROSS THE LEARNING SYSTEM?

Next, we dig deeply into the specific ways that teachers and principals must each work to adopt new ways of orienting to each other and the work. We situate them in the context of each specific space in the learning system described in chapter 3. We provide more specificity to the complementary ways that principals and teachers must show up in order to generate significant shifts in practice that change experiences and outcomes for students.

How Do Principals Learn and Lead in Learning Labs?

Recall that Learning Labs are immersive learning experiences during which teachers, usually in their grade-level teams along with a coach and principal, delve deeply into honing their instructional decision-making skills and practices. They provide the grounding experience for the commitments that teachers, coaches, and the principal will follow through with in Grade-Level Team Meetings, informal conversations, and Classroom Visits. For principals, this means being a learner and a leader right alongside teachers, *your* learners.

Fully Engage and Do What You Expect of Teachers "This is our work" is not a part-time conviction. It's a commitment to work alongside teachers to learn, try, fail, succeed, grapple, share, and celebrate. If teachers are learning, developing ideas, considering strategies, trying them with students, and revising in order to leave the Learning Lab with a shared plan, the principal has to be fully present and engaged in each step, right alongside the teachers (see figure 4.1). We can't overemphasize this point. And it's not about modeling for teachers; it's about learning with them so that the experience, questions, conclusions, and resulting commitments are shared. No one needs to explain it to anyone else later because you were all there.

Let's now dive into a Learning Lab. A grade-level team of teachers, the principal, and the coach come together at the beginning of a school day. They begin with some learning. Perhaps the group is digging into

Figure 4.1   Principals engage fully in learning with teachers

Source: Matt Hagen

standards together to examine what students need to know and be able to do to meet the standard. Then they sometimes individually engage in a task (e.g., a math problem or a student writing task) to explore what they each know about this content so that they can identify questions they have about their own content knowledge. If necessary (and it often is), they learn together about the content and the trajectory of understandings children need to progress through to build understanding. Next, they might think together about what their students can currently do in relation to these standards in an effort to identify what strategies and next steps would move students forward in their conceptual understanding. The group often reviews commitments to the Principles for Teaching, even informally, so that they stay true to the commitment to position students as sensemakers and engage them in meaningful dialogue to build community as learners who can share powerful ideas with each other. The group then considers what new task, practice, or lesson structure to try today in a classroom so that they can collaboratively learn and adjust with the intent of identifying what they will commit to moving forward in their instructional plans and practices. This is an important point because the group is committed to all students accessing the instruction they determine is most likely to support their growing conceptual understanding. By midmorning, the group plans the lesson and heads to a classroom to try it with students. Usually, the teacher of that class does not teach because it's a rare opportunity for her to observe her own students. Having planned together, the adults spread across the room, sitting with the students on the carpet to listen to their ideas, ready to jump in with a Teacher Time Out if helpful. After the lesson, they examine the student work or reflect on the student ideas shared during the class discussion. If there is time, they make adjustments based on what they learned and try it again in another room. This learning that happens together and with children develops shared knowledge about students, content, and instruction. This shared knowledge enables the group to end the day by identifying and committing to specific practices that are responsive to student learning.

We shared this rather long description because we want to help you notice a few important things—namely, that the teachers, principal, and coach are equally engaged in every step. All of them are:

- Present the entire scheduled time, without distractions
- Learning about standards
- Reflecting on and sharing their own developing knowledge of the content, and learning more about the content if necessary
- Examining students' current understandings
- Identifying what prevents some students from accessing instruction
- Learning new instructional strategies
- Considering what instructional strategies and decisions will support students in developing conceptual understanding and fluency
- Sharing the responsibility of deciding what to try today and coplanning it in an attempt to provide students with the most effective nudge
- Teaching and/or participating in the classroom visit
- Participating in the reflection by sharing observations and their own developing ideas
- Engaging in the planning of and commitment to the next instructional steps
- Walking away with a firsthand understanding of what was learned and how the team used that knowledge to make decisions about how to design student learning experiences moving forward

When principals fully engage alongside teachers, it shifts the relationship in powerful ways that support teachers in engaging in the work. It also provides the principal with very important opportunities to recognize and celebrate teacher engagement and learning.

"My principal is right there with me, learning the same thing at the same time and applying it right next to me. It makes me feel like I'm in this to learn. I'm not in this to be perfect; I'm in this to learn and do my best and reflect and try again, and there's my principal doing the same thing. So it makes me feel like we're in this together. Not that she's judging and watching over me and making sure that I'm perfect, but that she's showing me that I can be a learner.

Kindergarten teacher

My principal is there as a full participant and she tries everything out and she grapples with the content at the same intensity level that we're grappling with it. I think it's one of the many things she does that makes her really feel like she's part of our team versus a separate kind of figurehead above the team. I think it's also showing what a priority learning this stuff is, and again in terms of building that culture, we're all learning together. It does a lot for that too, in terms of she'll readily go up and fall on her face just like we will and try to learn from that. I think having a leader who's willing to do that has a huge impact in terms of how the whole community or team pulls into being able to do that or being willing to do that.

First-grade teacher

Position Your Students as Sensemakers and Be a Student of Your Students   In the Learning Labs space, more than any other, all three sets of principles must be authentically and intentionally integrated to inform the leader's participation. To create that partnership in which the teacher engages with the principal, the coach, and their teaching team to work together on shared practices, the principal must demonstrate her belief in the Principles for Teaching, especially being a student of your (adult) students and positioning learners as sensemakers. This requires the principal to manage competing priorities skillfully. While she must be authentically curious about teachers' questions, developing ideas, how they engage in new learning, how they support teammates, how they take up and enact new ideas, what it looks like when they experience dissonance, and how comfortable they are with dissenting opinions, she must also put them in dialogue with one another and hold them accountable for staying in relationship to the ideas and each other. Her moves must support everyone to make sense of the ideas and possible options. This requires her to convey the importance of the learning by shaping the actual experience of the learners in the moment. This means leaning in to address the questions, concerns, and challenges that come up along the way. This brings us back to the importance of leadership that attends to balancing the pressure and support. It's important to keep returning to the shared belief that this work is both important and hard, and that is why we're all in it together.

At the same time, the principal must maintain a learner's stance, curious about her learners—the teachers. To be a student of her students, she has to keep developing her understanding of how teachers grow, what supports that growth, what barriers arise, and how to mitigate them. By engaging in learning with teachers during the Learning Lab, she is able to actively observe and assess the process. This allows her to reflect and adjust in ways that teachers experience as collaborative and responsive, fostering the conditions that allow teachers to remain engaged even though the work is complex and iterative. This is a specific example of what we mean when we say that instructional leadership should be measured by the impact it has on student experiences; when a principal's actions support teachers in digging into and remaining engaged in the complex and long-term work of designing instruction and communities that provide all learners access, the impact should be evident in classrooms.

> " The principal is willing to come in here, she participates with us in the math Labs. She gets down and works with the kids, and we've all had chances to partner up with her. And she's asked questions and is willing to hear what we have to say. So it just lets me know that she's totally on board with what we're doing and values our instinct and our craft.
>
> *Kindergarten teacher*

It was going to help me gauge everything. How much pressure, what support, when to pull back, when to pause, when to say we're on the wrong track. So I just knew I needed to be in the Labs. That's the most interesting part to me, intellectually. When I'm sitting there, I'm constantly shifting back and forth between pressure and support. As I'm listening, I'm thinking all these things at once. One is, "OK, that's on the table now. That's something we're going to do now." Another one is, "Oh wow, we just overwhelmed them." And given this other contextual stuff, I'm going to say, "Let's wait until next time."

Principal

Use What You Learn to Inform the Plan Transforming practice takes place over time and requires repeated and intentional opportunities, and leading that learning requires the time and focus of the leader. When the Principles for Learning to Teach are guiding your instructional choices as the teacher of teachers, you are never more than a couple of steps ahead as you (and the coach) design learning over time. How teachers are taking up new ideas, how status and participation are impacting their engagement, the extent to which students are responding as predicted, and many other factors are constantly informing the design of the next learning experience for the teacher(s). Using what we learn from and about teachers to inform their future learning is predicated on leaders having clear learning goals for and being fully engaged in the teacher learning experiences. Teacher learning cannot be outsourced. Making instructional decisions based on someone else's observations of your learners is not going to work. In order to balance the pressure and support, you must pace the learning and connect the next experience to the last experience.

One principal looks back on how her practice developed and shared:

Either in PD [professional development] or in Grade-Level Team Meetings, I am with teachers 50 percent of my time. I think at first, it was just intuition like, "I have to know what they know. How can I help? How can I support? How can I pressure if I don't know what they know?" So, at first, it was just that. Now, it's clear to me looking back that this is the leverage point. If you're learning with the teachers, and you're really involved in their planning and reflection practices, that's when you can impact the future. If all you do is do data meetings, that's an autopsy. Maybe next year they'll change how they do it, but if you're in the formative data processes, where you're looking at and responding mid-unit, you are actually going to be guiding teachers toward practices that will change kids' outcomes.

Teacher learning is fostered when the leader is transparent about her intention to formatively assess progress and support momentum by responding. She doesn't hide the fact that she is two steps ahead and making it up as she goes along at some points because she is learning too. This might include pausing to plan a time to coteach with a teacher so they can see what students do next, or working with the coach to develop a quick assessment they can administer before the next Grade-Level Team Meeting. It might also mean pushing to clarify expectations and timelines if there is not obvious agreement across the group. The important point here is that leaders must own the role and the responsibility to shape this iterative plan responsively if they are to truly embrace the Principles for Learning to Teach.

How Do Teachers Learn and Lead in Learning Labs?

If teachers are mostly used to attending "sit-and-get" approaches to professional learning, engaging in a Learning Lab can (and should) feel very different. It's no longer possible to sit back and just listen or check their email on the side. Learning Labs are unique experiences for teachers, and yet they rely on teachers to embrace the opportunity to further their own learning. Under what other circumstances do teachers get to collaboratively plan something new and immediately go try it with students? To be part of a group of adults puzzling through how to support students' thinking in real time? To be in a classroom and focus so closely on how student ideas are unfolding in relation to teaching (without also having to pay attention to 10,000 other things)? To collectively debrief with teaching colleagues and leaders right after instruction? But to benefit from this, teachers have to show up with intentionality.

Be a Learner   Labs are all about experimenting together, so showing up as a teacher learner means being willing to take some risks with colleagues: throw out an idea that is half-baked, share how you're revising your thinking, be vulnerable about what is feeling hard, ask the question that you're worried you might be judged for, or dive into trying something during the classroom visit that you've never tried before. It's important to realize that showing up in this way doesn't only deepen the teacher's own learning. When teachers show up as learners, they support the learning of colleagues *and* contribute to fostering a new culture of collaboration and learning in the school. In our experience, whenever a teacher asks a question that she was nervous to say out loud, at least one other person nods or breathes a sigh of relief that someone asked it, and then that person is more likely to ask a question she's nervous about next time. So, during collaborative learning and planning, teachers have to ask their real questions, say things that they're not sure of, articulate what is starting to shift inside their heads, and lean in when others do the same. During the classroom visit, they must take risks—volunteer to try something new even though it feels a little uncertain and messy. During the debrief, ask questions: *How did others make sense of Abdi's idea? What question could we have asked that would have pushed his thinking in the direction we were hoping?* Teachers have to lean in to being the learners their students need them to be.

Engage in the Decision-Making   Learning Labs are also opportunities to make collaborative decisions. Good collaborative decisions depend on skilled practitioners putting forth their ideas, questions, and concerns. Students are not served well when teachers comply with an idea they don't think will actually work, or just sit through something in order to meet an expectation. Making decisions together also means that teachers cannot sit back and expect school leaders to have all the expert answers, which can feel unsettling at first. Instead, when teachers give leaders space to show up as learners alongside them rather than as the people who hold decision-making power, they are better able to consider options together. When teachers dive in with their ideas and listen closely to other ideas that surface, they can more capably consider ways to bring different ideas together. During the Classroom Visit, when teachers volunteer to try leading something or call a Teacher Time Out when they have an idea or question about what to try next, they offer valuable insights to the group. During the debrief, sharing honest thoughts and questions about what unfolded and actively participating as the group decides what to try next allows teachers to have a voice in shaping the commitments they make about what to do when they all return to their classrooms.

How Do Principals Learn and Lead in Grade-Level Team Meetings?

Because we view teacher learning and collaboration as integrally connected, the Grade-Level Team Meeting is an important space wherein the team works together on integrating new ideas initiated in Learning Labs into their individual practices. A second purpose is to continually work on the content and instruction of each unit of instruction, responding to what teachers and students are experiencing as the unit unfolds, carefully following students' progress. It is the time to share the unvarnished reality of how plans played out in actual lessons and share the responsibility to figure out the next steps. This presents both important opportunities and important responsibilities for principals.

Be a Student of Your Students It is always incumbent on the principal to hold true to her commitment to be a student of her (adult) students. Grade-Level Team Meetings are especially rich opportunities to keep growing your understanding of *your* students. Teachers are sharing their instructional decisions and their reflections on how they played out. They are revealing explicit and implicit beliefs and values. These are critical opportunities to learn about many aspects of their practice, from risk taking in sharing developing ideas to levels of comfort with asking for help. This is the formative information leaders need to design the "just right" next step and to inform how they balance the pressure and support that maintains the momentum of the individual's and group's efforts.

Facilitate Collaborative Decisions as a Means of Ensuring Equitable Access to Learning Because this is the time when teachers are collaborating to plan their immediate next steps in the design of student learning, it is also a critical opportunity to set the stage for and reinforce the commitment to making collective decisions that ensure students have equitable learning experiences. If the team identifies effective strategies to engage learners, then all learners deserve the opportunity to experience those strategies. It should not matter which teacher you have. That means supporting all teachers in enacting those decisions. This calls on principals in two ways. First, she must make it clear that the responsibility of enacting collective decisions applies to everyone; it's our decision, and we all own responsibility to do it, as well as the results. In other words, developing new practices means making best guesses, and when we decide it's time to try one, we all try it. As long as it's enacted as planned, whether the outcome is great or disappointing, we share the responsibility. This understanding locates the responsibility to execute the new strategy effectively on each teacher, but it absolves any one individual of responsibility if it does not go well. The leader's participation in these decisions by design implicates her in the shared risk, hopefully reassuring practitioners that failing is a shared risk. Second, holding her responsibility to know her learners, she is present and able to identify scaffolds that may be necessary to support an individual teacher to ensure that all students have access to the intended learning experience. The occasional need for temporary scaffolds is anticipated and normalized by instructional leaders who are committed to the Principles for Learning to Teach. This ensures equitable experiences for students while supporting teachers in developing independence as instructional decision-makers because they won't decide to try a strategy they do not feel they can enact.

How Do Teachers Learn and Lead in Grade-Level Team Meetings?

For teachers, showing up to a Grade-Level Team Meeting—often in the middle of a busy day—can feel challenging. Teachers have to be focused on all the things that just happened in their classroom and all the things they need to be prepared for when they return to their classroom. The purpose of the Grade-Level Team Meeting is to collaboratively reflect on and adjust the decisions made during the Learning Lab and previous team meetings. The reflection is based on what teachers have seen and done in the last few days; thus their voice in how to adjust is critical. How teachers engage in this real-time opportunity to learn from and with their team can powerfully shape the instructional decisions they are prepared to make in the next week.

Make Learning Public to Inform Decision-Making   We can only learn from what we each decide to put out there. Because teachers are closest to students' ideas and needs, their willingness to share specific examples about what they've tried, what happened, what went well, and what feels challenging is a critical factor in collaborative learning to respond to student needs. Teachers are uniquely qualified to contribute to these discussions because of their ability to identify and share when something is not working, when they pivoted and saw students take up a new idea, and when they are noticing a need across the team. Often in these meetings, the team makes decisions together about upcoming plans, including decisions about content, pacing, scaffolding, and adjusting. Teachers shouldn't view these decisions as something to receive. Instead, they must engage actively in these decisions, drawing on their deep and important knowledge of their own students and their learning. Then, once decisions are made, teachers have to follow through on what the team decides to try in order to bring back honest and open feedback about how they enacted it and how it impacted student thinking and work so that students' experiences are accurately being considered as instructional options are being evaluated by the team. When learning is public, it also provides a valuable opportunity to learn by being curious about colleagues' practices and experiences and by asking questions and viewing their reflections as learning opportunities. Finally, making learning public relies on teachers being vulnerable and vocal about what they're not sure about, what they're wondering about, what is feeling challenging, what they're excited about, what isn't working, and what they've changed their minds about. Teachers' willingness to fully participate in planning based on all they know is a critical element in supporting teams to learn together.

Bring Your Students into the Learning   Teachers know their students deeply as learners and understand how they are developing over time. Because Grade-Level Team Meetings are frequent and real-time decisions about how to adjust instruction are being made, these are important opportunities for teachers to bring their students into the room. Consistent with the Principles for Learning to Teach, we are driven by the belief that students' ideas and experiences should be central to teacher inquiry. Decisions should be responsive to student needs. We must count on teachers, who know so much about their students, to make sure students are represented in these collaborative spaces. This means bringing specific observations, examples of student work, or other data to collaborative conversations to support everyone's learning.

How Do Principals Learn and Lead in Classroom Visits?

Designing better experiences for children is our shared purpose. It's our *why*, and our strategy is doing it together in a principled way. So instructional leaders, the people who are one step removed but also responsible for the teacher learning, *must* know what is happening for students and teachers. It's not an exaggeration to say that the plan hinges on it. Classroom Visits are essential in supporting teachers and principals to engage in instructional decision-making together *in the moment* and *with students*. It is how they work together to enact all the ideas from the Learning Labs and Grade-Level Team Meetings.

Calibrate on Progress and Challenges   Only by being in classrooms can a principal both observe developing teacher practice and gauge the impact on and equity of student experiences across classrooms. This is a powerful opportunity for teachers and principals to observe together whether their shared purpose is being served. Being together to see, in the moment, how the plans you made last week actually impacted student thinking is energizing: if it worked, it's a powerful confirmation; and if it didn't, it's a powerful motivator to keep trying. Either way, they are sharing those conclusions, and this catalyzes the process they are mutually engaged in.

Those same moments can be just as valuable if they provide an opportunity to examine conflicting opinions, observations, or conclusions. In those moments, the teacher and principal have a real example to help them explore how they see things differently; they can examine if they are misaligned on the *why* behind the practice or their understanding of how it should be enacted. Either way, they can trust that the other sees how both teachers and students are experiencing the agreed-upon practices. Teachers knowing that their principal actually sees and knows what they see and know moves both the work and the relationship forward.

Share in the Expectation to Develop Instructional Skills The only place that teachers can grow in their instructional practice is in their classroom with students. When making practice public is a shared value, teachers seeing that principals are both willingly and authentically engaging in the practices they expect of teachers is non-negotiable. In addition, it puts the principal side-by-side with the teacher to face the complexities and puzzle through the challenges. And the power of students seeing that both teachers and principals are working together on designing their learning sets the stage for high expectations of everyone. There's nothing like a principal pausing to ask a teacher for a Teacher Time Out to drive home that we are all working on and contributing to the shared goal of creating schools and classrooms that engage all learners in powerful learning and supportive communities.

Give Frequent Feedback All three sets of principles that drive our work recognize the impact teachers have on students through the community they build and the instruction they design. Supporting teachers to grow better and better at that means deeply knowing how they are engaging in their practice and what impact it is having on students at this stage. When teachers are engaging in learning and collaborating, they need feedback. All learners need feedback, but teachers in particular are so deeply enmeshed in the relationships, the content, and the many, many influences that push and pull on their plans and enactment that it can be hard for them to see the direct impact they are having. A leader who is present to name and recognize the practices that teachers are lifting and the impact it is having on students is critical. Reciprocally, teachers also need to know that their principal is saying what she's thinking about their instructional efforts and the impact on students. This creates trust because teachers then have the opportunity to make the effort to grow in that area and be recognized for that effort. Enacting the Principles for Learning to Teach requires leaders to normalize giving feedback about areas for growth.

How Do Teachers Learn and Lead in Classroom Visits?

Often, when a principal, coach, or teaching colleague comes into a classroom during instruction, the teacher shifts into performance mode. It's natural to reflexively feel a need to prove to the colleague that we know what we're doing. But this shifts that teacher's focus away from her students and their ideas. Making space for others to learn with and from us requires that the teacher resist that common urge to change what she's doing or lose her focus on her original plan. Instead, we need the teachers to be real and stick to her plans when another adult walks into the room, resisting the urge to show other educators what we think they want to see. Teachers we've worked with describe a shift in their initial response to someone walking in the room from "Aaaah! They're going to judge me. How do I make this look good?" to "Ooh! Another person to think with!"

Invite Others In   Teachers understand most deeply what is going on for their learners—they were there ten minutes ago, and yesterday, and two weeks ago. It's important for teachers to recognize that a colleague, principal, or coach who is visiting is trying their best to make sense of what they see—it is an opportunity for them to learn, too. Teachers, inviting others in might include:

- If you're deep in facilitating a classroom discussion, invite the colleague in to be part of the instructional thinking with you in the moment through a Teacher Time Out.
- If students are working, share with your colleague what you are curious about, and you can both circulate and engage with students to see what you notice—either together or separately.
- If you have a moment to pull them aside, share something about what you're thinking about or noticing—this could be something that's feeling hard, unclear, or uncertain or something exciting you're noticing about students' thinking that you would love to celebrate (definitely don't be humble!).
- If there is something you're about to do (for example, lead a summary discussion to wrap up student work time), share something you are finding challenging and ask your colleague to puzzle through it with you as you give it a try.
- If what is happening right now is related to a previous discussion in a Learning Lab or Grade-Level Team Meeting, point out the connection. For example, maybe you recently discussed how to support students with a particular concept, and you're about to try one of the ideas that the team generated.

The learning and collaboration that can come from a Classroom Visit can be extended beyond the actual visit. Often, during the visit, we don't have time to really think together, as the focus is on the students and their learning. Making time later to more deeply discuss what you noticed, are wondering about, or are finding challenging can help to cement a new understanding and even reveal important ideas that should be shared with the whole team.

Support Adult Learning   The more we learn together, the better we can serve students. But coaches and principals don't have the same opportunities to practice that teachers do. Their learning also requires ongoing and coherent opportunities to make sense of new ideas and practices. Teachers' willingness to open their classroom up as a place for others to both observe and try out new ideas or instructional skills is a powerful driver of collaborative change. Inviting coaches and principals to coplan and teach together can help them to see the nuance and complexity of enacting a new practice, which they would have no other way of understanding. Teachers saying yes to allowing them to practice teaching a new instructional strategy and supporting them with Teacher Time Outs or clues about students to call on in the moment supports them in growing their own instructional practices. It also provides them critical perspectives on students and teachers that help to close that distance between teachers and everyone else.

Evaluation Spaces

Evaluation spaces are not a part of the professional learning system, but they are spaces teachers and principals must occupy together. Making the effort to think together about how the engagement in those spaces can detract from or compliment their relationship and collaboration in the other spaces is worth the conversation.

The difference in power and authority between teachers and principals is never more evident than in an evaluation meeting. These meetings and the processes that dictate them are often bargained. Principals are trained that evaluation is their job, that it is the primary lever they have for changing teacher practice. We are arguing that the opposite is true. Consistent with the belief that learning to teach takes repeated practice and must be coherent and sustained, no single conversation is going to change anything. Given its inherent formality, it can instead serve as a valuable chance to pause and memorialize what both teacher and principal already know about the current state of the teacher's practice. When the teacher and principal are working from their roles on the shared goal of developing more engaging and equitable instructional practices, formal evaluative feedback should no longer result in surprises. Instead, working together like this positions the principal to take this requirement and use it as an opportunity to document what she is seeing in the spaces across the professional learning system. Without scheduling a single observation, the principal has had many opportunities to observe and give feedback across all aspects of a teacher's practice in real time, such that she also gets to see the teacher reflect on and adjust her practice based on the feedback. The principal already gets to see both the effort and the outcome. In the context of a professional learning system, the pressure on the teacher to prove a level of proficiency or provide evidence is dramatically flattened because the principal is not only seeing every aspect of the teacher's practice, she shares the responsibility to assist in the development of more and more effective practices.

There is no denying that teachers still have to enact those practices effectively and create the relationships and structures that result in strong classroom communities. But when the principal sees the teacher leaning into opportunities to develop their practices and knows firsthand what challenges each individual teacher faces in the context of her trajectory of growth and current students' assets and needs, the principal already has a deep and nuanced understanding. That allows her to use the evaluative process to provide meaningful feedback rather than scrambling to construct adequate knowledge to meet the expectations of the arbitrary moment in time systems call "the evaluation." Instead, that required meeting becomes an opportunity for them to reflect, document progress, and plan together, rather than the date on which they both try to meet the expectations of the larger system.

> " *What do teachers say?*
> I also think our admin like really getting messy and dirty with us. It makes it so when they come in and do evaluations, they understand. They know our students more, and they also understand what it could look like.
>
> *Third-grade teacher*

[Being in the other spaces with us] lets him see us in a different light. It lets him see how we interact with our peers. It lets him see for the most part how prepared we are. I think he could get a really good picture from that. For me, it's really helpful. It makes the whole evaluation process so much easier. I feel like you have to submit less evidence, like formally, because he's seeing it.

Fifth-grade teacher

What do principals say?
Two principals new to leading in the context of a professional learning system reflected: "It's the first time that I felt like the evaluation conversations were actually useful for teacher learning. Because I'm in Grade-Level Team Meetings, classrooms, Learning Labs." Similarly, the other noticed that by participating in teacher learning spaces, she had developed new content knowledge in math, which supported her to "feel more confident about what I'm saying during evaluations because I understand. I feel like I can go a little bit deeper."

If teachers and principals are already routinely engaged in the shared work of developing better instructional practices, they can leverage the knowledge, ongoing feedback cycle, and outcomes being generated over time to more authentically partner to document the teacher's practice using the locally agreed-upon process. The positionality the process likely creates will still be present, but you can work together to:

- Leverage the partnership that exists in spaces across the professional learning system. Bring that into the evaluation space. Don't let your orientation to each other shift just because this requirement is being satisfied. If your relationship is safe and predictable in other spaces, this should be a foundation to make the evaluation space safe and predictable.
- Let go of old expectations. Talk in advance about what this means for each of you and how to prevent surprises. Acknowledge that you're

both expected to be honest and accurate in the context of your system's evaluation framework.

- Recognize that while you may have different roles or responsibilities based on your local requirements, you share the responsibility to construct an accurate record of current practice. If questions or discrepancies surface, maintain your learner's stance and lean in to learn more together.

NORMALIZING THE PARTNERSHIP ACROSS THE SCHOOL

Typically, principals (and coaches) only "work with" teachers when there is an identified need to improve or when there's a new initiative or curriculum implementation; in either case, it's temporary and outcome focused. Once the practice has improved or the new thing is implemented, that collaboration ends. This problem-centered approach to teachers, principals, and/or coaches working and learning together reveals a belief: teachers should be capable of teaching and learning autonomously—they should only need support or collaboration when there's something new or when they struggle. Leadership based on the principles we ascribe to is in direct opposition to this. We assert that in addition to organizing the time and interactions in schools to create an ongoing context for collective learning, principals must also be intentional in creating the space for partnerships that support teachers. Further, those partnerships must focus on the impact on student experiences, not problematize teacher practice. Again, when the adults focus their work on the same goal, the work *can* align in ways that have the power to change student experiences.

ROLE OF ASSISTANT PRINCIPALS AS LEADERS OF SOCIAL EMOTIONAL LEARNING COMMUNITIES

Recognizing that schools have a variety of leadership configurations, it's important to address the role that these leaders play in enacting the principles. Schools fortunate enough to have two administrators have more options for distributing support for both students and teachers.

In most of the schools we have collectively supported, there has been one assistant principal and two content coaches. Because coaches are so enmeshed in the work of supporting shared instructional practices, we devote significant space to elaborating their role, but if there is a second administrator in any form, that role has the potential and responsibility to provide similarly powerful leadership.

The communities of learners we describe in this book require teaching practices that prioritize relationships, shared power, and student voice. They require a commitment to providing students opportunities to develop and practice the social and academic skills that foster independence in all aspects of students' development. Getting children to learn by any means has resulted in harmful experiences, especially for Black and Brown students. It leads to a reliance on compliance and control over community.

Because community is foundational to enacting the principles to which we ascribe, intentional efforts must be made to build those classroom communities. This cannot be fully learned during teacher preparation. It is rarely supported by an adopted curriculum. It is not a tested skill. It is, however, an essential element of the school experience all children deserve, and a required context for Black, Brown, and all students experiencing poverty or significant trauma; if we want to change the outcomes schools have predictably produced for more than two hundred years, we must change the classroom communities such that all students are supported to take intellectual risks, make meaning, learn to reason, and develop the skills to persevere in making the effort to reach high expectations. Even great instruction will not accomplish this if every student is not invited in and made to feel valued in the community. This is the important part community plays in creating equitable classroom experiences.

Having a school leader who has the skill and capacity to support this aspect of teacher practice is a tremendous advantage. In the schools we have supported, leaders have reimagined what and how they lead. As principals devote their practice to supporting teachers in learning and collaboration focused on instruction, assistant principals provide the parallel support to develop and sustain the vision of the classroom communities students need and deserve. Assistant principals lead a whole body of work that includes examining what is meaningful student engagement, how students develop the social and emotional skills that allow them to engage in instruction designed to position students as sensemakers, what explicit instruction and practice must be designed to foster community building, how adults and students both develop the capacity to stay emotionally regulated and in relationship, and how rewards and punishment erode community.

Developing strong classroom communities is deep, messy, personal, and adaptive work. Schools are designed to expect and promote compliance, and almost every teacher is a product of that system. Examining the impacts of systemically requiring compliance and learning trauma-informed practices to replace that is a commitment most educators did not explicitly sign up for. It can feel beyond the scope of what should be required of us, and yet so many of us have seen and been heartbroken by the alternative, and as a result, committed to doing something different. We have recognized that if we want different outcomes for children, we will have to do something differently. The teachers who work in schools committed to this, and their students, benefit tremendously from leadership dedicated to supporting their efforts to do the work to build equitable experiences in classrooms rooted in relationships and community.

And this has important leadership implications. In schools where there is an assistant principal leading this area of practice, similar to coaches and principals, the assistant principal's efforts must be aligned to those of the other Instructional Leadership Team (ILT) members. This work is one aspect of a larger vision, but if teachers experience it as separate or in conflict in any way with the instructional practices they are working on, that dissonance creates a distraction. This is why assistant principals are essential members of the ILT and play a critical role in supporting how all adults in a school enact the principles by creating experiences for students across multiple settings.

The impact of the assistant principal's leadership extends across the school community. While the principal is spending the majority of her time in teacher learning and collaboration spaces, the assistant principal is leading, supporting, and supervising support staff, lunch and recess schedules, student behavior systems, substitutes, volunteers, special programs and special services, and real-time problem solving, often including families, in addition to supporting teachers' classroom community building. The leadership across all of these spaces has a huge impact on how the principles are enacted by adults, as each decision made by the assistant principal will often have a ripple effect across many adults. This supports schools in creating a consistent experience for students and families because the vision is shared and all adults are developing the skills to enact it.

Of course, in schools where there is a single administrator, leading the social emotional and community building, as well as the schoolwide programs and supervision is held by the principal. But in schools where the work is shared by two leaders in the division of labor described here, we have seen huge benefits to the adult and student learners. When both administrators hold their areas of responsibility in principled and aligned ways and carefully coordinate their messaging and expectations, the school community thrives.

IDEAS FOR GETTING STARTED

Principals and Teachers: Examine Your Biases

The changes necessary to shift the teacher/principal relationship to a true professional partnership represent a significant adaptive change. In considering how you might engage in this change, it's important to assess your readiness. We all have deeply ingrained ideas about what it means to be "competent" or "good" at our role *and* what it means for others to be "competent" or "good" in their roles. These shape how we interact with each other. A good place to start is reflecting on your own beliefs. Do you have any biases that might get in the way? Next, we suggest some possible reflection prompts to consider. We encourage both principals and teachers to take a stab at jotting down some thoughts (related to both roles) and then try sharing your reflections with each other.

Principal

- What does a good principal spend most of her time doing?
- What does a good principal do during teacher professional development?
- How does a good principal respond to teacher questions or concerns?
- What does a good principal do during teacher collaborative time?
- What does a good principal do when she comes into a teachers' classroom? How does she decide *when* to come into a teachers' classroom?

Teacher

- What does a good teacher spend most of her time doing?
- What does a good teacher do during professional development?
- What does a good teacher do if she isn't sure about something, she has a question, or something is challenging?
- What does a good teacher do during teacher collaborative time?
- What does a good teacher do when she comes into another teacher's classroom? How does she decide *when* to come into another teacher's classroom?

Look through what you jotted down.

- What connections do you see between good enactments of these roles? How do they perpetuate each other?
- Are any of the biases you identified getting in the way of your learning and collaborating?

Groups: Develop Norms That Support You to Show up Differently

When you read the descriptions of how you should show up across the professional learning system spaces, what "buts" pop into your mind? Perhaps you thought, "But what about . . ." or "But I could never . . ." or "But I'm supposed to . . ." or "But that feels . . ." or "But that would make teachers [or my principal or my coach] think X about me," or "But my colleagues would never . . ."

Being curious and empathetic and open to sharing your "buts" can lead to new ways of being together. Make time to have conversations to help each other more deeply understand what "buts" are actually getting in the way. Then develop an initial set of norms to support you in showing up differently.

Principals: Find the Time

We imagine that one of your "buts" was, "But I simply don't have this much time to spend with teachers." That will have to change, so consider setting aside a few minutes at the end of each day for a month. Use this time to reflect on how you spent your day and how it impacted teacher and student learning. You're looking for things you can trust others to do or just stop doing:

- What could you delegate to someone else?
- What could you just do less of or do more quickly?
- What could you condense or restrict to certain times (e.g., checking emails, returning phone calls, or recurring meetings)?
- What could you entrust to the assistant principal, office manager, counselor, custodian, or district staff?
- What just doesn't need to be done?
- What could you push back on (e.g., district expectations or process requirements that are inefficient or unnecessarily time consuming)?[6]

5

Teachers and Coaches in Partnership

COACHING AND COLLABORATION WITH TEAMS OF TEACHERS

New ideas continually emerge in education: new models of instruction, changing expectations about what children can and should learn, richer ideas about building on children's and communities' funds of knowledge. A fundamental message of our book is that teachers need time, space, and trusted colleagues to engage in taking on these new ideas and to be creative and curious, while maintaining a deep commitment to the principles of teaching and creating an excellent educational experience for the communities and families they serve. Delivering on these commitments in multilingual, racially diverse communities that have historically experienced deficit instructional practices in US public schools requires ongoing collaboration and collective learning among adults in schools. Teachers need a lot more support than is typically provided to create thriving classroom environments that consistently position students' ideas and experiences at the center of teaching. Taking on this scale of change requires equally robust learning environments for teachers.

A Change from the Typical Model of Coaching

In most US schools, coaching is aimed at individual teacher improvement. Coaches work one-on-one with teachers, often toward goals that the teacher has identified.[1] What the coach discusses with one teacher is often completely different than what the coach discusses with another teacher. For example, one teacher may choose to work on the pacing of lessons, while another teacher may choose to work on asking rich questions to students. In individualized coaching, teachers across the school are typically not working toward a common instructional vision. And teachers do not have the benefit of learning alongside and from other teachers.

Our approach to coaching is different.[2] It involves organizing the coach's work around teams of teachers based on the foundational belief that schools must serve as learning organizations for adults as well as children.[3] Coaching is grounded in the Principles of Learning to Teach, which means that this approach to coaching supports change across the entire school system, creating learning experiences for teachers that are sustained, connected, and coherent over time and designed to position teachers to learn from and with one another. We think of coaching as a key lever in supporting system changes rather than just enabling individual teacher improvement.[4] We conceive of the coach as a learner who is on a journey alongside teachers to figure out the best ways to create meaningful learning experiences for children. Being on this journey together allows everyone to share in the excitement of exploring children's thinking and experiences, as well as taking on the complexities, tensions, and dilemmas that arise in teaching that don't have easy answers.[5] This conception positions teachers and coaches to think and work together to experiment with solutions and to partner in making sense of how they shape students' thinking and experiences.

What does it mean to coach a team of practitioners? It means entering a partnership in which coaches and teachers regularly work *together* on planning, teaching, and reflecting on how they can create rich social and intellectual learning experiences for children.[6] The coach facilitates ongoing learning for teachers in many different spaces across the school, attending to teachers' developing knowledge and a grade-level team's capacity to learn, reflect, and adjust together. The coach, as a subject matter specialist, also helps the principal, who is also part of the team, to understand the priorities and opportunities for content instruction at each grade level in the school. Because the coach is guided by the Principles for Learning to Teach, she is attending to the adult learners' opportunities to orient to each other and students' developing ideas, to practice and make sense of what they are learning, and to look at how each is experiencing the learning, with the goal of making it coherent and responsive. Coaching provides a team with access to another dimension of collaboration, learning with and from other teachers. This kind of coaching provides teachers with someone to help them unpack problems of practice, explore their students' needs, dive deeply into their own knowledge and beliefs, and then expand their practice as learners on the journey of meeting their students' needs.

Consider this example from a Grade-Level Team Meeting that took place early in the 2021–2022 school year, after students had returned to in-person learning after the COVID-19 pandemic:

The second-grade teachers shared that they were noticing that their students seemed to have progressed more in their reading skills than their writing skills during remote instruction. Because teachers had weekly Grade-Level Team Meetings facilitated by the literacy coach, they had time to really dig into samples of student work that they had collected and share their observations to see if they could identify the underlying cause of this discrepancy and collectively decide how to respond.

They discovered that students could decode appropriately and were able to read text relatively well. However, students struggled to encode words and even common second-grade spelling patterns were troublesome. In addition, students also needed support with the mechanics of holding a pencil and forming letters. The joint challenges of encoding words and the mechanics of printing caused significant obstacles to composition, resulting in a discrepancy between reading performance and writing performance. The team suspected that during remote learning, it may have been easier for students to progress in reading development than writing development.

At first, teachers felt very disheartened that students seemed on track in reading but had not yet developed some key understandings important for writing. The Grade-Level Team Meeting provided a space for teachers to collectively process what they were noticing and consider how to move forward. The coach, having a broader perspective on the kindergarten through second-grade writing progression, provided an article about writing development and how to position students to have agency in writing. The discussion about the ideas in this article supported the teachers and the principal to deepen their thinking about the reciprocal impact of reading and writing development and actively consider what specific instructional adjustments would advance students' progress within the K–2 grade band.

As the team tried to understand how they could support students to draw on the skills they had developed in reading to support their writing, they identified multiple instructional activities they wanted to use with students. Teachers identified the need for students to engage in more interactive writing and more practice with writing using whiteboards. The teachers also felt the need to give more specific feedback to students to improve their ability to form letters when physically writing and to encourage students to use elaborations to improve the content of their writing. Because teachers had noticed that the students had not yet developed strong writing identities, they wanted to support students to feel confident in their writing. And they wondered what instructional moves would support their students to build up stamina and volume in writing.

The coach looked at the upcoming instructional unit to identify where teachers could provide additional learning opportunities for students and considered how to shift the pacing timeline. To support the teachers in making these instructional shifts, she planned to introduce strategies for using interactive writing with students in the upcoming Learning Lab. In the Lab, teachers, along with their principal and coach, explored how to support *students to get their rough-draft sentences written, then go back and listen for particular sounds or words, then check for accuracy. This strategy, regularly used by kindergarten teachers, would support the development of the second-graders' writing skills.*

What we want you to notice in this example is that teachers are the leaders of the instructional decisions. It wasn't the coach, principal, or someone at the district office identifying skill gaps based on data generated by a computer program. It wasn't just a matter of making sure that all students reach a learning target by looking at an end-of-unit quiz and identifying what to reteach. Teachers are directly engaged in identifying student needs and in designing responses that they believe will work, based on their observations of and interactions with students in their classrooms. The partnership between teachers and their coach is responsive to both student needs and teachers' questions. Teachers, together with the coach, focus on students' thinking and engage in examining teaching practices to continue to refine and hone strategies that support children over time. And note that teachers felt responsible for all the students across their grade level, not just those assigned to their classrooms. This shared ownership compels them to contribute their ideas about how to best support students and fosters a shared urgency to respond to the needs of all students.

Teachers had purposeful conversations with their students and analyzed their work in an effort to uncover their current understandings. This collective inquiry resulted in an actionable realization: students needed more support in writing. But they did not view this as a gap in some students' skills that should be addressed by intervention groups. Further, the principal and coach trusted the teachers and their expertise to create a working theory about what might be the root issues and what students needed in order to move forward. Because the coach had a deep understanding of how students progress in the writing process, she drafted new lessons that provided specific strategies like the one mentioned here and worked with the team to create flexibility in the curriculum pacing to be responsive to student needs.

> “Teachers are the instructional decision-makers. It isn't me, as a coach, telling them what to do. It's me coming alongside them as a person who has some resources and some information and some things I've tried in the past, along with their information and knowledge of kids. During Grade-Level Team Meetings, we share with each other and then we just adjust. I think the powerful piece of why it works is because it isn't about any one person being an expert. It's about together, we know more, so we can make decisions. Then I figure out how to provide space for them to tweak their instruction. It isn't about "Oh, my gosh, that didn't work." It's about "We tried this, this isn't working, let's do something else." It's an ongoing conversation.
>
> *Literacy coach*

CREATING THE PARTNERSHIP BETWEEN COACHES AND TEACHERS

In chapter 4, we argued that in order for it to become "our work," teachers and principals both must engage with each other and the work differently. This requires intentional efforts to each authentically engage in opportunities to learn and lead together. The parallel need exists if teacher-coach relationships are to evolve into partnerships focused on improving student learning through teacher practice. This means recognizing and leveraging the unique contributions that each brings to the process of generating and trying new ideas in service of the common goal. The coach brings specialized knowledge and a perspective on collective learning across the school. Teachers bring knowledge of their students, including their identities, how their students are making sense of ideas, and how they engage in the learning community. The act of trusting and inviting these valuable contributions from each other creates the fabric of the partnership. Together, coaches and teachers collectively design and create instructional responses based on their collective understanding. How they show up, make space for others, and stay focused on designing what students will experience next is the work of the partnership (see table 5.1).

Nurturing Mutual and Reciprocal Relationships

The individual relationships between the coach and each teacher are pivotal for the health and effectiveness of the team. This calls on both teachers and coaches to develop authentic relationships that honor the expertise that each brings. This relationship only develops with intentional effort over time. Being thought partners means appreciating that they bring complementary perspectives and actively lend their expertise. It also means being able to honestly share questions, ideas in progress, and challenges that emerge in the work of being a teacher. We don't view coaches as all-knowing experts, but we do recognize and value them as subject matter specialists. They bring a deep and current knowledge of children's subject matter development and the teaching practices and curricular resources that elicit and build on children's ideas. Their position also provides them a unique perspective on practices, experiences, and progress across classrooms and grade levels.

Because a coach's time is not tied to the student schedule as a classroom teacher's is, the coach has the benefit of continually learning from and with many teachers and can convey new insights from one teacher to

Table 5.1 Coach-teacher partnership roles and responsibilities

Coach	Teacher	Together
• Designer and facilitator of learning for teachers, informed by knowledge of teachers, students, and content • Subject matter specialist who brings knowledge of content, curricular resources, and teaching practices • Coordinator of shared knowledge and practice across the school	• Leader of instructional decisions and classroom learning space • Source of knowledge of their students; deeply understands the social and emotional dynamics of the classroom community • Holder of perspective of students' experiences and teaching practices across content areas	• Thought partners and cocreators of instructional responses that result in meaningful and equitable learning experiences for children

another and from one grade level to another. What they observe and learn as they spend time with teachers across the school allows them to raise questions and invite teachers to examine what they are noticing and learning from their own students in ways that teachers seldom do alone. Reciprocally, teachers bring detailed knowledge of their own students and practices that are working and not working in their classrooms across content areas. They see how students access and respond to classroom tasks in every subject matter. They understand how their students are participating in the academic and social life of the classroom across the school day. Teachers deeply understand the social and emotional dynamics that are at play among their students and will be the first to identify the ways that a new curriculum lacks opportunities to leverage students' cultural diversity. Together, the teacher and coach as partners are powerfully qualified to respond to student needs.

> I don't see it as the coach coming in to my classroom to judge me. She's coming in to try to help me figure out how to best get the kids to where they need to be. And that means jumping in and having a conversation with me. Or jumping in and asking the kids a question that I haven't thought of. Or coming up to me as the kids are working and suggesting something or asking a question. It's really cool to have that relationship.
>
> *Second-grade teacher*

> If you approach all of this work as a grand adventure that you get to do together, if you can get excited about the adventure and joining them on this exploration together, it captivates everybody. You know? Coaching is not something I do to you. It's like, look, we get to wade through this together. This is really cool. What are we going to see together? What problems are we going to encounter that neither of us have the answers to? Let's see if we can figure it out together.
>
> *Math coach*

Developing Trust through Partnership

Even between highly qualified professionals, trust is vital to productive partnerships and must be built over time based on shared experiences working and learning together. Collaborating to create learning experiences for students involves emotional investment. Trying and succeeding at something new can be invigorating. Conversely, trying and possibly failing is scary. Learning includes being vulnerable while taking risks and managing the feelings that come with stumbling, making mistakes, and sometimes failing. Creating an authentic partnership between teachers and coaches means navigating the emotional highs and lows of learning and creating together. Coaches and teachers both have to show up to learning spaces with curiosity and willingness to experiment, embracing the stance that making public the challenges, demands, and anxieties of teaching will advance their work in service of students.

Trust is also fostered over time as coaches share in taking risks with the ideas they generate with teachers. Coaches too have to try out new ideas in front of students and then reflect with teachers about how they affect and benefit students. In fact, it's very important that coaches are equally willing to be the first volunteer to try something new. When a teacher and a coach develop a new idea, the coach's role is to support the teacher in reflecting on whether an instructional decision benefited student participation and learning. By volunteering to try out the idea in front of students, the coach assumes the risk so the teacher can focus on observing and reflecting, which prioritizes the teacher's opportunity to deepen and gain instructional decision-making skills. The coach's willingness to assume a bit of risk in trying a new idea also nurtures a shared understanding of what it means to learn from, with, and for students. Some risk taking is foundational to the commitment to create more equitable experiences for students. The partnership between teacher and coach serves to normalize risk taking and foster developing trust in service of designing better student learning experiences.

> ❝ The person that I want to be for my students is the person that my coaches are for me. Everything from helping me plan and just see the road that I'm supposed to be on, to talking me off the cliff. And when I'm ready to give up, they encourage me. So there's this personal relationship that we have. They helped me believe that I can do what I'm doing. And then the other part is that they're showing me how to do it. And so they are, for me, what I hope to be for my own kids.
>
> *First-grade teacher*
>
> And because they see themselves as learners, the coach will never say that she's mastered everything in math. And so when you have a coach who's supposedly the content expert, and a principal who's supposedly, the person who runs this whole ship called "school." When you have those two people who are willing to say, like, "Hey, I don't know. Let's experiment, let's learn from the kids." That's huge.
>
> *Fourth-grade teacher*

CREATING RESPONSIVE TEACHER LEARNING GOALS AND EXPERIENCES

While the partnership between coach and teachers is essential, it is important to recognize that each plays a unique role in the learning spaces in which they are the leader. In classrooms, this is unequivocally the teacher. In the collective teacher learning spaces across the professional learning system, this is the coach. The coach is the principal designer of the adult learning experiences, and as such plays an important role in enacting the Principles of the Adult Learning Context across the professional learning system that supports teachers, coaches, and principals to work together in ways that intentionally focus on developing practices that better serve students. In addition, we have previously elaborated on how we see learning to teach as a continual process of knowledge, skill, and identity development, which the learning system leverages by providing timely, embedded, and logical opportunities for educators to collaborate on instructional decisions and practices. But this will meaningfully support teachers only if the learning and collaboration opportunities are crafted by a reflective, skilled, and intentional leader.

The coach's role is to deeply understand current student learning, be in productive relationships with teachers, ensuring that she knows their developing practices so that she can design experiences that support their learning across the system. Next, we unpack the work coaches do with and for teachers in service of designing collaborative learning experiences that support collective growth. Some responsibilities require that coaches work directly with teachers to identify or develop ideas or goals, while others rely solely on the coach to orchestrate a coherent, long-term strategy. Both depend on and have the potential to deepen the close and interdependent partnership between teachers and coaches.

> I think of the coach as kind of like the teacher role. Presenting questions. Bringing us something new to learn. I think it's important that the coach provides us with something new to learn, or something related to what we've been talking about.
>
> *Third-grade teacher*

As stated earlier, coaches have a privileged, even cherished perspective, in that they get to see teachers' instructional decisions play out with students in classrooms across grade levels and across the school. Teachers and coaches are in continual conversations about what to work on next to deepen and enrich instruction across the school. These conversations inform the goals that drive the coach's work with teams. Coaches formulate goals as they watch teachers' instructional practices, listen to their ideas and concerns, and talk with them about how their students are engaging in learning and sensemaking. Teachers see that coaches recognize, value and position them as competent, trustworthy sensemakers and decision-makers. This trust is critical because there should be no secrets about what is getting worked on. Our experience suggests that in the context of this kind of partnership, teachers develop a trust in the coach's ability to identify learning goals that are valuable for the whole team.

Although we are elaborating the coach's role in this chapter, it's important to remember that all Instructional Leadership Team (ILT) members are invested in and continually working to foster the schoolwide vision and Principles for Teaching and Learning to Teach. In chapter 6, we explain in greater depth how teacher learning goals are thoughtfully developed through discussions during the ILT as coaches and principals reflect on their conversations with teachers and in light of student learning across the school. In her role as a content area specialist, the coach is continually reflecting on questions like those we list here, to identify immediate and long-term learning goals for teams:

- How are students progressing toward the instructional goals we have for them at each grade level? What are the content standards and big ideas of the current or upcoming unit? How deep is each teacher's understanding of this content?
- What do teachers need to know and reflect on to make sense of what is happening for students in their classrooms?
- How do the teaching practices in our classrooms and how we engage children reflect our Principles for Teaching? How are students being positioned as sensemakers? Are we seeing differences in teacher decision-making and its impacts on students that are worthy of reflection and group consideration?
- How are students showing up in the classroom? How do they see themselves? How are they demonstrating agency and independence? What's making sense to students right now? How are they showing understanding and engagement through their words, models, pictures, and other modes of communication?
- How are teachers feeling about their instruction and how children are accessing and engaging in learning opportunities and advancing in their learning?
- How are teachers responding to and taking up the most recent new learning that we have been engaged in as a group? Are there any

constraints or obstacles that teachers are running into as they try on new ideas?

- How well are the curricular resources supporting teachers in making instructional decisions that position students as sensemakers?
- What support might individual teachers and teams need as they try out new practices or dig into new content?

The coach's reflections on these questions, combined with her conversations with teachers and members of the ILT, help her assess whether and how to continue and deepen work on current ideas or move on to new ideas. Her reflections also help her determine the scope and pacing of new goals.

The identification and development of adult learning goals shape every aspect of the work that adults do across the learning system. We provide the following examples next to illustrate how they emerge as a product of the professional learning system in which coaches, teachers, and the principal collaborate in classrooms, Grade-Level Team Meetings, and Learning Labs:

- In a Grade-Level Team Meeting, one of the fifth-grade teachers shares that many students in her classroom are not participating in literacy Hands Down Conversations, which are student-centered conversations that students engage in without raising their hands.[7] The other two teachers share a similar concern. They reflect on questions like: Who are the students who are not participating? Do they participate in math conversations? What might be possible reasons they do not participate? They realize that participation in discussions across contents is not as robust as they would like and decide to explore strategies that increase participation in a range of conversation structures in the upcoming Learning Lab. The coach listens in on Hands Down Conversations during several Classroom Visits to better understand what teachers are noticing. After another discussion with the team to calibrate the specific behaviors that are affecting student engagement, the coach synthesizes what she now understands in order to determine goals for the upcoming Labs.

- As the mathematics coach visits multiplication mini-lessons across third-grade classrooms, she notices that two of the teachers represent students' multiplication strategies using a grouping model, while the third teacher's representations also include number lines and area models. She notices that student conversations about multiplication differ depending on the classroom because of these instructional choices about what to record on anchor charts. The coach invites teachers to discuss these instructional decisions at the following week's Grade-Level Team Meeting and consider how and whether it's making a difference in students' understanding of multiplication.

- The school has adopted a new science curriculum that foregrounds scientific modeling and inquiry in line with the Next Generation Science Standards. Teachers will need time and support to dig into the scientific concepts involved in the kindergarten unit on the water cycle and figure out how to meaningfully connect the ideas in the unit to children's lived experiences. The coach plans to work with teachers in a Learning Lab and several Grade-Level Team Meetings to support the implementation of this new unit.

- The fourth-grade teachers have shared with the coach that they would like to engage students more deeply in learning mathematical argumentation. Since this is a big mathematical practice, it requires a long-term engagement over a series of Learning Labs. Given that the fourth-grade team has been working together for a number of years, she agrees that this would be a good year to do a deep dive into mathematical argumentation, so she begins gathering the foundational texts and tasks that will provide the basis for designing a series of Learning Labs and Grade-Level Team Meetings.

In these examples, notice that goals are emerging and being considered as coaches interact with teachers and the principal across various teacher learning spaces in the school. As we explained in chapter 3, each space in the professional learning system has a different purpose. In the Learning Lab space, coaches introduce new ideas, give teachers opportunities to practice something together, and explore students' thinking around a new disciplinary idea. In the weekly Grade-Level Team Meetings, coaches can support teachers to continue to develop and deepen new learning as they discuss how it can inform their instructional decisions. They work in real time to respond to students' current ideas and progress, reflecting on past teaching and planning for upcoming teaching. In the individual Classroom Visits, the coach and teacher can think together in the moment about what specific instructional decisions to make. Depending on the adult learning goal, the coach is able both to choose the logical space in which to introduce or practice a goal and to support the ongoing learning about that goal by intentionally weaving the work on a goal across the spaces in ways that make sense for teachers and students. This combination of well-chosen goals and intentionally designed work on the goal—in the spaces where teachers actually do the thinking and reasoning of planning responsive instruction—is what powerfully supports the growth of new practices. Teachers are supported in the course of their work based on what their students are doing, processing developing ideas and addressing challenges as a team with coach support.

> I use the coach's knowledge to guide our approach to how we present information to kids; about what we focus on. And she's so instrumental in clarifying for us what the most important parts of this specific lesson is or what the key parts of a standard is. Having her there to streamline what we do as the fourth-grade team allows us to be consistent across the classrooms. It allows us to be consistent in how we're presenting information. And it's just really nice to have someone who can listen to everything that the three of us say and process it, then re-present it to us. So it's really nice to have [the coach] there to focus us and take our different experiences and kind of mesh them into something that works for us.
>
> *Fourth-grade teacher*

RECOGNIZING THE NEED FOR RESPONSIVE TEACHER LEARNING EXPERIENCES

As we asserted in chapter 4, there is a belief that teachers should be capable of teaching and learning autonomously—they should need "support" or collaboration only when there's something new or when they struggle. In what other industry do we train a professional one time and then expect them to develop into skilled practitioners without ongoing opportunities to refine their craft? This is simply denial of responsibility. To create the rich, intellectual, and asset-focused learning communities we want for all children, teachers need and deserve routine, embedded, intentional, and responsive learning opportunities. Content coaches, in the context of a professional learning system led by a principal who is equally committed to teacher learning as a key lever of student learning, can partner with teachers to meet this need. When we stop acting surprised and recognize ongoing teacher learning as a responsibility, we open ourselves to the possibility that we can work together in new and more powerful ways to create the schools we want for students and the schools we want to work in.

CASE STUDY: LEARNING SPACES IN ACTION

This case study is intended to provide you with a snapshot of how a coach and a group of teachers work in a productive relationship with one another across the learning spaces to support teaching that nurtures students' capabilities and curiosities (see figure 5.1). We offer it to highlight how both coaches and teachers use the learning spaces across the system to leverage each other's expertise. Each plays critical roles in the creation of new strategies and practices. As the facilitator of teacher learning, the case illustrates how the coach brings intentional goals into each space and actively supports coherent experiences for teachers. Just as important, this case provides a view into the teachers' critical role as learners, partners, and innovators.

Figure 5.1   A student works on a mathematics problem

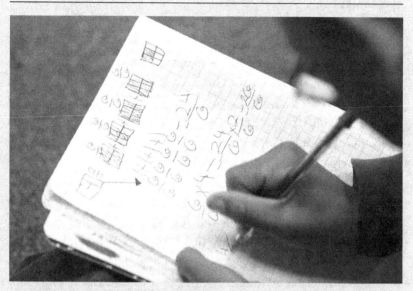

Source: Matt Hagen

The case study spans a little over a week, beginning with the fourth-grade Learning Lab on January 7 and ending with the Grade-Level Team Meeting on January 15 as the team works together to begin a fractions unit successfully. We include dialogue to help you picture how we take an asset-based approach to teacher and student learning by bringing students' sensemaking and their affective and social experiences into the space. Along the way, we pause and offer commentary on the things we think are important to notice. While this case study is based on data and real events from our research, it is a composite narrative inspired by our experiences across many years and schools. This strategy allows us to distill many complex accounts into a single, more digestible situation that conveys the big ideas and insights that we have gained from our work together. It also serves to maintain the anonymity of participants. All names are pseudonyms.

Planning for the January 7 Learning Lab

Tara, the mathematics coach, is planning her Lab for the fourth-grade team: Val, a teacher who has taught fourth grade at the school for three years; Tia, a veteran teacher at the school who just moved from first to fourth grade this year; and Maya, who joined them this year after teaching fourth grade at another school. Julie, the principal, participates in every Learning Lab.

This Learning Lab is taking place just prior to the start of a fractions unit. Tia and Maya have each had several conversations with Tara. They feel anxious about the approach to teaching fractions, which is new to them, and have questions about this unit. Tia has also checked in with Val who, three years ago, shared the same anxieties about fractions. Val is eager to support her teammates as they learn to anticipate the ideas and strategies that their fourth-grade students are likely to bring to the unit.

Tara draws on her knowledge of how fractions are taught in third grade and her conversations with the fourth-grade team to identify the learning goals for this Lab. In third grade, students work on developing an understanding of fractions using language that connects the size of the piece and the name of the fraction. For example, picture a child cutting a square in half and then cutting just one of those halves in half (see figure 5.2). The square now has three pieces, and the child may incorrectly identify the pieces as "thirds." If the teacher orients the child to think about how many of those sized pieces fit into the whole, it supports the child to recognize the smaller partition as a fourth-sized piece because four of those equal-sized pieces fit into the whole.[8]

Third-graders apply these ideas about naming fractional quantities in the context of fair sharing problems. For example, to figure

Figure 5.2 A square partitioned in three parts, but not thirds

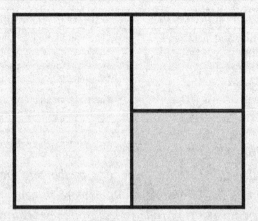

out how much pizza eight people would each get if they shared three whole pizzas equally, students could say, "Each person would get three-eighths, or three eighth-sized pieces."[9] Third-graders also explored simple equivalent fractions and compared fractions with the same denominator or the same numerator. Val and Tara want the new fourth-grade teammates to be prepared for the range of ways that students are likely to interpret fraction quantities so they can recognize and work on how to use instructional questions to advance students' ideas.

Tara has selected a familiar activity called True-False Equations, which asks students to compare two fractions and determine if the equation is true or false, allowing the team to listen to the language and strategies students use to make sense of fractions. Table 5.2 lists the goals she has identified for the Learning Lab. She will share these goals with the teachers at the outset of the Learning Lab. Just as we state in the Principles for Teaching, effective instruction requires clear instructional goals. As the coach thinks about her learners, the teachers, she needs to be sure that she has intentionally identified the goals that will guide their time together.

Table 5.2 Learning Lab goals for teachers

Teachers' Practice Goals	Teachers' Content Goals
• Listen carefully and make sense of student thinking in order to ask responsive questions.	• Listen and probe to learn how students make sense of fractions and the strategies they use to compare fractions. • Use fractional language to support students' understanding of fractions.

What to Notice

Tara scheduled this Lab just prior to a challenging unit to provide teachers time to dig into content and explore students' understandings. As she planned, she considered key grade-level content, as well as the teachers' individual and collective knowledge and practices.

Tara has identified two kinds of goals: practice and content goals. She is mindful that Tia and Maya will encounter significant new learning as their thinking and ability to talk about fractions develop. As they dive into fractions, Tara wants to foster curiosity about student thinking rather than teaching procedures to drive instruction. With two new members on the team, Tara also wants to ensure that Tia's and Maya's voices are present. Her decision to enlist Val is designed to orient the team members to each other and help the new members engage in learning from colleagues.

Learning Lab on January 7

As described in chapter 3, Learning Labs are an anchor for introducing and experimenting with new ideas in the ongoing effort to develop specialized capacities for teaching. In Labs, teachers develop a shared vision of instruction and the learning communities they are trying to foster by designing, enacting, and debriefing a lesson together. Throughout the Lab, students' ideas and experiences are central. Everyone takes a learner stance since learning is messy and almost never linear, for both children and adults.

Phase 1: Engaging in New Learning

In the first phase of the Lab, teachers engage in new learning. Tara provides teachers with an opportunity to work together to place index cards with fractions (8/16, 1/3, 3/4, 8/8, 2/9, 6/10, and 9/6) on a number line. The quantities are more challenging than the quantities that their students will work with; the added complexity supports the development of teachers' own content knowledge. The teachers are tasked with hanging these fractions on an actual clothesline. The team stands and hangs them one at a time, shifting their positions to approximate where the fractions would be in relation to each other on a number line. There's a lot of negotiating and laughter as the team reasons through the relationships and spatial placement, revising their thinking multiple times along the way. As they place the fractions, Tara presses teachers to justify their thinking, recording their ideas on chart paper as they share. Tia places 8/8 at the end of the clothesline saying it's one whole.[10] Maya goes next and, chuckling, says, "Now what do we do with 9/6?" Tia laughs, "Oh I see, how cool, we can just move 8/8 to the left" (see figure 5.3).

Maya worries that students won't understand 9/6 because it is an "improper fraction." Val explains that fourth-graders last year read 9/6 as "nine sixth-sized pieces." Val begins a drawing to demonstrate how students would show 9/6. She draws two rectangles on chart

Figure 5.3 Placing and moving fractions along the clothesline to show relative positioning as new quantities are considered

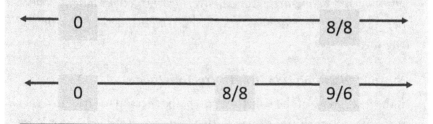

paper, dividing each into six equal-sized pieces, and explains that students would shade in nine of the pieces and say that nine-sixths are more than one whole. Tia and Maya begin to get excited about how the language supports students' understanding. Tara recognizes an opportunity to elaborate on the fractions language that is used at their school: the "denominator" tells what is being counted, referring to the size of the piece; and the "numerator" is the counting number, referring to how many equal-sized pieces we have. Julie, the principal, shares the progress that students across the school have made in their understanding of fractions. The conversation has really piqued Tia and Maya's curiosity about how students will work with fractions today.

What to Notice

Tara selected a task that set the tone for the Learning Lab: mathematical work that could be approached with curiosity, in a lighthearted and relaxed manner. Notice how the teachers engage as learners of the actual content, doing an instructional activity together rather than just reading about the activity or unpacking the standard and learning new vocabulary. This supported them to engage with curiosity, asking one another questions and pressing for justifications. As the teachers explored math ideas together, Tia and Maya encountered unfamiliar ways of thinking about fractions and had the opportunity to explore them without embarrassment. Val, as a returning teacher, was invited in as a resource. Instead of introducing vocabulary upfront, Tara deliberately waited, layering in fractions language once they developed a readiness to see the importance of the precise language.

Phase 2: Planning a Lesson to Try Together

In the next phase of the Lab, the team plans a lesson to enact together in a classroom. Tara explains that she has selected True-False

Equations, a familiar instructional activity, for the teachers to enact because it will allow the team to listen to the language and reasoning students use to compare fractions, a key goal of this Learning Lab. The team sets to work planning, thinking carefully about the pairs of fractions they will use.

Tia:	I think our first number sentence should be one that kids will be able to make sense of like 3/8 < 7/8.
Tara:	Do you think they'll say it's true or false?
Maya:	Definitely true.
Tara:	What do you think students might say?
Val:	I think they might say that three eighth-sized pieces are less than seven eighth-sized pieces, and they'll tell us to draw a picture to prove it.
Maya:	The picture will help anyone who isn't sure.
Tara:	What if a student says "True, because 3 is less than 7." What question could we ask to uncover what they know about fractions?
Tia:	We could ask, "Three what?"
Val:	Or "What's the size of the piece?"
Maya:	Oh yeah, I love that. That's really making sense to me.

The teachers select three more fraction comparisons to try with students. They anticipate how students might reason through each inequality and brainstorm questions they might ask to uncover how students are making sense of fractions, plus ways to support them to use fractions language.

Next, the team discusses the flow of the lesson. Val and Julie offer to lead today's lesson so Tia and Maya can listen to the language of fractions and students' ideas. Since they will be visiting Maya's class today, she shares a bit about her students. Four students are new to the school, so this approach to fractions will likely be unfamiliar to them. Three students are learning English, so opportunities to talk with their partners in any language they choose will be especially helpful. Just as they had explored the ideas together at the start of the Lab, the teachers want to be sure their students are all invited into the task; minimizing status differences based on language or newcomer status to the school is important. In the lesson, Val and Julie will seek to ensure that the students are oriented toward one another as they grow ideas together through discourse.

What to Notice

Because the planning portion of the Lab is constrained by time, Tara preselected the instructional activity that they would try out in the classroom, but she left the selection of which fraction quantities to compare up to the teachers in order to provide opportunities to make instructional decisions and provide rationales for those decisions. The teachers made decisions about the quantities, representations, questions, and language used in math instruction. This provided an opportunity to practice reasoning publicly through instructional decisions. Because they are going to teach together, it's important for everyone to own the lesson, being invested in what they are trying to accomplish and learn from their students.

Phase 3: Trying out the Lesson

In the third phase of the Learning Lab, the team goes into a classroom to try out the lesson. As the team enters the classroom, the students are seated on the carpet. Teachers and students wave at each other as the teachers find seats alongside the students. The students count the number of teachers coming into the classroom and exclaim with delight as they recognize who is joining them. Julie, the principal, greets the class and thanks the students for helping the teachers learn today. Tia explains to the students that they will be doing some True-False number sentences today, but instead of thinking about whole numbers, they will be thinking about fractions.

Val writes 3/8 < 7/8 on the chart paper and asks the students if the statement is true or false; she reminds them to signal by putting a thumb on their chest when they've decided. When the students have signaled, she tells them to turn to their partners and share what they think and why. After the turn and talk, Val asks students to share their thinking. The students eagerly do so. The students agree that the statement is true, and they guide Val to draw pictures of brownies to justify their thinking. Val repeats this process with the next inequality, 2/8 < 2/3. After spending time to reflect on the inequality independently, most of the partners agree that the number of pieces (numerators) is the same, but the size of the pieces (denominators) is different. A few students grab whiteboards to show their partners how eighths are smaller than thirds.

Val passes the pen to Julie, who writes 3/2 < 4/8.

Julie: Place your thumb on your chest when you have an idea about whether this is true or false.

Students slowly put their thumbs to their chests. Some students look uncertain.

Julie: This seems like it's a tricky problem, and there might be a lot of different ideas out there. Would you show me what you're thinking? Right here on your chest, put your thumb up if you think it's true, thumbs down if you think it's false, or thumbs sideways if you're still thinking about it.

The class is divided, with about a third signaling true, a third signaling false, and a third signaling uncertainty.

Julie: We have a lot of different ideas. Would it be OK with you if the teachers do a Teacher Time Out?

Students smile and say "Sure!" Julie looks at the teachers.

Julie:	Should we have students share their ideas or talk with partners first?
Val:	Getting lots of different ideas out first would surface the many different ways the kids are thinking about fractions.
Maya:	Talking with partners first would support those who are uncertain, but fewer ideas might be shared.
Tia:	How about both? Let's have a couple of kids share ideas, and then turn and talk? It might provide some different ideas that the partners will want to discuss.

Julie turns back to the students.

Julie:	Thanks, everybody! We'd like to hear what you're thinking. Would someone who is unsure share what makes this number sentence tricky? Elijah?
Elijah (student):	Well, the number of pieces are different *and* the size of the pieces are different. So how can we compare them?
Julie:	Yes, this number sentence is different from the others. Who has an idea about whether this is true or false, and how do you know?

Julie asked Elijah to share what made this number sentence tricky in order to prompt the students to think about the number of pieces and the size of the pieces. After a couple of students share, Julie asks students to turn and talk with their partners. The classroom buzzes with excited conversation as the teachers lean in to listen in on the partners' conversations. A couple of students grab whiteboards to draw pictures. After several minutes, Julie calls the students back together and asks them to share. Sahra, who is new to the school, shares that she knew that 4/8 is equal to 1/2, and her partner drew a picture and showed her that 3/2 is more than 1, so 3/2 is greater than 1. Several students signal that they agree.

What to Notice

Before and during the Classroom Visit, the principal participated in the professional learning and took a risk, trying something new in front of the students. By volunteering to be one of the lead teachers, the principal took a learner stance, modeling her desire to experience the joy and messiness of learning while developing her own teaching practice alongside the teachers. She took the initiative of calling for a Teacher Time Out, consulting with the team about the option that would best allow students to wrestle with the problem and provide them the opportunities they are seeking to hear how students are thinking about and able to describe their strategies for comparing fractions. Notice, also, how the teachers made space for the principal to be a learner and rely on their expertise. This is an example of the power of collaboration during a Lab where teachers, the coach, and the principal get to slow down and analyze their decision-making process.

Phase 4: Reflecting

After the Classroom Visit, the teachers begin the fourth phase of the Learning Lab, debriefing the visit and thinking about what they have learned. Tara asks the team what they think students understood about fractions. They agree that most of the class remembered the language of fractions and were able to compare fractions when the size of the pieces was the same, and that pictures helped them think about the size of the pieces. They discuss how the pictures serve as a scaffold. They decide that they will need to keep this in mind as the unit progresses and be mindful that they don't overscaffold by relying too much on pictures.

The teachers are eager to share what they had heard in the partner conversations, noting that the turn and talk opportunities supported students in accessing the mathematical ideas. Maya excitedly shares that one student explained, "Two halves are a whole, so three halves are more than a whole." Tara also asks the teams to reflect on their choice of quantities, as well as their instructional moves. Tia and Val are eager to try the lesson the next day, staggering the times so that Tara and Julie can join both classrooms.

What to Notice

The teachers positioned the children competently, sharing how the children made sense of the ideas of fractions. They were genuinely curious about the students' thoughts and ideas. Their reflections focused on the students' ideas rather than what students did not know or could not do. They named the instructional decisions and considered how they can provide students with access to ideas and build their knowledge. They also recognized the impact of scaffolding and how it can inhibit student independence.

Day-to-Day Conversations and Informal Check-in on January 8

In a school where teachers are learning together, people are always in conversations about what is happening in their classrooms related to teaching and student learning. It's not unusual to find teachers in the hallway at recess chatting about how a particular lesson went.

In Tara's school, the coaches' desks are in a space called "the Teachers' Classroom." Students will tell you that it's the place where the teachers go to learn. Just inside the door is a single-serve coffee machine and snacks for teachers. The day after the Learning Lab, Maya stops by to get coffee and chat with Tara about the lesson they'll do together today. Maya asks Tara to write the students' ideas on chart paper as she leads the discussion. They do a quick rehearsal of the lesson and agree to use Teacher Time Outs to think together during the lesson.

A bit later, a fifth-grade teacher pops in to talk about representing decimals on a number line. A third-grade teacher stops by to share with the literacy coach the ideas that students shared in yesterday's Hands Down Conversation.

What to Notice

These informal conversations play a crucial role in building a culture of collaboration and experimentation. With the coaches in a central location, with coffee and snacks available, the Teachers' Classroom is a convenient and welcoming place for teachers to stop by for these informal chats, allowing them to continue to think together about students' developing ideas and teacher's instructional responses.

Individual Classroom Visits on January 9

After the Learning Lab, the teachers launch the fractions unit. The initial student goals include:

- Understand that a fraction is a number and the denominator represents the size of the pieces or number of equal-sized pieces that fit into the whole, and the numerator represents the number of those equal-sized pieces.
- Use pictures, reason about the size of the pieces, and relate the quantities to benchmark fractions such as 1/2 and one whole in order to compare and order fractions.

Tara visits all three classrooms in the week following the Lab. She adjusts her support to fit the needs of each teacher. Having taught at the school for several years, Tia is skilled at asking questions and listening in order to learn what students understand. So Tara's support will focus on building on the content learning goals from the Learning Lab as Tia incorporates fractional language and uses questions to uncover students' partial understandings.

During a visit, Tia and Tara walk around the classroom together as students work on a task involving comparing and ordering fractions. They are curious about how students are making sense of the size of fractions. Anthony, who is new to the school, has his head down on his desk. Tia wants to ensure that he feels part of his new community and to find ways to spark his engagement and curiosity. Tia and Tara walk over to him, and Tia starts a conversation with him.

Tia:	What's up, Anthony?
Anthony (student):	I don't know how to put these [fractions] in order. *(He points to a set of fractions: 3/6, 3/8, 3/4.)*
Tia:	What do you know about these three fractions?
Anthony:	I know that they all have three pieces.
Tia:	Yes, I also see that all the fractions have three pieces. *(She points to each numerator and then points to 3/6.)* What else do you know about this fraction?
Anthony:	It's three-sixths. It's a half.
Tia:	How do you know that?
Anthony:	'Cause I learned about halves in third grade.
Tia:	*(points to 3/8)* What do you know about this fraction?
Anthony:	It's three-eighths.
Tia:	Is it greater or less than three-sixths?
Anthony:	Maybe bigger, since 8 is more than 6?
Tia:	How could you check?
Anthony:	Maybe I could draw pictures.
Tia:	That's a great idea. What will you draw?
Anthony:	I'll draw a brownie and cut it into eight pieces and color in three.
Tia:	Could you draw a brownie to show each of these fractions?

Tia asks questions to uncover what Anthony understands about fractions and learns that Anthony thinks of fractions as two separate numbers. He understands that the numerator tells him how many pieces, but he's unsure about what the denominator means. Tia's goal is to help Anthony think about the size of the pieces. She knows that drawing pictures of the fractions will help him see that eighths are smaller than sixths because the brownie is cut into more pieces. So she encourages him to draw each quantity.

As Anthony begins to draw, Tia and Tara step away to talk about what they are seeing.

Tara: Your questions uncovered what he understands and what's confusing him. Encouraging him to use drawings will support him to make sense of the quantities.

Tia: He knows that the numerator indicates the number of pieces, but he thinks that the denominators are just numbers. Although when he thought about drawing, he knew that he needed to cut the brownie into six pieces.

Tara: What question could you ask to help him to think about using the size of the pieces to compare fractions?

Tia: I'm not sure what you mean.

Tara: *(Tara looks over at Anthony's drawings.)* Anthony drew a brownie and divided it into six equal pieces, so the size of the piece was sixths. And now he's drawing another brownie and dividing it into eight equal pieces, so the size of the pieces is eighths. What could you ask to help him focus on the difference between sixth-sized pieces and eighth-sized pieces?

Tia: Oh, I see what you mean now. I could say, "You shaded in three pieces in each of the brownies. Here, you shaded three sixth-sized pieces. Here, you shaded three eighth-sized pieces. And here, you shaded three fourth-sized pieces. Which one has the smallest amount shaded?" And I can ask why they're smaller.

Tara: Let's try it and see how this supports his understanding.

Tara affirms the way Tia asked questions to find out how Anthony is making sense of fractions. One of the lesson's goals is to move Anthony toward thinking about the denominator as the size of the pieces and using the size of the pieces to compare fractions. When Tara asks Tia if there's a question they could ask, Tia is unsure. Tara sees the opportunity for Tia to deepen Anthony's understanding of fractions by connecting his drawings to the language of a number of certain-sized pieces. She offers this idea, and Tia formulates a plan.

Tia and Tara return to Anthony.

Tia:	Hey, Anthony, I see that you drew some brownies. Can you tell me about them?
Anthony:	This one is 3/6, and this one is 3/8, and this one is 3/4.
Tia:	I get it! Here, you colored in three sixth-sized pieces. Here, you colored in three fourth-sized pieces. And here, you colored in three eighth-sized pieces.
Anthony:	Yeah.
Tia:	Which brownie has the smallest amount shaded?
Anthony:	3/8.
Tia:	Why do you think three eighth-sized pieces are the smallest?
Anthony:	Because the pieces are super-small.
Tia:	Which brownie has the largest amount shaded?
Anthony:	3/4
Tia:	Why do you think it's the largest amount?
Anthony:	Because the pieces are bigger.
Tia:	Oh, so eighth-sized pieces are smaller than fourth-sized pieces! Could you share your thinking with the class during our strategy share?

What to Notice

The purpose of the coach's visit to the classroom is to support teachers by engaging in instructional decision-making together in the moment and with students. At the heart of teaching is a myriad of decisions made in the moment. Tara's role is to ask questions and to think with Tia as she makes an intentional decision, based on a specific rationale. Tia's role is to reflect on what she's noticing and to think with the coach about next steps. The coach might join the teacher as she interacts with students during independent work time, as Tara did with Tia. On other occasions, the coach might join a mini-lesson to listen to children and serve as a thought partner for the teacher using Teacher Time Outs. Other times, a teacher might invite the coach into the teaching by "passing the pen," asking for help recording a student's thinking. Occasionally, the coach might lead the discussion with students so that the teacher has the opportunity to sit with her students to listen deeply to their thinking. There are so many little things that emerge as teachers attempt to put their commitments into practice. The coach's partnership with teachers enables them to continue to experiment with and refine their instruction.

The work that Tia and Tara do together in the classroom is grounded in two important principles for learning: children are sense-makers and teaching includes becoming a student of your students. Tia and Tara are genuinely curious about how Anthony is making sense of fractions rather than just trying to help him get the right answer. Tia doesn't tell Anthony that when the denominator is larger, the pieces are smaller; instead, she encourages him to draw pictures. She then uses the pictures to engage Anthony in thinking about the size of the pieces, supporting him in the work of developing conceptual rather than procedural understanding. And yet Tara does not assume that she knows exactly what to do to support Anthony's learning; instead of telling Tia what to do, she asks questions. Equally important, Tia is the person who knows her students and is doing the hard work of planning, teaching, and making decisions every day. Together, Tia and Tara have a partnership built on trust, which enables them to share ideas and try things without judgment or the fear of being wrong. This kind of partnership develops over time. Engaging in this kind of partnership is not easy. It requires transparency and vulnerability, as both the coach and teacher grapple with problems of practice. It also requires a clear understanding of the emotional work involved as trust develops. Questions like "How did that feel?" or "Did that feel helpful?" provide opportunities for candid discussions about this joint endeavor.

Grade-Level Team Meeting on January 15

At the heart of Grade-Level Team Meetings is the belief that curiosity about students' developing ideas, collaboration with colleagues, and commitment to our own learning results in changes in our instructional practices. Teams do this each week by digging into content, reflecting on student thinking and instructional decisions, sharing the rationales for these decisions, and then planning together.

After the Learning Lab, Tara and Julie joined Tia and Val in enacting the lesson from the Lab in their own classrooms. In addition, Tara visited all three classrooms in the past week to support teachers. She uses her observations to plan this week's Grade-Level Team Meeting.

As Tara visited individual classrooms, she noticed the strategies students were using and the challenges that were surfacing. Most students drew pictures to help them compare and order fractions, but they struggled to make accurate drawings when the fractions were smaller than fourths. Recognizing the limitation of drawing pictures as a strategy, she concluded it would be helpful to move students toward reasoning abstractly about comparing fractions. At the

Grade-Level Team Meeting, she plans to share what she's noticed so that the teachers can think together about the following:

- How pictures support student understanding of fractions initially but can confuse them if they struggle to draw more complex fractions accurately
- How to move students toward reasoning about the size of the pieces to compare and order fractions.

After greetings and checking in with the team, the conversation begins.

Tara:	How are things going with the new fractions unit? What are students understanding, and what are they able to do?
Maya:	They understand that the numerator is the number of equal-sized pieces and the denominator is the size of those pieces.
Tia:	They can identify fractions that are greater than 1 or less than 1.
Val:	And they have an easy time comparing and ordering fractions with the same denominator because they know that the size of the pieces is the same.
Maya:	Some kids know that if the numerators are the same, they can just think about the size of the pieces, but most need to draw pictures to make sense of it.
Tara:	When I was visiting Tia's room, Anthony was struggling with that idea. I asked her to bring his work here so we can look at it.

Tia sets Anthony's work on the table.

Tia:	When Anthony started out, he thought that maybe 3/8 was the biggest because 8 is greater than 4 or 6. But when he drew the picture, he decided that 3/8 was the smallest because eighths have the smallest pieces and fourths have the biggest pieces.
Tara:	Anthony's initial reasoning makes sense when kids look at fractions as two separate numbers. The pictures that Anthony drew helped him see that 3/8 is smaller than 3/4. I remember you saying to him, "Oh, so eighth-sized pieces are smaller than

fourth-sized pieces!" You used his picture to help him think about the size of the pieces.

Val: It helps the kids when we keep saying "the number of pieces" and "the size of the pieces."

Tara always begins the Grade-Level Team Meeting with questions focused on student learning. This is important because without it, it's very easy for the conversation to wander toward a myriad of other topics—everything from field trip details to discipline issues. The teachers identify what students understand and can do. As Tia and Tara discuss Anthony's work, they focus on his sensemaking—how he made sense of denominators.

Tara: I noticed that most kids are using pictures to compare and order the fractions. When are pictures helpful, and when are they not as helpful?

Maya: It's helpful when the numerators are the same but the denominators are different, like in Tia's example.

Val: But it's not helpful if the fractions are really close in size and their pictures aren't accurate. Like this. (*Val draws a picture of 3/4 and 5/6, but because the squares are divided unevenly, the shaded portions look identical.*)

Tia: Maybe we should work on teaching the kids to draw accurate pictures.

The teachers briefly explore this idea.

Next, Tara guides the conversation toward considering a new idea—the limitations of using pictures to compare fractions.

Tara: Supporting kids with accurate drawings would definitely be helpful, and we can certainly think more about this. But I'm wondering if it would be OK to put that idea on hold for the moment. Let's think about the kids who have begun to reason without pictures. Maya, you mentioned that some kids know that if the numerators are the same, they can just think about the size of the pieces. As long as they are in relation to the same-sized whole, of course.

Maya: Oh, like Ella! She ordered these fractions (2/3, 2/10, 2/6) without pictures. She wrote, "2/10 is the smallest because tenths are tiny-sized pieces. 2/3 is the biggest because thirds are big pieces. And 2/6 is in the middle because sixths are medium-sized pieces."

Tia: In my class, Javier knew that 1/10 was smaller than 1/4 because he said with tenth-sized pieces, the cake is cut into ten pieces; and with fourth-sized pieces, the cake is cut into four pieces. The more equal-sized pieces a whole is cut into, the smaller the pieces are.

Tara: As I visited classrooms, I wondered how we could support more students to think about the size of the pieces, like Ella and Javier. Then yesterday, when I was in Val's class, she wrote an inequality and asked two questions before she drew any pictures. She asked, "What's the size of the piece?" followed by "How can you use the size of the piece to help you figure out which fraction is bigger?" Val, can you tell us more about this number talk?

Val: Well, pictures aren't always helpful for comparing fractions, so I wanted to see what would happen if we just thought about the size of the pieces. So I wrote 7/12 < 7/20 on the board.

Tara: Why did you select these two fractions?

Val: I wanted the fractions to be unfamiliar and difficult to draw, so that they would need to think about the size of the pieces. Then I said, "When you talk with your partner, talk about the size of the pieces and how it could help you figure out which fraction is greater."

Tara: How did this change the partner conversations?

Val:	Well, instead of drawing pictures, it focused their conversations on the size of the pieces.
Tara:	When you came back together, what did they say?
Val:	Everyone agreed that it was false. Imran explained, "Twentieth-sized pieces are a lot smaller than twelfth-sized pieces because if you cut a cake into twenty pieces, the pieces are super small." We checked our thinking with pictures just to be sure.
Julie:	Getting kids to think about the size of the pieces first was really helpful.
Maya:	That could really help my students, especially the kids who draw pictures to compare fractions, even if they don't need to! I'd like to try it with my kids.
Julie:	It would be really interesting to try this in all the classes to see how it changes kids' thinking. When do you think you'll try this? I'd love to join in on the discussion.

Tara prompts Val to share instructional decisions she made that moved students from dependence on pictures toward reasoning, and her rationale for making those decisions. The team plans a number talk using this idea and agrees to try it out before next week's Grade-Level Team Meeting. By having all the students across fourth grade engage with these ideas, the teachers will be able to get a better sense of how students begin to move from concrete models to reasoning strategies when comparing fractions.

What to Notice

Tara's overarching goal for teacher learning in Grade-Level Team Meetings is to invite the team to reflect on their instructional decisions. To accomplish this, she shares what she's noticed across the Classroom Visit and encourages the teachers to share the why behind their decisions.

During the discussion, Tara has an instructional decision to make. She evaluates the potential of continuing the conversation about drawing more accurate pictures versus the potential of supporting students to begin to rely on reasoning instead. Even though the teachers are interested in exploring picture accuracy, she chooses to shift the conversation toward her original goal of moving students toward the more powerful strategy of reasoning about the size of fractions. To accomplish this, Tara first affirms that it would be helpful to support students with accurate drawings. She then intentionally shifts the conversation to discuss the reasoning that she believes students are ready to develop, based on her Classroom Visits. She heard students using reasoning strategies, so she knew that teachers would have examples to share. She recalls an example that Maya gave earlier, encouraging the teachers to think about other students who are also reasoning about the size of the pieces. Notice that Tara's goals for teacher practice and student learning evolve in response to students' developing ideas and teachers' developing practices.

Tara also pays attention to the dynamics of the team to ensure equity of voice, knowing that full and equal participation in collaboration creates more equitable experiences for both teachers and students. To foster this, she comes ready with questions to prompt teacher participation. The team has a high degree of trust and respect for one another, but because of the varied experience of the team, Tara wants to ensure that all teachers have a chance to share their thinking and ask questions.

Finally, notice how the teachers are fully engaged. All three teachers fulfill the important commitment to bring their own and students' ideas and voices into the learning space. The teachers come prepared and share general observations about their students' learning and specific examples, as Tia did in sharing Anthony's work. The teachers make their practice public by sharing specific examples from their *classroom about what they've tried, what happened, what went well, and what feels challenging, as Val did when she shared how she changed her questioning strategy. Finally, teachers engage in decision-making, as they did when they made an agreement to try Val's questioning strategy in their classrooms, reinforcing their commitment to making collective decisions that lead to equitable learning experiences and ensuring that all students have access to effective practices, no matter which classroom they are in.*

IDEAS FOR GETTING STARTED

Coaches

- How would you describe your role as a coach? (one-on-one coaching, mentor for new or struggling teachers, curriculum specialist, interventionist, something else)
- When you visit a classroom, what is your purpose, and how do you typically spend your time? (collaborating, modeling lessons, giving feedback, working with students)
  - What might you do differently in your Classroom Visits to support teacher learning more effectively?
- How do you get to know teachers' instructional practices and come to understand how they are thinking about instruction?
  - Focus on one grade-level team's instructional practices, reflecting on how they think about instruction individually and collectively.
- How do you nurture collaborations with individual teachers? With groups of teachers?
- Look through your calendar for the past two weeks and create a list of the times you worked directly with teachers. Was the work primarily with groups or individuals in classrooms,

professional development, or meetings? How did the interaction change teacher instruction or student outcomes?

- Imagine a perfect week, focused on teacher learning. What would it look like? Where and how would you spend your time? Based on this reflection, what is one small change that you could make in your schedule that would support teacher learning?

Grade-Level Teams

Think back on your team collaborations for the past month. What was discussed, and what was the impact of the collaboration on your instructional practice?

- In what ways were student ideas and voices brought into the conversations?
- How was practice made public? In what ways did you share what you tried, adjustments you made, and challenges you experienced related to instructional decision-making?
- What collective decisions and/or commitments were made?
- How did these interactions result in changes in your instruction or in your students' learning?
- Is much of your time together centered on planning and logistics? How might the time be reorganized to shift the focus to instruction and student learning?
- How did you attend to equity of voice to ensure that everyone's ideas and questions are heard?
- How did your team think about the responsibility to ensure equity of access to effective instruction across classrooms?
- Did you collaborate with a coach to work together on a specific challenge or practice?

Considering your reflections, identify one area in which your team is willing to set a goal and work together and with a coach to refine your practices.

Coaching Resources

Here, we list coaching resources that we have found helpful in conceptualizing what it means to coach teams of teachers. These resources align well with the model of coaching described in this chapter and provide more specific guidance for how teachers and coaches work together. Although they are all focused on mathematics content coaching, we think that the ideas apply to coaching in any subject area.

Courtney Baker and Melinda Knapp, *Proactive Mathematics Coaching: Bridging Content, Context, and Practice* (Reston, VA: NCTM, 2023).

Lynsey Gibbons, Melinda Knapp, and Teresa Lind, "Coaching Through Focusing on Student Thinking," *Teaching Children Mathematics* 25, no. 1 (2018): 24–29, https://doi.org/10.5951/teacchilmath.25.1.0024.

Nicora Placa, *6 Tools for Collaborative Mathematics Coaching* (Portland, ME: Stenhouse, 2023).

Visit Teacher Education by Design (tedd.org) to explore resources for leading Learning Labs.

6

Leading Teacher Learning and Collaboration

In chapter 2, we discussed the idea that the school context we create either supports or constrains both teaching and learning to teach. We elaborated on our assertion that decisions must be driven by deep and well-examined beliefs about teacher learning, and we shared the three sets of principles that inform our work. In chapter 3, we shared the professional learning system that provides the platform of opportunities to actually do the work together.

This chapter elaborates how leaders continually shape the adult learning context. We unpack how leaders can develop the practices necessary to pay constant attention to what people are experiencing and design responsive learning experiences that sustain the teacher and student learning experiences we desire. We examine how leaders can ensure the coherence of the adult learning across all spaces in a professional learning system through intentional instructional team practices.

Together, coaches and principals are primarily responsible for designing teacher learning and providing coaching, guidance, and feedback on teachers' efforts to enact shared practices (see figure 6.1). The Instructional

Figure 6.1 Ongoing communication and collaboration among coaches and principals are vital as they design for teacher learning

Source: Matt Hagen

Leadership Team (ILT) space provides them the opportunity to plan that learning, share what they individually see unfolding across classrooms, and calibrate in order to align how they will respond when they are in different spaces, striving to ensure that teachers experience coherence in the feedback they receive. The ILT is partially the huddle between plays that allows the leaders to make the small adjustments to the immediate plan, and partially the opportunity to step back and reflect on the overall progress toward the vision.

We recognize that school leadership teams are configured in many different ways. Whether your school or district supports teachers with a principal and a part-time district facilitator, a principal and assistant principal, or a principal/coach team, our intent is to support the development of their principled and intentional practices because the challenges and tensions described in this chapter are the same across schools and must be attended to by your ILT, whatever its composition.

WHAT IS THE INSTRUCTIONAL LEADERSHIP TEAM?

The ILT is both a group of people and a space. As a group of people, this team includes the school-based leaders who are responsible for supporting teacher learning. In our schools, the ILT includes the principal, assistant principal, and two to three instructional coaches. As a space, the ILT is a weekly meeting where the instructional leaders have dedicated time to monitor the learning conditions of the school (for both teachers and students) and plan the ILT's response in the coming days and weeks. ILT is where leaders step out of the fray to ask: Are we doing the right work *in alignment with all of our principles*?

> Are the *Principles for Teaching* guiding the way we design student learning experiences?
> Are the *Principles for Learning to Teach* guiding the way we design teacher learning experiences?
> Are our plans and decisions in alignment with the *Principles for the Adult Learning Context*?

To continually enact all three sets of principles described in chapter 2, the ILT has two primary purposes:

- To plan teacher learning and collaboration
- To determine how to address the tensions that commonly and predictably impinge on the work as they arise in real time

Both are necessary. Both must be intentionally planned. Note that we place equal weight on both the planning and the adjusting functions of this team.

OPERATIONALIZING THE COMMITMENT TO CREATE THE CONTEXT FOR ADULT LEARNING

Each week, ILT members prioritize spending sixty to ninety minutes together to assess, reflect, adjust, and coordinate the instructional cycle they are responsible for leading. The ILT is an ongoing conversation informed by observations and questions about what is currently happening in classrooms and across the professional learning system. It is an opportunity to respond to teacher and student experiences. Having a timely and nuanced understanding of current conditions, practices, and perceptions is essential to the function of this team, so we start with how to effectively prepare for this weekly meeting. We follow this with a careful examination of the leadership practices that support effective teacher learning and collaboration across the professional learning system.

Teachers, our hope is that reading about what principals and coaches are doing in the ILT space helps you to understand the ways that the members see and prioritize their work in service of your work. This is an opportunity for them to operationalize their belief in the Principles for Learning to Teach as they identify and develop specific ways to support you as sensemakers and learners. The purpose of this chapter is to guide the leadership practices of ILT members to support them in best supporting you. As you read this chapter, please note that the leadership practices are driven by and in service of fostering our vision for all learners, including you.

> ❝Our coach and principal work so well together, understanding that at the center of everything we do is kids and their conceptual understanding. I think they're such an integral part of what we do. I don't think that what we do is possible without a coach and principal, working that closely together to support a staff. They've been such a huge support, because they work so well together.
>
> *Fourth-grade teacher*

Preparing for a Productive ILT

Each ILT member has a different perspective on teacher practice, school culture, and individual teachers. In addition, by virtue of their roles, coaches sometimes see more of a teacher's vulnerabilities, assistant principals tend to see more sides of teachers' community building practices and family interactions, and principals have a view of the system, as well as how the parts and the whole are fitting together. With members bringing different but equally important perspectives, taking steps to prepare for the ILT meeting can significantly increase the productivity of the team. Table 6.1 lists examples of how different needs merit different preparation.

Each member should think in advance about any priorities, concerns, and opportunities, as well as upcoming events (e.g., new units, report cards, conferences, state testing) that they anticipate will affect teachers or students and therefore plan to bring up at ILT. They should also assess whether they and/or other ILT members need to do anything in advance to be fully prepared to discuss this topic. This ensures that as many relevant perspectives as possible will inform the design of next steps.

ILT LEADERSHIP PRACTICES

Adult learning is still learning. It requires clear instructional goals, knowledge of your learners, careful instructional planning, and responsive adjustments along the way. This section elaborates the practices principals and coaches use to support ongoing teacher learning and collaboration across multiple topics and teams. They are listed in table 6.2 for your reference. In addition to the practices we offer, we want to highlight that how we enact these practices must align with our principles and vision.

Assess and Reflect: *How Are Instructional and Collaborative Practices Developing?*

Consistent with the Principles for Teaching, the leaders must position teachers as competent learners and design experiences that support them as sensemakers. So ILTs frequently begin with sharing what we are seeing across the school. What follows is a comprehensive list of what ILTs must pay attention to over the course of, perhaps, a few weeks. We don't suggest using it as an agenda; however, it might help in prioritizing what feels

Table 6.1   Example of ILT preparation

Need/Issue/ Opportunity	Preparation for ILT	Discussion at ILT
If you . . .	*Preparation might include . . .*	*In order to . . .*
Have a Learning Lab coming up for a team	The coach looking ahead at upcoming content, thinking about teacher and team learning goals, and visiting classrooms to assess current practices and needs	Be prepared to share initial ideas for teacher learning with the rest of the ILT
Have a concern about the alignment of content or practices across classroom experiences on a team	The coach and principal spending time in each of the classrooms	Note the alignment and misalignment to support the ILT to more specifically identify the challenges that they are attempting to address
Observe a new practice really gaining momentum and teachers sharing insights that could support other teams	Asking other members of the ILT to notice and consider what can be learned from them	Identify what conditions or developments can be learned from and shared in support of other teams
Hear from a teacher or team that supervision at recess is becoming punitive or resulting in issues that distract students once they return to class	Asking for other teachers' observations, reviewing current playground and classroom behavior data, and having the assistant principal observe recess over the course of a few different days and times	Identify what is occurring, who is affected, and what else you need to know to identify what problem you're really trying to solve
See a need to support an individual teacher	Asking other members of the ILT to observe in either the classroom or collaborative spaces	Allow each member to draw their own timely and informed opinions before you share your wondering or suggestions
Have a whole-staff learning opportunity coming up	Asking the ILT members to each identify and prioritize some needs that they see as potentially high leverage	Get all perspectives on how the time can be best used and to look for priorities that are common across the ILT members, and therefore high leverage

Table 6.2   ILT leadership practices

Assess and Reflect
How are instructional and collaborative practices developing?
In the process of assessing and reflecting, consider: • Different perspectives on teacher practice provide important insights. • Take principled actions to provide a bridge from where we are to where we want to be. • Embrace learning to lead.
Plan and Adjust
What do teachers need now and later?
In the process of planning and adjusting, consider: • Keep the principles at the center of planning.
Intentionally Coordinate
How will coaches and principals enact next steps?
In the process of intentionally coordinating, consider: • Balance pressure and support. • Messaging matters.

important this week, as well as a tool for identifying what the team has not reflected on in a while.

We attend to the following:

- How are teachers engaging
  - In Learning Labs?
  - In Grade-Level Team Meetings?
  - In individual coaching or feedback interactions?
  - In instructional planning aligned to the Principles for Teaching?
- How are teams taking up recent learning and developing independence as instructional decision-makers? (See figure 6.2.)
- Are there teams making particular gains and insights that we can learn from?
- Are there discrepant practices or inconsistent progress within a team?
- Do teachers or grade-level teams bring up needs for support
  - With content?
  - With instructional practice?
  - With data or assessment practices?
  - With classroom community and student engagement strategies or practices?

Figure 6.2 This may be a useful visual for analyzing what might be affecting teacher practice. For example, if a teacher is leaning toward overscaffolding, it's helpful to explore if they understand the approximations that students make along the way as they progress toward a specific standard. Or perhaps the teacher is not yet familiar with the curricular resources or assessment practices that might better reveal what students know.

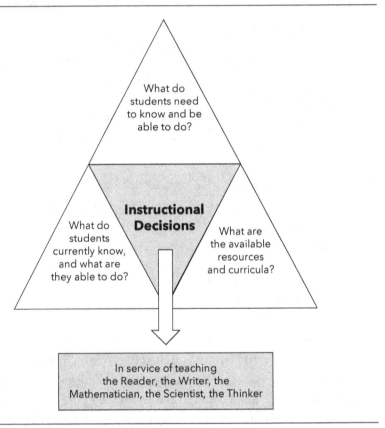

- How are team dynamics such as status, content knowledge, or experience impacting teacher instructional or collaboration practices?
- Do we need to differentiate for the teachers on a given team?
- Are there personal situations impacting teachers?
- Are there individual students impacting instruction or the classroom community?

- Are teachers positioning students as sensemakers with the goal of teaching the reader, the writer, the mathematician, and the scientist?
- Are we seeing evidence that teachers know their learners and are looking for the nudges that continually lift students as sensemakers?
  - Is conferring happening?
  - Is the scaffolding appropriate?
  - Is data being gathered about student sensemaking and used to drive decisions?

We must discuss these observations with genuine curiosity and intentionally lean in to explore what teachers are experiencing and how we can better shape their experiences. We must humbly acknowledge that *they* are the practitioners who create the learning experiences for students. Our work in ILT is to design the learning that supports their growth in effective instructional decision-making. The goal is to help them reason better, *not* to follow a plan better. Teachers have to improvise a thousand times a day; our value is in helping them to develop the capacity to make principled decisions based on student responses. We want teachers to have agency, but all teachers are in different places on their trajectories, so we must be students of our students to effectively scaffold and differentiate their learning.

In the process of assessing and reflecting: Different perspectives on teacher practice provide important insight   Supporting the growth of each teacher requires leaders to know each teacher's practices in multiple areas. For example, if the principal observes a teacher only while she is teaching or collaboratively planning writing, the principal cannot assume her practice is at the same level in mathematics. She may have very different content knowledge of or experience in teaching mathematics, both of which affect her instructional decisions, and therefore students' experiences. To support this teacher's growth, *her* teachers must know her in order to identify just the right nudge, and that nudge may be very different in different areas of practice. This is the value of content area coaches, principal, and assistant principal all coming together to share their perspectives on teacher practices. Leaders demonstrate their commitment to the Principles for Teaching and the Principles for Learning to Teach by carefully attending to practitioners as both learners and teachers. In order to position teachers as learners who must be provided opportunities to practice and construct meaning, leaders benefit from the opportunity to share their knowledge with each other. By taking a stance of genuine curiosity and looking for the approximations teachers make as they work to grow their practice, coaches and principals can inform each other's practices and enhance their collective impact.

An example of the importance of perspective

At ILT, the literacy coach shares that she is working with a fourth-grade teacher on strengthening her conferring practices during reading. Following the midyear reading assessments, the teacher was disappointed at the growth of some of her readers and asked the coach for support. Today, the coach shares that the teacher is really leaning into building student independence during independent reading so that she is able to support small groups, and it's starting to shift how students are engaging during reading, improving her ability to both confer and teach small groups.

Because the literacy coach has a level of content expertise that allows her to speak to the teacher's subtle approximations of growth in literacy, she is able to share a perspective on this teacher's practice that may not even be apparent to other ILT members. And because this whole team sees this teacher as their learner, knowing that this teacher is trying new things in literacy, demonstrating agency and perseverance, and taking up coaching suggestions resulting in improved student learning is critical information. This knowledge provides the team an opportunity to consider how each member can best support this teacher's efforts. For example, would it be helpful if the principal stopped in to notice the new practices? Or, perhaps the assistant principal, who is providing feedback on reengaging students after recess across that grade level, should avoid her literacy block for now to protect the teacher's focus on the work with the literacy coach.

Here, we have listed more examples of role-specific perspectives that can inform the ILT's collective response:

- The principal might share that a teacher has confided that status among the grade-level team members is impacting her ability to share ideas. As the newest teacher, she doesn't feel like there's space for her to share. This provides a hint about how to disrupt that dynamic. Perhaps coaches will invite her to share first at the upcoming Grade-Level Team Meeting and visit her classroom at the next Learning Lab.

- The literacy coach shares that during Classroom Visits across first grade, she is noting that parts of the instructional block are taking too long and teachers are not getting to independent practice. This prompts the ILT as a team to examine why this might be. Is it understanding of the pacing of each part of the block? Is it a lack of preparation to teach the first section? Is it overscaffolding during instruction out of fear that children won't be able to engage in the independent practice? Is it a lack of understanding about the role practice and feedback play in developing independence? In this example, the ILT might decide to have each team member observe this week and see if they can better understand the teacher and student experiences in each of the classrooms.

- The assistant principal mentions that recently, a teacher is calling for behavioral support most days during the math instructional block. This may provide a glimpse into a struggle that no one knew the teacher was experiencing. They might explore: Is there a student who becomes dysregulated during this content and disrupts instruction? Is the teacher less familiar with the content in the current math unit? Have recent changes in the support schedule for multilingual students resulted in students returning from groups at a time that disrupts the independent practice in her math block?

- The principal mentions that while observing fourth-grade mathematics, she is noticing that a teacher is facilitating discussions that elicit student thinking and that students are very engaged during class discussions, which is typical of this teacher's practice. But just in the last couple of visits, she's noticed that a once a student shares a more efficient or sophisticated strategy, the teacher has shifted to asking students who previously shared if they want to revise their thinking rather than asking questions that allow students to connect their ideas to that strategy and therefore construct how this makes sense to them. The literacy coach is surprised by that, commenting that this teacher's classroom discussions in literacy are very supportive of student sensemaking. The math coach reminds the group that this teacher is new to fourth grade, and the fractions unit has just started, and that it is a very complex set of standards. She wonders if the teacher's knowledge of how students develop conceptual understanding of fractions is getting in the way of her facilitation of classroom discourse. She commits to connecting with that teacher to support how she's making sense of the new unit.

As facilitators of adult learning, coaches and principals are constantly monitoring growth in teacher practice. Like any teacher, leaders must deeply understand the trajectory of growth teachers progress through so that they can recognize approximations of new practices, attempts at approximations, misconceptions, and barriers. And it bears repeating that how leaders position teachers impacts how teachers position students.

How teachers experience the actions of coaches and principals is, of course, also critical. If teachers perceive that coaches and principals are labeling, targeting, or discussing how to "fix" teachers, the trust needed to share and grow their practice will be lost, which robs students of the benefits of all the adults working together to better design their learning experiences. But when principals and coaches stay true to all three sets of principles, our experience has been that teachers perceive the efforts of the ILT as support.

In the process of assessing and reflecting: Take principled actions to provide a bridge from where we are to where we want to be Each week, the ILT must attend to multiple dimensions of the school context as they both respond to student and adult learning needs *and* continue to push practices toward the long-term vision. Taking principled action means ensuring that each member's actions position teachers as sense-makers and create coherence across spaces while nudging the work forward. This means leaving with a plan for what each ILT member will do and how they will do it.

In the process of assessing and reflecting: Embrace learning to lead Leaders are learners too, and they need to get better and better at leading teacher learning. ILT provides members opportunities to support each other's growth in this area, especially the important skill of recognizing the approximations teachers make along the way as they grow. This dimension of leadership develops in the ILT; we support and challenge each other to learn together about recognizing teacher learning by:

- Embracing the messy, nonlinear way that learning progresses and being patient
- Keeping an asset-based approach by
  - Pushing each other beyond noticing surface-level or technical shifts
  - Attending to our language in describing teacher practice—holding ourselves accountable for getting underneath "they aren't/they can't" statements
- Holding ourselves accountable to see and consider multiple perspectives of a teacher's or team's practice—resist allowing one observation or perspective to define our thinking
- Learning together:
  - How to recognize the small shifts in teachers' learning as they progress along their learning trajectories
  - How to design the "nudges" and next steps that will support teachers' growth
  - How to balance the pressure and support that we collectively provide teachers and teams
- Recognizing and acting on the opportunities to celebrate progress
- Asking: What's our evidence of how our leadership is impacting teacher and team growth?

What's listed here is, in part, what we mean when we talk about leaders holding the responsibility to be the "lead learner." Learning to lead should parallel the Principles for Learning to Teach. If developing as an instructional leader means getting better at the practices that support teacher growth, then taking the position that leading is something that can be learned and there is value in making your leadership practice public is powerful—*if you make the effort to do that.* We offer that ILT members can and must hold each other accountable for doing just that.

Leaders, try reading the Principles for Learning to Teach, but substitute "leading" for "teaching" and "leader" for "teacher." We think you'll see that approaching your own leadership practice in this way supports you in authentically embracing and enacting the role as the lead learner. The ILT space provides you a context in which to do this routinely.

Protecting ILT as a time to plan teacher learning and collaboration

Schools are incredibly busy places, and because student schedules determine when adults can connect, we often walk around with a list in our head about what we need to talk about when we see someone. It will be tempting to bring those items, or your stack of actual sticky notes, and start with, "Can we just quickly discuss . . ."

Like every hour in a school day, the ILT time will go by fast, so in order to be as prepared as possible to make principled moves in the next week, it's worth protecting this as time to reflect and plan intentional next steps. It helps to have an agenda that members have added to in advance; a calendar of upcoming events on hand, such as staff meetings, testing windows, upcoming breaks, and scheduled professional development (PD); and a list of the teaching teams so that you reflect at least briefly on each individual and each team every week. It also helps to establish what the ILT is *not*.

We suggest you avoid:

- *Lingering on the problem*: The problems have to be unpacked, but if the conversation veers away from examining what the adult learning needs are and how to design an opportunity for growth, reground it in the appropriate set of principles.
- *Venting*: This work is hard for a thousand reasons, and let's be real—we all need to vent and have our frustrations validated by people who understand. But if you do that here, the critical work of planning the upcoming teacher learning and collaboration won't happen, and you still have to lead it—possibly later that same day. Help each other to maintain a learner stance and work to position teachers competently.
- *Getting caught up in technical challenges*: If the challenge is simple, identify the next step and move on quickly. If the challenge is complex, take the minimum time necessary to schedule a meeting to deal with it outside of the ILT meeting.
- *Trying to solve or plan a response to every issue during the ILT*: Some next steps that you identify will be too much to plan for in the moment. It's not uncommon to conclude you need to plan a follow-up meeting with a subgroup of the ILT (and possibly other people) to delve more deeply into a topic, get more information, and ensure that adequate time is set aside to plan. Don't let an entire ILT session become that meeting. But do take the opportunity to schedule that follow-up time while you are all in the same room.

Plan and Adjust: What Do Teachers Need Now and Later?

Ultimately, the time that leaders spend together in the ILT meeting should support teacher engagement, learning, and collaboration. Leaders must identify the specific shifts they will make to strike that balance of responding to current needs and keeping the momentum of collective change in practices moving toward the vision. Practically speaking, in the course of this meeting, ILTs need to identify the next steps or adjustments to:

- *Upcoming teacher learning*: Is a grade-level team ready to take on a next step, or is there a practice the whole staff will benefit from digging into? When is there an opportunity to do this together? Will it supplant prior plans? What's the priority?
- *Upcoming teacher collaboration*: What is the highest-leverage way we can spend this time? Do teachers already perceive the need to work on this, or will we need to provide some information in advance? Will the Grade-Level Team Meeting this week be enough time? Will teachers need to prepare anything? Do ILT members need to meet again to plan for that/those specific grade-level teams?
- *Long-term strategies or collective practices*: Is this adjustment a predictable next step that won't surprise teachers, or is the first step to engage teachers in the discussion? Is it more technical or deeply adaptive, and therefore it requires a pause to assess readiness?
- *Specific support for individual teachers*: How will we scaffold support? How are we attending to relationships? How will we monitor our efforts to foster independence in teachers as instructional decision-makers?
- *The balance of pressure and support*: Is this adjustment in alignment with our principles? If we are removing a scaffold or increasing the expectation of independence, have we differentiated appropriately? If we are increasing support or slowing the pace of expectations, have we weighed how this will impact students?

The plans we make and how we enact them reveal our leadership. If they are principled and relational, people will develop trust, share their honest reactions, and engage in the messiness of creating new practices together. This level of engagement is a lot to ask of both teachers and leaders. As leaders, the urgency is something that must be managed. As the ILT identifies the work each week, it's critical to ensure that you are intentionally attending to relationships, balancing the pressure and support, and enacting the principles, *while* relentlessly pursuing better experiences and outcomes for students. This means investing in teachers as instructional decision-makers. The growth in their practices is what changes outcomes for children.

In the process of planning and adjusting: Keep the principles at the center of planning   In the process of planning for your adult learners, hold each other accountable for making principled plans by asking:

- Are our plans in alignment with the Principles for Learning to Teach?
- Are we using what we know about our learners to inform our goals for them?
- Are we building on teachers' developing ideas and understandings?
- Are we designing instruction that is aligned to learning goals?
- Are we designing learning in ways that allow them to measure the impact that their efforts are having on their progress?
- Are we recognizing and providing feedback on their progress?
- Are we designing opportunities for teachers to orient to and learn with and from each other?

Intentionally Coordinate: How Will Coaches and Principals Enact the Next Steps in Ways That Foster Sensemaking?

Principled leadership is about helping people to reason better, not helping them to enact a plan better. Toward this end, positioning teachers as sensemakers helps them to make better instructional decisions for our students and should guide ILT members as they establish not only what needs to be done and when, but also who will do it and how it will be communicated. To operationalize this, in the course of the meeting, ILTs need to identify:

- *Who will engage the teachers or teams?* Will the coach adjust an upcoming teacher learning agenda to incorporate this? Will the principal bring it to a Grade-Level Team Meeting? Is coordination necessary along the way?
- *How will this plan or shift be messaged?* How are the coach and principal intentionally framing this? How will they make the

reasoning for this transparent and connected to the principles? Does the principal need to frame this for the whole staff before the coach engages teachers in teams?

In the process of coordinating: Balance pressure and support As leaders, members of the ILT must hold each other accountable for positioning teachers as sensemakers who benefit from the opportunity to understand why something is a priority. This is one aspect of attending to how teachers are experiencing the work. Changes in plans, timelines, or even technical aspects of what is expected of us can be distracting and impact our sense of being in sync with each other. The responsibility to balance the pressure and support teachers feel is a larger topic that is addressed more fully in chapter 7, but in the process of ILT members coordinating how they undertake their next steps, it's important for them to examine how teachers will experience the plans they are about to enact. How changes, even those intended to be supportive, are perceived often depends on the framing, timing, and clarity of roles and expectations.

In the process of coordinating: Messaging matters The coach and principal's intentionality in messaging the *why* behind the work is an important factor in how teachers experience schools that are organized to enact these principles. On the one hand, it sounds great to organize schools around teacher learning and collaboration. But it could feel to the teacher as though there are lots of people observing, making suggestions, adjusting plans, encouraging reflection, and expecting a lot from her and her students. And that would completely defeat the purpose because how teachers experience their schools is hugely impactful on their willingness and ability to engage in the work of changing the student experiences they design. This hinges on the principal and coach very intentionally attending to the relational aspects of this work. The responsibility to clearly, transparently, and continually message the reasons behind suggestions, decisions, pacing, new practices, and even uncertainty is essential in nurturing the shared vision. Intentionality in messaging the *why* behind decisions helps people connect back to the principles that drove the decision;

this creates coherence over time and across the school context, from the staff meeting to the Grade-Level Team Meeting, for example.

SUSTAINING THE VISION IN DAILY PRACTICE: COACHES AND PRINCIPALS MUST COORDINATE TO ADDRESS MULTIPLE CHALLENGES ACROSS THE SCHOOL

Even with the best-laid plans and a coherent learning system in place, the reality of teaching and leading in schools is *hard*. We all know that the complications, distractions, competing priorities, and ever-present demands teachers and schools face are real and predictable, and they can be the death of innovation. If we're serious about creating the schools where this is not the reality teachers face, leaders must anticipate, identify, acknowledge, and come alongside teachers to address the barriers that prevent, distract, or pull teachers in other directions.

What follows are challenges that have routinely arisen in the schools in which we have worked. We offer them as real and complicated examples of the ways that ILT members must thoughtfully and intentionally work together to coordinate their responses to the systemic challenges that can kill meaningful change.

Challenging the Privacy of Practice

Resisting the norm to go in my classroom and close the door One of the central Principles for Learning to Teach is that there is value in making teaching public through ongoing, collective opportunities to experiment with new ideas and instruction. However, teaching has been a private practice historically, with the individual teacher making decisions for her students as they teach behind closed doors. In the early days of Learning Labs, it may be difficult for teachers to experiment with new ideas and practices alongside colleagues. When the principal or coach visits classrooms, teachers may experience a level of self-consciousness or defensiveness. The Grade-Level Team Meetings discussed in chapter 3 require a level of transparency and vulnerability that can be uncomfortable.

> Learning Labs were a bit nerve-wracking at first. Seriously, most of us would rather teach a whole room of children than a small group of our peers. At least that was the way it felt in the beginning. Since it was new to all of us, I could give it a go, since I didn't have an expectation that I was already supposed to know all of this. It was a process, though, to keep the anxiety down. It came down to focusing on the reason for what we were trying to do. We were doing what we were asking the kids to do: think, explain our thinking, be able to repeat another person's learning, ask questions, extend each other's thinking, add on, etc. As we got better at doing this, I think we got better at nurturing that in the classroom, because the matter became the learning, not the intelligence or abilities of any one person. We also were allowed to revise our thinking and grow in our understanding, so in the end, I relaxed and was able to learn more.
>
> *Fourth-grade teacher*

To foster this kind of adult learning, everyone must take a learner stance, valuing experimentation, vulnerability, and curiosity. This begins with the principal and coach working alongside teachers, trying out those same new practices in Learning Labs and in the classroom. As we explore together, leaders must model that we learn and grow together. Both the principal and the coach must give a unified and consistent message, both spoken and modeled: learning is messy, and "you can't look good and get better at the same time."

Confronting the Barrier of Deficit Thinking Driven by Test Scores

Resisting the temptation to fill gaps and chase test scores rather than teach for sensemaking The systemic pressure to use test scores as a measure of success is endemic to schools. Whether the particular metrics examined are state test scores, standardized diagnostic results, or simple end-of-unit tests, the priority of instruction routinely shifts to "getting kids to standard" and an inclination to fill gaps in discrete skills. This shift prompts teachers to view students through a deficit lens. Deficit thinking explains low academic performance by attributing it to something lacking in students, their families, or their cultural or racial communities.[1] Deficit thinking causes teachers to focus on what students are missing rather than on the whole child. Focusing on deficits unintentionally leads to lowered expectations and shows up in the form of ability grouping, interventions that decrease access to grade-level instruction, and other attempts at "fixing" students. Chasing achievement gaps overshadows our essential responsibility to provide students with multiple entry points and time to process that will enable them to actively construct meaning.

Even as we prioritize teachers' learning and collaboration aimed at designing joyful, inquiry-based classroom communities, deficit thinking often surfaces from time to time, hidden behind conversations about homework, a student's behavior, or how to respond to the latest assessment results. To confront the challenge of deficit thinking, the principal and coach must be cognizant of the times and situations when this thinking may surface. For example, at a Grade-Level Team Meeting, teachers look at data from an end-of-unit assessment and are dismayed by the number of students who struggled with different parts of the assessment. It would not be surprising if the conversation turns to teachers considering skill-based intervention groups or returning to the unit for another week or two. Before responding to this tension, it's important for the principal and coach to consider what might lie beneath teachers' concerns. Is the concern based on deficit thinking, focusing on what kids don't know rather than what they do know? Does the unease come from a lack of deep content knowledge or a linear view of learning, believing that concepts or skills are sequential and must be mastered before proceeding to the next concept or skill? Or is the desire for interventions or slower pacing based on what's been done in the past? While acknowledging the importance of the standards, the principal and coach must continue to emphasize our commitment to positioning children as sensemakers and offer alternative ways to measure success, shifting conversations away from what students can't do toward what they are trying to do and how they are making sense of ideas.

To explore the reasons for teachers' concerns, the following questions could be posed during the Grade-Level Team Meeting for everyone to consider:

- *"How did students approach the tasks?"*
- *"What do students understand? How do you know? What else do they need to understand?"*

These questions shift focus from the content and what kids don't know or can't do to how students are making sense of ideas.

- *"What conceptual pieces have to be in place to access new content?"*
- *"What else can we do besides squeezing additional lessons into an already overflowing pacing calendar?"*

Consider alternatives such as conferring or small groups during independent work time, using mini-lessons to revisit topics, and ongoing practice during the workshop time.

ILT members can guide conversations to focus teachers on becoming students of their students, seeking detailed knowledge of their students' evolving ideas, and encourage teachers to reflect on the changes they see in their students' identities as readers, writers, mathematicians, and scientists. Teachers understandably want to ensure their students make the most progress possible. An important role that coaches and principals play is to maintain a focus on supporting students as sensemakers and independent learners in service of the broader goal of disrupting historically inequitable access to learning.

Resisting the Temptation to Develop Formulaic Answers

The challenge of maintaining the teacher's role as instructional decision-maker   Inevitably, there are times when instruction is particularly challenging and adults wish for and may be tempted to design step-by-step guides to avoid getting stuck. For example, when teachers trust coaches and value their deep content expertise, it can seem reasonable at the end of a grade-level team discussion that resulted in more questions than answers, that a teacher might ask, "Just tell me what to do!" And coaches, recognizing how hard teachers are working, may be tempted to take on some of the decisions by providing preplanned content. Similarly, teachers may try to help students by providing formulaic strategies or mnemonics to guide them through complex processes. In both cases, these scaffolds and shortcuts rob teachers and students of opportunities to productively struggle as they make sense of complex content. As we feel ourselves or teachers drifting away from positioning learners as sense-makers, it is essential that ILT members help each other and teachers stay grounded in our commitment to teach the learner, not achieve a goal. Developing independence is our goal for all learners. For teachers, that means supporting them in staying engaged in making the multitude of in-the-moment decisions, based on students' understandings that help them get better at instructional decision-making—even when they are exhausted and we just want to help them.

As this temptation surfaces in Grade-Level Team Meetings in response to particular student struggles or the team's desire for more explicit instructional guideposts, the principal and coach can highlight the importance and challenges of instructional decision-making that fosters productive struggle. They can support teachers to lean into rather than away from this challenge by offering additional support. For example, the coach might visit daily for a few days to coteach with each teacher. The principal or coach might offer to provide coverage during the mini-lesson portion of instruction so that the teachers can teach with a colleague. They could plan to pull a small group of students into their next Grade-Level Team Meeting to confer with them so they can diagnose and problem-solve together based on what they hear.

Addressing the Balance Between Collaboration and Autonomy

The challenge of ensuring equitable access to instruction We collectively transform the way we teach in order to provide equitable learning experiences for all students. This requires collaborative decisions and agreements about specific instructional routines and practices, how we are going to support students to engage in robust discussions and orient to each other's ideas, and how we develop common language and understanding of content across classrooms. These collaborative agreements and practices do not mean the end of teacher agency, creativity, or improvisation, or that every classroom looks the same. But it does ensure that all students have access to the full range of instructional strategies and routines that the team has collectively developed and identified as effective, no matter which teacher they have.

In order to create equity of student experience and coherence across classrooms, teams make decisions related to content, such as the language we use and the strategies we use to develop student understanding. But what if a teacher prefers to teach something the way she has always taught it or decides that a particular strategy or routine doesn't fit her teaching style? This tension between collective decision-making and teacher autonomy requires a coordinated response between the principal and coach. Depending on how this challenge surfaces, the coach or principal might have a candid conversation with the teacher to clarify what lies beneath her preferences. For example, a teacher's resistance might be related to uncertainty about the instructional practice, a need for deeper understanding of the content, or a worry that her students won't engage in the same way as the other students in this grade level. After identifying what is challenging to this teacher, the teacher and ILT members can determine what additional support might be helpful. Perhaps the coach could go in and coteach until the teacher feels more confident. If the teacher is afraid that "it won't work" or that the students will not make progress, the principal may be the best person to coteach and provide reassurance that any specific strategy may not work, but trying the ideas that we collectively identify is what results in powerful collective learning.

Navigating Competing Demands

The challenge of protecting teachers' time to focus on learning   Even when Learning Labs are fostering new ideas and experimentation, teachers are trying new practices in their classrooms, and collaboration is at the heart of grade-level decisions, the everyday demands of schools compete for attention. Some of the demands, such as family conferences, are important; but combined, they can feel overwhelming and distract teachers during the collaborative time specifically set aside to focus on student learning progress and instructional decisions. Curriculum nights, special events, field trips, report cards, teacher evaluations, testing schedules, problems on the playground, and many other important issues require our attention. This challenge of navigating competing demands creates a tug-of-war between the focus on teacher learning and everything else.

Gatekeeping the continual onslaught of demands teachers face becomes a leadership function. Principals and coaches must be vigilant in identifying upcoming or emerging distractions and strategize how to mitigate the impact on teachers' attention. While we cannot eliminate all demands, ILT members can support teachers to focus continually on student ideas and experiences, even as they address the ever-present list of other important issues. Through intentional planning and coordination across all the teacher learning spaces, the ILT can determine the time and space to discuss these topics, while protecting the focus on student learning during Grade-Level Team Meetings. For example, a staff meeting might be divided to include whole-group time to discuss the logistics of conferences, as well as team time to discuss grade-level specific issues. While teams occasionally may need to discuss an upcoming event during a Grade-Level Team Meeting, it's important that the purpose of those meetings remains clear. Leaders must provide a coherent and consistent message that both protects and reinforces the focus of our work—teachers as learners focused on student thinking. When all the people who support teachers consistently protect the focus on students growing ideas in a strong learning community, teachers feel supported and are better able to stay focused on honing their practice in creating those communities in their classrooms.

CONCLUSION

When we start our teaching journey, we hope to work in a school where the adults are continually engaged in the collaborative process of creating better and better experiences for students—a place characterized by curiosity, excitement, commitment, encouragement, and joyful inquiry. But few schools approach this description. In this chapter, we have endeavored to share what we have learned about *why*, what's missing in the very architecture of schools. Building better schools starts with leadership designed to support that curiosity, commitment, and collective community. We must disrupt the belief that a "good" teacher can learn on her own in her spare time, support the revolving door of new teachers who will become her partner year after year, and figure out how to collaborate with colleagues across the school who may or may not share her eagerness to keep growing their individual and collective practices to meet the changing needs of students. Ensuring common planning time once or twice a week is not enough. Adult learning requires just as much intentionality as student learning. It shouldn't matter what teacher a student gets; all children deserve teachers who love them and the work of meeting them where they are. All teachers deserve the same. Our public schools have work to do to meet this need, and it starts with principled leadership.

ILT CASE STUDY

We turn now to a case study that has three parts, which correspond to the ILT practices: (1) assess and reflect, (2) plan and adjust, and (3) intentionally coordinate.

This case study, like the one in chapter 5, is based on data and real-life events from our research, but it is a composite narrative inspired by multiple experiences across many ILTs and schools. As a reminder, this strategy allows us to distill many complex accounts into a single, more digestible situation that conveys the big ideas and insights that we have gained from our work together. It also serves to maintain the anonymity of participants.

The case study describes what happens over two months as an ILT supports teachers to deepen their discussion facilitation practices (see table 6.3 for an overview of its sections). We intentionally include dialogue to illustrate how leaders interact with one another as they seek to understand

Table 6.3   Overview of sections of the ILT case study

ILT Practice	Corresponding Events in Case Study
Assess and reflect: How are instructional and collaborative practices developing?	Part 1: • ILT meeting on January 9 • In between the January 9 and January 16 ILT meetings • ILT meeting on January 16
Plan and adjust: What do teachers need now and later?	Part 2: • ILT meeting on January 16

Intentionally coordinate: How will coaches and principals enact the next steps?	Part 3:
	• ILT meeting on January 16
	• Between January 16 and February 13
	  • Email
	  • Staff meeting
	  • Learning Labs
	  • Grade-Level Team Meetings
	  • Classroom Visits
	  • Weekly ILT meetings
	• ILT meeting on February 13

challenges and act on opportunities to drive the work forward. To help you track how the members work together, we refer to people by their roles rather than by their names.

CASE STUDY, PART 1: ASSESS AND REFLECT

ILT Meeting on January 9

On Monday, January 9, the ILT sits down for their first meeting after winter break. The Principal opens up the conversation by asking the group (the Assistant Principal, the Literacy Coach, and the Math Coach) what they had seen during Classroom Visits.

The Assistant Principal shares that she had done a round of Classroom Visits focused on classroom meetings.

Assistant Principal:	I have seen at least one class meeting in every classroom. I noticed that students are raising

their hands more often instead of using the schoolwide hand signals we've agreed on. It feels more competitive and teacher-centered because the kids aren't orienting to each other. They are talking to the teacher instead of sharing their ideas and making decisions together.

The Principal responds by inviting related observations.

Principal:	What are the rest of you noticing about how kids are orienting to each other and growing ideas together?
Math Coach:	This feels connected to something that came up in my last Third Grade–Level Team Meeting. The teachers wanted to reset some discussion norms because kids were talking over each other during number talks and math discussions. It was like "Yay! The kids are talking! But no one can hear each other." *(group laughs together)*
Principal:	Did the team make a plan for how to reset discussion norms?
Math Coach:	It came up towards the end of the meeting, so I added it to our next agenda.
Literacy Coach:	I've been visiting classrooms during reading and writing conferences, and I've seen teachers frequently position students as sensemakers. Our teachers are really bringing genuine curiosity as they ask really rich questions and listen carefully to students.
Principal:	That's exciting to hear, especially since we spent so much time working on this as we launched the school year.

After listening to everyone, the Principal summarizes and reframes it as a problem of practice, explicitly naming the complexity of it.

Principal: We've laid a pretty solid foundation with the intentional work last year around the kinds of teacher moves that facilitate student-to-student talk, and I don't want to lose momentum. Teachers have been excited about how kids are orienting to each other. If what we're seeing isn't isolated to a single classroom or team, I think it's worth digging into this schoolwide. We've seen a pretty significant and exciting shift away from the competition in classrooms and teachers being positioned as the arbiters of good ideas. It makes sense that this kind of adaptive shift will have some ups and downs. But this really goes back to our commitment to students being positioned as sensemakers; they have to be oriented to each other—growing ideas together. It sounds like we need to resume a focus on this.

Before jumping into making a plan, the Principal checks in with the team.

Principal: Do we feel like we know enough? Like, do we understand what's actually happening around discussion in each classroom and across content areas?

While the team acknowledges that they have lots of experiences to draw upon, they haven't necessarily paid close attention to discussions in their recent work with teachers.

Literacy Coach: Since I've been trying to get into classrooms during reading and writing conferences, I haven't seen much discussion during my recent Classroom Visits.

Math Coach: I can speak to how number talks have been going across classrooms, but now I'm wondering about the summary discussions at the end of math lessons. Those discussions can be tricky for lots of reasons, and I'd be curious to check in with teachers and visit some summary discussions before we make a plan.

| Principal: | I want to check in with a couple of veteran teachers. I wonder what they are seeing with kids, and I'm curious if they intuitively retaught discussion expectations after break. I'm always humbled by what they just do and don't think to mention at Grade-Level Team Meetings. I also don't want to surprise anyone if we decide to revisit talk moves as a whole group. |

This ILT meeting concludes with everyone agreeing to focus the Classroom Visits over the coming week on learning more about discussion practices across the school.

What to Notice

This ILT meeting illustrates some important ways that leaders work together in this space.

First, anyone in the group can raise a problem of practice. In this instance, the problem of practice is first suggested by the Assistant Principal. While not illustrated here, problems of practice can also be raised by teachers, who share them with leaders.

Second, as the team makes sense of the problem of practice, they position the teachers as learners, sensemakers, and decision-makers. In addition to talking about the challenges that are coming up, they highlight the growth that has happened and the strengths across classrooms. The challenges are not framed as "things teachers should be doing," but rather as learning opportunities for everyone in the school—leaders, teachers, and students.

Third, the leaders check in with each other to see if there is additional information they need before they make a plan. The group is honest about what they know and don't know at this moment in time. Note that the group decides they need to spend some time visiting classrooms and checking in with teachers, with a focus on discussions so that what they plan is responsive and relevant. They want to hear from teachers directly about what they are seeing in their discussions with students and how they are thinking about their instructional decisions.

Finally, the Principal plays an important role in both facilitating (asking questions, restating big ideas, and keeping the conversation grounded in the principles) and participating in the discussion.

In Between the January 9 and January 16 ILT Meetings

In the week between the January 9 and January 16 ILT meetings, all four leaders spend time visiting classrooms. They each make it a priority to get into classrooms when discussions are happening:

- The Principal focuses on seeing discussions across all grade levels and content areas and checking in directly with a couple of veteran teachers.
- The Assistant Principal continues to focus on class meetings.
- The Math Coach focuses on summary discussions that happen after students have explored a mathematical task.
- The Literacy Coach focuses on reading mini-lessons and asks teachers in Grade-Level Team Meetings to do some reflecting on writing mini-lessons.

What to Notice

The work that ILT members do between meetings is connected to the focus determined in the ILT discussion: learning more about the discussion practices and experiences across the school.

Note that this work is not turned over to a single leader (e.g., a coach) with the expectation of that person reporting back to the whole group. Each leader also demonstrates agency in determining what they are curious about and how they explore that in relation to the focus set in the ILT meeting. And in this effort, they both intentionally seek teacher perspective and transparently engage teachers in their inquiry, talking with teachers after Classroom

Visits and in Grade-Level Team Meetings about their questions surrounding this topic. We can also see how the existing learning spaces support the leaders in learning more about classroom discussions.

ILT Meeting on January 16

A week after the January 9 ILT, the group meets again to share what they learned over the previous week. The principal makes two important moves as she opens up the discussion. First, she asks the group to start by sharing what they learned; she does not immediately solicit "solutions." Second, she positions the leaders as "students of the teachers" when she asks the group what they learned. This creates space for the leaders to share both successes and challenges that came up as the group focused their learning on classroom discussions.

Literacy Coach:	I was excited to see a range of talk moves being used across the classrooms of our returning teachers. I am wondering how we might support our new teachers, though. I didn't see the same range of talk moves in their classrooms yet.
Math Coach:	When I started to use talk moves, I definitely just sprinkled them into lessons randomly. I felt successful if I got all the different moves into a single discussion. *(laughs)* It took time before I understood the power of using particular talk moves intentionally. Like, how I could ask a student to repeat as a way of positioning them as a sensemaker or to orient kids towards one another.
Principal:	That was something I got curious about this week too—how teachers are thinking about the purpose of the talk moves. We found a bit of time to talk about this at the second-grade literacy meeting.

Math Coach:	What did they say when you asked?
Principal:	There were a range of reasons that people shared related to selecting and using talk moves. Some were more technical, like using a variety of talk moves to keep it feeling fresh or trying to use moves they are less familiar with. Other reasons seemed to show an internalization of talk moves as a tool to responsively shape student engagement in the moment and keep the focus on the instructional goal.
Assistant Principal:	Oh, that's interesting! Talk moves are fairly new to me, and I haven't really thought about how they could be used in such different ways.
Principal:	One teacher talked about using the repeat move when a student shared an idea that was related to the instructional goal, how repeating could slow down the lesson to linger on that idea, giving kids a chance to hear it more than once. Another teacher talked about asking for agreement or disagreement after hearing a range of ideas in a turn and talk as a way of eliciting ideas in a student-centered way, rather than sharing the range of ideas herself. I'll see what the teachers remember about how they learned to use talk moves in these ways.
Literacy Coach:	I'm glad we asked that question to the second-grade team because that discussion revealed for me that we—myself included—need to do some work moving from a generic turn and talk that might look the same across every mini-lesson to more deliberate use. I'm wondering how to support more intentional planning of discourse moves and strategies.
Principal:	Let's hold on to that question. Before we dig too far into it, though, I'm wondering what else we learned this last week.

Assistant Principal: During class meetings, I tried to pay attention to what competitiveness looked like in action beyond seeing more hands raised. I noticed some more subtle things. Sometimes kids show a thumb when they have an idea, but they hold the thumb up high instead of in front of their chest, or they thump their fist on their chest in a way that disrupts the thinking of everyone around them. Or kids do the disagree hand signal before the person sharing has a chance to share their complete thought.

Principal: So kids are doing what we've asked them to do, but how they are doing it is not getting us closer to creating communities we want. Kids need time to think and space to engage in sharing ideas with each other. I'm glad I talked to two of our veteran teachers because they are two steps ahead of us. They both reviewed the discussion expectations and pushed kids to think about why we use quiet thumbs to give everyone thinking time and how important it is to be able to repeat what the speaker says. I swear, those kids could run a discussion without an adult. Our veteran teachers are really internalizing their responsibility to position students as sensemakers, and that's why they are so focused on kids' engagement during discussions. They both said that it's really been worth the planning time and instructional time helping kids understand their role as learners and thinkers during discussions. I even asked them if they'd help us plan, and they said yes!

Math Coach: That's great! My goal was to get into classrooms for the discussion portion of the lesson. I'm noticing three challenges. The first was that summary discussions aren't happening consistently across all classrooms.

Principal:	Hmmm. That's an important part of the math block. Were you able to learn more about what's getting in the way?
Math Coach:	In fifth grade, their math block is sandwiched between specialists and lunch, so even though their math block looks like sixty minutes on paper, they are lucky if they get fifty minutes. They really need sixty minutes.
Principal:	Yeah, that is a problem. Let's look at the master schedule tomorrow to see what we can do. What other challenges did you see?
Math Coach:	In some classrooms, students are staying at their desks for the summary discussion. This impacted engagement because students were spread across the room and had more distractions at their desks. I talked to a couple of teachers about that decision, and one teacher said her carpet space feels cramped. The other mentioned that the transition to the rug takes too long, and they could maximize discussion time if they eliminated the transition.
Principal:	OK. And the third?
Math Coach:	I have to preface this one with something I was really excited to see. Across classrooms, teachers are doing a lovely job of representing kids' ideas during discussions. The work we did in August and our first round of Learning Labs seems to have impacted how teachers are listening carefully to students' ideas and capturing their thinking in a public record.
Assistant Principal:	That's awesome!
Math Coach:	Agreed! Unfortunately, a lot of the recordings are not being captured in a way that is lasting and public.

Assistant Principal:	What do you mean?
Math Coach:	Ever since remote learning (during COVID), and then when the smart boards were installed, a lot of the representation of students' ideas during discussions is now done on the screen, and it disappears once the lesson is over. In the past, the recordings were done on chart paper and hung on the wall as a resource for future lessons, discussions, and independent practice.
Principal:	Ah, I see. So, let's get back on track. We will definitely need to come back to the schedule impact on summary discussions in fifth grade, students staying at their desks during discussions, and the shift away from recording student thinking in ways that foster independence. Those are all really important, but it seems like we confirmed that working on discourse practices would benefit our teachers and students schoolwide.

What to Notice

This ILT meeting builds on the conversation started the previous week. The team continues to assess and reflect before jumping into making a plan. As the team unpacks their observations and reflections, new and deeper understandings emerge. This deep investigation and reflection on the problem of practice honors the complexity of what teachers are working on with their students. It gives leaders a chance to affirm what teachers are trying to accomplish. It also yields a list of things that the ILT could focus on. Most important, it properly equips the team to engage in the work at the ILT: prioritizing, planning, and messaging what's going to happen next.

CASE STUDY, PART 2: PLAN AND ADJUST

ILT Meeting on January 16 (continued)

After sharing what they each learned as they visited classrooms and talked with teachers, the Principal shifts the group into planning and making adjustments to existing spaces and roles.

Principal:	We'll tackle the fifth-grade schedule one outside of this meeting. What about the time for transitions and the cramped carpet space? Is that a widespread challenge?
Math Coach:	No, and my hunch is that both of those can get re-solved pretty quickly with some support.
Assistant Principal:	I can take that on. I'm in those classrooms often and have a strong relationship with both teachers.
Literacy Coach:	[The Math Coach] and I could introduce talk moves to our new teachers during our session for new teachers on Friday morning.

The Principal then engages the group in prioritizing what's next for the school as a whole, based on what they know and understand from their experiences in classrooms and conversations with teachers.

Principal:	That leaves us with these three: increasing the intentional and responsive use of talk moves, how hand signals orient students to each other's ideas, and using anchor charts to engage students with each other's ideas across lessons. Does that list seem to capture the discussion-related challenges that we're seeing across multiple classrooms? (*The group nods.*) As I think about these things, I keep coming back to the underlying *why*. We know our teachers want to

create communities where kids are sensemakers and have time to think, and space to engage in sharing ideas with each other. Before we jump into planning a response, can we take a minute to make clear for ourselves, what seems most important right now? What would we want to see in classroom discussions six weeks from now, or at the end of the year?

Assistant Principal: I think resetting the use of hand signals is a priority. When I see students using those consistently, the discussion just feels different. There is a patience that students have for each other and feel *from* each other because they don't have a reminder waving in their face that someone else wants a turn.

Literacy Coach: I would agree that using hand signals is a strategy worth prioritizing. I would add on that when students are using different hand signals, it also provides helpful information for teachers. In a Grade-Level Team Meeting last week, a teacher mentioned how kids' hand signals sometimes help her decide what to do next. For example, if there's a student who indicates they want to add on to another student or a student that indicates they have a different idea, the hand signals are a way for students to communicate with teachers and each other.

Math Coach: I agree with you all. I know I brought up how anchor charts are being used, but that doesn't feel as important to work on as a whole school. I could look for opportunities to embed this in some of our planning conversations or my Classroom Visits.

Principal: So I think we've narrowed it down to a couple of strategies that we want to focus on so that we see more classroom discussions where teachers are facilitating student-to-student talk and supporting participation in discussions.

What to Notice

In this part of the ILT, the group shifts from sharing and reflecting to prioritizing what will get worked on and who will support it. The list is initially pared down when they acknowledge that a couple of things apply to only a subset of teachers and can be worked on by one ILT member in an existing space (e.g., the Assistant Principal working on transitions and carpet space with individual teachers). The group also considers what can wait (e.g., the Math Coach suggesting that the use of anchor charts is less important to focus on as a whole school right now). Prioritizing and lifting out the heart of the work that feels "next" for the school are important step before the team plans and coordinates how they will position teachers as sensemakers and instructional decision-makers.

CASE STUDY, PART 3: INTENTIONALLY COORDINATE

ILT Meeting on January 16 (continued)

Next, the principal invites the group to start thinking about how they might coordinate across the learning spaces and their roles to engage teachers in working on discussion practices.

Literacy Coach:	The next round of Learning Labs starts in two weeks. We could focus them on discussion.
Math Coach:	But some teams won't have their Learning Lab for almost six or seven weeks. That feels so far away.
Assistant Principal:	What if we modified the Learning Lab schedule so that the next three weeks are half-day Labs? Two grade levels in one day—one in the morning and one in the afternoon. Can we do that?

Principal:	That's up to us! I mean there's no formula. We'll need to make sure we update the substitute requests but otherwise, it shouldn't be an issue. This could really help to build momentum quickly. It's hard when some teams get to start on things several weeks before others.
Literacy Coach:	I like that idea! Maybe we could do a second round of half-day Learning Labs to build on what we do in the first round.
Math Coach:	*(laughing)* Woah there! We haven't even planned the first round.
Literacy Coach:	I know, I'm just getting excited thinking about how we could have two Learning Lab touch points around discussion . . .
Math Coach:	. . . with some supporting Grade-Level Team Meetings in between!
Principal:	OK, so I think we have some energy around this idea. We're going to need to find some time to do some additional planning for those Learning Labs. What else?
Literacy Coach:	I wonder if we should do some messaging in person. This feels like a pretty big focus for the next several weeks. I think we want to help teachers understand why we're working with talk moves and hand signals again. If we aren't really clear, I could see some teachers feeling like they are doing something wrong. But it's more about how we take what we've started and grow it.
Math Coach:	Is there room in the agenda to say something in this week's staff meeting and then follow up with an email and the calendar changes?
Principal:	Hmmm, let's think about this. Maybe I'll start with an email thanking everyone for the

conversations about how discussions are going, and name that it's amazing to see the progress we've made in shifting kids' orientation to each other and how they are learning to grow ideas together. I want to share the story about the second-grader asking another student to repeat her idea. I'll mention that we're going to take some time at the staff meeting to unpack this further while we're all together, so if they have other thoughts or ideas to share, definitely let one of us know. This will give people a little time to process or ask questions in advance.

What to Notice

These two ILT meetings illustrate some of the important and complex ways that leaders work together to understand the challenges that teachers are facing and develop a plan to support teachers and their students.

First, the leaders stay in inquiry. They don't try to solve a problem immediately. They take time to understand the problem of practice and then develop a plan that takes into consideration everything ranging from logistics to the needs of different teams to differences between content areas. They craft a plan that is responsive to the problem of practice in their context and do not seek out a formulaic response.

Second, as the leaders make sense of the problem of practice and construct their plan, they continue to position the teachers as learners and decision-makers. For example, as they set out to learn more, they talk with teachers and seek out their voices and experiences. And, as the leaders thinks strategically about different ways of messaging their plan to teachers, they consider ways both to give teachers time to process and to invite their input.

Finally, the ILT navigates the challenge of balancing problems that surface in the moment alongside long-term strategies and practices that move toward the vision. For example, the ILT did attend to things like scheduling challenges and cramped carpet space, but they did not allow those things to derail the group from determining the next steps for the school as a whole. ILT meetings are an important vehicle to shape and reshape the learning content and context.

Using the Learning System Spaces

Across the next month (i.e., between January 16 and February 13), the plan developed in the January 16 ILT meeting comes to life through various strategies and across spaces: messaging from the Principal, Learning Labs, weekly Grade-Level Team Meetings, Classroom Visits, and subsequent ILT meetings. We provide a brief summary of each of these to show how the decisions made in the ILT meetings guide the work in the different learning spaces.

Principal Email to Staff on January 17

The day after the January 16 ILT meeting, the Principal sends an email thanking teachers for the recent conversations about how their classroom discussions are going. She shares a couple of anecdotes from classrooms to celebrate the hard work and progress to this point. She also shares a couple of the challenges that teachers had named in their conversations and connected those challenges to the kinds of classroom communities the school is committed to creating for their students. She closed by saying that the next round of Labs would be an opportunity to work on these challenges together and invited teachers to ask questions and share their ideas and thoughts.

Staff Meeting on January 18

Two days after the January 16 ILT meeting, the staff gathers for a regularly scheduled staff meeting. Toward the end of the meeting, the Principal shares that they will be focusing their professional learning on discussion practices in the coming weeks:

> Next week is the start of our next cycle of Learning Labs. I shared in an email yesterday that we're going to build on the discussion work that we started last year. So far, we've really focused our professional learning on using talk moves as a strategy for inviting students' voices and ideas into lessons. And I have to say, I continue to be so impressed with how different our classrooms feel. Our kids have *so* much to say! In fact, some of you shared with me how that has created a new problem of practice! (*Laughter across the group*) So now that we're really familiar with the range of talk moves, we're going to dig into how we can use them as a tool to responsively shape the student engagement in the moment and keep the focus on the instructional goal. That's what we're going to dig into together at the upcoming Labs.

The Principal quickly shares that the ILT made changes to the Learning Lab schedule so that all grade levels could have a Lab experience in the next three weeks, and she closes by positioning teachers as partners in the inquiry cycle that the school is entering:

> I encourage you to start noticing how discussions are going in your classroom. Are you seeing kids engage in sensemaking opportunities during discussions? How are you deciding which talk moves to use? What's going well? What's feeling tricky? I know that each of us has things that are going well *and* things that feel hard, and this next few weeks is going to be a great time for us to learn from and with each other.

Learning Labs on January 24, January 31, and February 7

Each grade-level team participates in a half-day Learning Lab focused on discussion practices. The Lab is facilitated by either the Math Coach or the Literacy Coach, who coplanned the Lab. The

Principal participates with all six grade levels, and the Assistant Principal joins one grade level so that she has a similar experience to the other leaders and all the teachers.

Weekly Grade-Level Team Meetings

In the Grade-Level Team Meeting that follows each Learning Lab, the Math Coach and Literacy Coach plan opportunities for teachers to reflect on their discussion practices and engage in coplanning around discussions. This is intended to support teachers in pulling new learning into their practice immediately. Here are some examples of what this looks like:

- At the end of the Learning Lab, each teacher shares a goal for her own practice. The Literacy Coach opens the next Grade-Level Team Meeting by asking each teacher to share what she has tried in relation to her goal, how it went, and any challenges she encountered.
- After examining student work, the Math Coach asks the group to coplan the number talk for the next day. As they plan, the Math Coach asks teachers to share their ideas about which talk moves could be useful and why.
- The Principal repeats parts of her initial message to reinforce that discussion strategies are a priority and focus for teachers and teams across the school.

Classroom Visits

During the four weeks, the Principal, Assistant Principal, and both coaches focus their Classroom Visits on times when students will be engaged in discussions. Sometimes this visit is more formally scheduled; other times, they aim to drop in when a discussion is likely to be happening. The leaders use the Classroom Visits as an opportunity to support teachers and students as they try out new things and practice ideas and strategies from recent Learning Labs. They are there to celebrate when exciting things unfold, as well as serve as thought partners when new challenges and problems of practice pop up in the moment. The Classroom Visits are also an important means of ensuring that leaders are in sync with teachers and aware of how things are going in classrooms.

Weekly ILT Meetings

During this time, the ILT continues to meet weekly. They don't stop meeting once they have a plan. It is important that they are regularly checking in with each other so that they can assess, reflect, adjust, and coordinate. The team also has to manage new and/or unrelated challenges that arise—deciding how each challenge does or does not fit into the work that is currently happening. In other words, new cycles of assess and reflect, plan and adjust often begin before another has concluded, and the ILT is responsible for coordinating, managing, and pacing these cycles.

What to Notice

The problem of practice that was identified in the January 16 ILT meeting is the focus of the professional learning in Learning Labs and Grade-Level Team Meetings for several weeks in a row. Instead of each space taking on a new idea or practice, leader and teacher learning is supported over time, offering multiple opportunities to practice, reflect, and refine strategies and practices.

There are also opportunities for the leaders to check in with teachers, visit classrooms, and adjust the plan in response to how ideas are taken up and what new challenges emerge. Because there was no formula to follow when the team started planning on January 16, the ILT members relied on what they were learning from and with teachers and stayed open to making adjustments along the way.

IDEAS FOR GETTING STARTED

Getting started can be as big or as small as your school context allows. But any way you get started is a start! Launching a pilot can provide a starting point as you develop your professional learning system. It provides a way to simultaneously develop the spaces and the practices that support all three sets of principles. The suggestions below are not meant to imply that you have to secure every role and resource listed before you start. The following ideas may help you think about what assets you can start with and how to shape your initial agreements as you begin to collaborate to intentionally enact the principles.

1. Identify your ILT members: Who are the people who shape teacher practice in your school?

   An administrator who:
   - Shapes the school's goals and plans
   - Provides evaluative feedback to teachers
   - Communicates with district and union leaders
   - Has managerial discretion over teacher schedule/use of time, budget, and resources
   - Can commit time each week to collaborating with the facilitator to assess and reflect, plan and adjust, and intentionally coordinate and to participate with teachers in Grade-Level Team Meetings

   A facilitator/coach who has:
   - Significant content knowledge
   - Time to:
     - Collaborate with an administrator to plan, reflect and adjust, and intentionally coordinate
     - Be in classrooms
     - Plan and facilitate teacher learning
     - The professional respect of the teachers

2. Identify a teaching team: Who is willing to work together on teacher and student learning goals?
   Teachers who are:
   - Willing to collaborate with colleagues and leaders
   - Prepared to learn, practice, and reflect together, including teaching in front of each other
   - Open to Classroom Visits
   - Willing to sustain the work over several weeks
3. Create time each week for teachers and leaders to collaborate:
   - Identify regular times for the teaching team to work on their learning goals facilitated by the coach; try to have time for reflective conversations, as well as planning and coteaching which includes:
   - Explicitly sharing the learning goal for the group
   - Documenting what gets worked on each week during collaborative time, and being clear about what the team members have decided to try out in their own classrooms
   - Be sure that the facilitator/coach and administrator visit the classrooms of each teacher between the weekly meetings and engage with teachers as they try out the commitments from the weekly meetings
   - Find weekly time for the leaders to get together in an ILT meeting to assess and reflect, plan and adjust, and intentionally coordinate
   - After two to three weeks, check in with everyone to see how the team members feel about the work they are doing together. What new insights are emerging? Does the team need to make any revisions to how they are spending their weekly collaborative learning time?
4. Reflect on the successes and challenges of the pilot by considering:
   - Was the learning goal substantive and focused enough to guide the collaborative learning?

- How was time spent during the weekly meetings? How well did the meetings prepare teachers for their classroom experimentation?
- What benefits did the team experience?
- What was the impact on student experiences and learning outcomes?
- What challenges arose, and how did you manage them?
- What would you keep the same or do differently in the next pilot?

7

Shared Intentions Means Sharing Challenges

To organize our schools as workplaces where we keep students at the center of collaborative adult learning, we have to change most dimensions of what we do and how we do it. Because we are changing how adults relate to each other and to children, new challenges will emerge. New expectations for working together will reveal people's underlying beliefs and challenge inconsistencies that may have coexisted peacefully.

To help you in anticipating and responding to the challenges of engaging in this adaptive change, we offer four examples of tensions that may emerge as the work progresses. It's reasonable to expect that these or similar tensions will arise. Regardless of the particular challenges, when tensions arise, it will be necessary to examine and address them collectively so they don't distract from, or worse, derail the work. There is never a straight path to adaptive change, but anticipating it, carefully identifying what the problem is and working to ensure that everyone stays connected to your shared vision, your *why*, will allow you to embrace these tensions as opportunities to examine your vision and deepen your commitments. This approach can help your school move through these growing pains productively and diminish the risk that either competing interests or the pressure to maintain status quo will distract from the work of better serving all students.

WHY WILL IT TAKE MORE THAN GOOD INSTRUCTION TO CREATE EQUITABLE EXPERIENCES FOR CHILDREN?

High-quality instruction is essential. But our children are more than the sum of their content knowledge. The premise of this book is not that we must design the best lessons for students; the goal is to design the best school experiences for students. Our responsibility for children doesn't end at the classroom door. The inequitable outcomes we persistently see reflect the experiences, knowledge, and conclusions children draw about themselves and others throughout their time in school. Again, if we want different experiences and outcomes for children, we must accept responsibility for doing things differently. Further, we assert that as educators, we must develop and adhere to a deeper belief that *how* we design children's days across all the spaces they experience must align with how we hope to change the conclusions they have historically drawn about themselves, others, learning, and power. And we cannot say yet that schools are experienced well or equally by all children.

At the heart of this potential tension is the question: Do the adults accept the responsibility for designing schools in which children experience each other's brilliance and develop a shared respect and responsibility for their community as a place where they can get and give the care they need to learn and grow? This question cannot be skirted; it creates significant tension when some embrace this responsibility and others don't. It pushes on beliefs about what teachers see as their role, responsibility, and even identity. Comments such as "They should know this by now," "Parents should teach them . . . ," "What happens on the playground is not my problem," and "Someone has to deal with their behaviors—I just want to teach," are windows into the beliefs and biases adults bring to the work. They indicate the degree to which some adults believe their responsibility for children's experiences are confined to what happens in their classroom during instruction. This underscores the importance of having and staying committed to evolving your shared vision collectively because, as we move toward a new vision, the old, more traditional beliefs and mindsets can linger and arise. When they do, don't shy away from recognizing them; examining adult beliefs is one of the hardest parts of working together to change student experiences, but it can be a powerful driver as your vision evolves.

We attend to how students experience the learning community *all day, in all spaces across the school,* because children are always observing, learning, and making decisions about the world and about themselves. The learning community children experience extends beyond the classroom; it is the sum total of their experiences across the day at school. As such, we must examine and develop this community in service of our goals for students that are beyond rich academic learning. Constructing this larger vision of your school's learning community presents a challenge that schools face when they try to organize the workplace to keep students at the center of collaborative adult learning. Tension will arise if adults have differing responses to the question: How do our most aspirational goals and hopes for children shape the way we design their school experience during and outside of instructional time?

Our response is that it means teaching in ways that orient children to each other, explicitly teaching social emotional skills and providing opportunities for children to practice over the course of years so they see and feel seen so powerfully that they never accept less. Whether you are already having these conversations or just realizing that this may be an unexamined tension among adults in your school, the following descriptions of adult beliefs, goals, and practices may help you to examine and develop your own thinking or facilitate the conversation. It provides a glimpse of how schools that are deeply committed to creating equitable experiences for students can operationalize that commitment.

Social emotional terms

A basic understanding of these terms and concepts may be helpful as you read this chapter.

Trauma-informed: Being trauma-informed is a mindset educators use to approach all children. It requires us to recognize the profound impact of trauma on a student's well-being and learning. This approach is not about labeling or diagnosing trauma, or about fixing kids, as they are not broken. Instead, trauma-informed practices are about addressing broken, unjust systems and structures within education that continue to exclude and marginalize students. Trauma-informed educators cultivate classroom environments that prioritize safety, empathy, cultural sensitivity, regulation, and the development of trusted relationships. Through these consistent practices, all children have an opportunity to learn skills that provide them the opportunity to develop and sustain relationships and resilience.

Self-regulation: Self-regulation is a person's capacity to manage her emotions, behaviors, thoughts, and reactions effectively across different situations.

Dysregulated: When people are dysregulated, they have difficulty managing their emotions and behaviors. In these moments, their responses to situations can be unexpected, disproportionate, or inappropriate. During dysregulation, access to the prefrontal cortex, known as the "thinking brain," is limited. Reactions come from the most primitive part of the brain, the brain stem, and include freeze, fight, flight, and fawn. Dysregulated behavior may include emotional outbursts, impulsive actions, difficulty concentrating, or withdrawal. Learning is not possible.

Restorative discipline: This is an approach to behavior management and conflict that prioritizes accountability, empathy, and the repairing of harm among individuals both directly involved and within the broader community. In contrast to punitive responses, which require students to pay for their mistakes, often resulting in exclusion, restorative practices emphasize open communication, active listening, engagement in the process of repairing harm, and collaboratively finding solutions that foster healing and provide opportunities for skill-building.

Resiliency window: Sometimes referred to as the "window of tolerance," this represents the space between a person's regulated best self, when she can effectively engage in learning and with the community, and the point when she becomes overwhelmed or loses control. This window is not fixed. It will stretch or shrink depending on the circumstances. By practicing regular self-regulation exercises, both adults and students can increase their ability to remain within this regulated state and increase their capacity to learn and interact effectively.

In-relationship: In the context of a trauma-informed classroom, the term "in-relationship" refers to the establishment of positive, supportive connections between educators and students and between students and their peers. It requires the development of strong, empathetic, trust-based relationships in the classroom setting. Safe, trusting relationships and a sense of belonging in the classroom community are fundamental for engagement in learning.

Adults Must Accept Responsibility for Teaching Those Things That "They Should Know by Now"

Accepting the responsibility for creating learning communities in which all children can learn means embracing that if you expect students to have social emotional skills, you have to teach them. It means prioritizing these skills as you would any other content area skills by devoting instructional time to teaching them. Many schools have character development or social skills curriculum, and they fit in lessons here and there, or the counselor makes the rounds of classrooms in some grade levels to provide lessons. This approach falls well below the level of what we have seen work. Done well, this body of content is taught to and practiced with children by their teacher in the community in which they will use it and build their skills—namely, their classroom. There is an agreed-upon curriculum that includes a scope and sequence, resulting in equitable and coherent instruction for students. (This also serves as an important foundation for the shared terminology and expectations that must be in place across the school so students have a consistent experience.) This curriculum is trauma-informed and can be used responsively by teachers and teams to respond to their students' learning needs.

As with all good instruction, students are provided thoughtfully designed opportunities to practice, and there are standards-based assessments embedded that allow teachers to identify necessary scaffolds. But supporting social emotional skill development also requires that children be provided many, many opportunities to practice. This happens in the context of relationships during unstructured times—such as on the playground or while book shopping—as well as during structured times—such as solving a conflict that arises between discussion partners or addressing class problems during a class meeting. Seeing "conflict" or "behaviors" as an opportunity to practice skills development calls on adults to expect and take an active role in supporting students in this learning in restorative rather than punitive ways. It requires an approach that is informed by an understanding of child development, but far more important, a commitment to know each child as a whole person. Supporting all children in developing self-regulation and communication skills that broaden their resiliency window in service of increasing their ability to engage in learning is the goal. Schools that aspire to create a community where children have the opportunity to stay in-relationship as they learn from their mistakes and see others make and recover from their own mistakes design instruction and practices that provide children the chance to see themselves and their peers as capable of learning, approximating, experiencing the results, getting feedback, trying new strategies, revising their developing thinking, and trying again without feeling shame or being excluded from the community. This changes how children see their relationships within their community and improves their access to learning opportunities.

> *Things to consider*: This means that clip charts, points that could be pub-licly earned, school currency systems, awards for compliance, and putting kids "on the bench" at recess are off the table. These practices are not trauma-informed; they promote compliance rather than community and keep power in the hands of adults. This is likely where tensions will arise, but these awards-based and punitive practices predictably dysregulate children, so we must examine their use if we are holding ourselves ac-countable for the goal that we have stated here.

Adult Social Emotional Skill Building Must Be a Shared Goal of the Adult Community

Embracing that "conflict" is an opportunity for children to practice devel-oping social emotional skills is a significant departure from how most schools approach "behavior" issues. Discipline practices are designed to provide adults with the authority to determine when behaviors are dis-ruptive and what consequences will result. Shifting toward viewing behaviors as communication and regulation skills as things that can be learned puts very different demands on adults. In the schools we are describing, teachers have worked very hard to design instructional experi-ences that orient students to each other and rely on rich discussions in which students grow and compare ideas, and teachers understandably want their students to have the opportunity to engage in the learning they have designed. When disruption or conflict prevents this, teachers experi-ence the very human emotions one would expect: frustration, anger, pow-erlessness, and blame. Holding the dual goals of engaging children in this type of instruction *and* providing them with opportunities to grow their social emotional skills in the context of their community challenges teachers as humans who have their own constellation of skills and experi-ences that shape their responses.

This dimension of the work, the goal of creating classroom learning communities that can withstand some disruption and still support learners with very divergent goals, all in the span of one instructional block, requires teachers to possess and exercise significant self-regulation skills. Let's consider an example.

Imagine students working in pairs on the carpet discussing their ideas about why the character in their book is or isn't changing, when one student named Avi gets up and gathers blocks from a shelf, brings them back to the carpet, and begins building a tower. Her partner shifts to join the pair next to them instead. As students stop their discussions and turn to look, the teacher reminds them that Avi's goal today is to be at the carpet listening, and she's doing that. The teacher reminds all the students that their goal is to think about their character and share the reasoning behind their opinions. When it's time to share out, Avi continues to interact with the blocks as the teacher prompts students to wrap up their discussion and turn to face the front. During the share-out, the teacher asks if anyone else would like to share something their partner said that makes them think about the character in their own book, and Avi blurts out that she heard Neela say that her character was selfish, but he's growing up. Neela and her partner show a connection signal, and several other students put quiet thumbs to their chests, indicating that they have an idea to share.

This is an example of a community that has developed the skills to withstand what some would call disruption. This community develops among seven-year-olds only when teachers consider it their responsibility to teach social skills and to develop their own reflection and regulation skills. This teacher and the students in this example could not continue with the lesson at the beginning of the year. Avi did not always remain quiet or even stay in the classroom. It took many failed attempts and painstaking effort for this teacher to stay regulated herself, to ask for help to ensure the class kept learning when she needed to speak to Avi in the hall, and especially to find it in herself to stay in-relationship with Avi, even when Avi repeatedly frustrated her attempts to teach and meet the needs of all her other students.

And this would not have been possible without the support of the adult community. They have practices in place to support both the teacher and

Avi. They accept that students do come to school with needs such as Avi's, and they embrace that they are responsible for creating a place where she can learn the skills that she lacks in service of their goal: *Supporting all children in developing self-regulation and communication skills that broaden their resiliency window in service of increasing their ability to engage in the learning.* As a result, there is explicit professional learning for all adults to identify and support the development of practices that teachers need. There's acknowledgment that this is hard, and teachers aren't going to learn enough in teacher preparation programs. There's a shared understanding that the belief that if we want something different for children, we are the ones who have to do something different extends to developing the personal capacity to deal with this in productive ways. Adults must develop the self-regulation skills necessary to support children who don't yet have them.

> *Things to consider*: The pressure test of the adult beliefs about their responsibility to support each other in staying regulated and in-relationship is how others respond when the teacher in this example walks into the staff room crying, furious, or hopeless. It's absolutely human to empathize with her. It's also totally reasonable to fear that this will be you one day. The community that sees this as a hard but important part of the job empathizes, comforts, and cares, but does not problematize Avi or blame anyone. When this teacher is ready, the community helps her get curious, identify the next steps, ask for support, and recognize her effort and progress in supporting Avi. They help the teacher remember that we don't give up when children struggle to learn to read, and social emotional skills are no different. Having an adult community that supports and holds its members accountable for this dimension of student learning experiences is essential, and it often quickly reveals each member's personal area of growth.

Adults Are Products of the System *and* the Ones Shaping the System for Students Today

Most educators grew up in schools in which you had no choice but to leave most of your identity at the door if you were Black, Brown, Indigenous,

Asian, not straight, nonbinary, not able-bodied, or even female. School was about getting children to do the right things. Teaching was about getting students to master skills. Identity didn't factor into these goals. In fact, it was a distraction, and thus we were taught compliance so personal differences wouldn't get in our way, and they could more easily shape us into the better standard we were all supposed to become. When we decided to become teachers, we may have hoped to do it differently, but lots of this schema of what school is and how roles are enacted have permeated our identities. (That was the point, after all.) Fast forward to today, and many of us are products of this system who now want to disrupt this very dynamic. We recognize that despite decades of reform efforts, how you look when you walk through the door continues to be a very accurate predictor of your experience and success in school, and this is not acceptable.

Modern pedagogy has evolved to explore and endeavor to attend to how students develop identities as readers, writers, artists, mathematicians, scientists, and thinkers. We now prepare teachers to recognize the importance of students developing skills and exercising agency, voice, choice, perseverance, problem solving, argumentation and metacognitive skills such as analyzing and responding to feedback, and monitoring their own learning goals and effort. Many of us have studied and aspired to create classrooms that support the vision of independent learners that Zaretta Hammond describes.[1] And even as we work so earnestly to create these experiences for our students, we remain limited by what we know based on our experience as mostly white, middle-class, public school–educated people. This acknowledgment alone bothers some readers, and we understand that. Most of the authors of this book fall into this group, and we remember when statements such as these felt accusatory and in direct opposition to how we saw ourselves—namely, as devoted teachers of our mostly Black and Brown students in Title I schools. What we and many others have learned over time is that good instruction, strong classroom communities that support social emotional skills, and truly caring teachers will not be enough if students still have to leave their identities at the door.

If you're still with us at this point in the book, you're probably already thinking (hopefully with a team) about the complexities of shifting so many aspects of the work at once. Depending on your identity, some readers are now beginning to recognize (and some have always known) that there is ambivalence at best, and often reluctance, from school systems to directly address how identity affects access to learning. Given this, you may be on your own to learn and grow together to understand what students need and what adults need in order to meet them there.

Identifying the learning adults need and how to meaningfully and realistically engage in learning together is a problem of practice we anticipate you'll face. The principles described in chapter 2 can support you. Learning to teach is a continual process of knowing, doing, and becoming, in that learning unfolds along a complex trajectory of knowledge, practice, and identity development. Principled decisions about how to engage in learning together combined with a commitment to stay focused on your evolving vision of what you want for students will support you in codeveloping beliefs and practices aligned to your goals (see figure 7.1). Grounding your efforts in your hopes for children and your developing adult learning community can help you to identify what learning you could engage in together to identify some practices to start with. Remember, there's no magical right answer or best course of learning. Start with a student need you can agree on, find a reading or two that help you learn more about your students, spend time talking with your students and families about how they are experiencing school, and/or consider a new way to engage students in this topic, and try it out together. Be students of your students; listen for their experiences and voices as you iterate your practices.

Here are a few belief statements that might help you get started. React to them individually and then reflect on the degree to which the group agrees. Use areas of disagreement to identify what new learning the group could engage in.

- If children don't grow up in the context of a community that sees them (not just *includes* them) and expects them (not just *allows* them) to show up as their authentic selves, then they learn that this is acceptable and expected—or worse, that it is just the cost of access to learning.

Figure 7.1 Third-graders make sense of a problem situation

Source: Matt Hagen

- Intersectional equity is affected by students' school experiences.
- We are deeply committed to examining our beliefs and practices and identifying those that may be well intentioned but are actually biased or assimilationist.
- Our students are able to bring their full intersectional identities into their learning communities.
- Adults are able to bring their full intersectional identities into the adult learning community.

Things to consider: This is a polarizing topic. We anticipate that some people will read this section and wonder what took so long and why this subject isn't addressed more specifically throughout the book. Others read it and feel unfairly implicated or react negatively to the terms in the belief statements. These feelings existed before the questions were posed; if present, they are regularly shaping the ways we interact. All of us have complex identities; it's never a single dimension, and it changes over time. Recognizing that we can impact how students' identities develop over time provides us with an opportunity to examine how we impact that development. All five of the Principles for Teaching underscore the importance of knowing our students in service of designing instruction that will effectively engage them. The extent to which your team develops and shares an understanding of and commitment to doing that lies at the heart of this problem of practice. Strive to create communities in which authenticity by all is expected; doing so does not mean teaching any specific values, but *not* doing so has implications that must be examined.

HOW DO YOU ATTEND TO STATUS AMONG ADULTS?

The people who are in the space when decisions get made impact those decisions. In the journey to create schools that prioritize student experiences, we are working together to make decisions with much greater frequency. From learning together to make collaborative instructional decisions to responding to behavioral data to reflecting on adult learning needs, we are intentionally collaborating far more across roles to keep student experiences as our common goal and the driver of decisions. These collaborations bring more adults from across the school into spaces to influence the developing vision and the decisions that are made along the way. While this brings more adults into alignment in terms of how we support students based on our vision, it can challenge people's beliefs about who should "stay in their lane."

Consider these examples:

- When the first-grade team is ready to analyze the data that resulted from the recent phonics assessment, the special education and multilingual specialists join the Grade-Level Team Meeting to evaluate what strategies may need to be implemented in Tier I (instruction that all students experience) and Tier II (targeted instruction for identified students delivered by a classroom teacher or a specialist). Although they are not "their students," such specialists are part of the collaborative instructional decision-making process, even when discussing Tier I instructional strategies.

- The data team that is responsible for monitoring and responding to discipline data and identifying Tier I and II needs across the school is co-led by the PE teacher and the assistant principal. The composition of the data team is heavy on specialists. Because they serve students from across the school and they do not have the responsibility of two Grade-Level Team Meetings each week, they have the capacity to bear a greater portion of the responsibility for analyzing and responding to school-level behavioral data.

- At an all-staff meeting during a delayed start time, the paraeducators who supervise recess and lunch present two problems of practice that are affecting students on the playground and lead staff in analyzing and responding to data. In the course of the presentation, they share that they feel that students are perceiving that their status as support staff is lower than teachers and this is a factor in student behavior.

In all these examples, educators who are not the classroom teacher are meaningfully engaged in decision-making processes that have implications for classroom teacher practices. This is necessary if we are working to create schools where all adults share the responsibility and have the skills to foster the experiences we want for students in all spaces across the school. Yet as these shifts in roles progress, it's wise to anticipate that people's conceptions of authority and scope of influence will shape how they show up in different spaces and what they expect from the professional community. The problem of practice is not the conceptions themselves—that's to be expected and will likely continue to evolve as the school shifts its practices. The problem of practice might be better framed as: How do we attend to perceived adult status and any impacts, directly or indirectly, on student experiences?

Attending to people's conceptions of the following ideas may help your community to reflect on and address them should the need arise.

Hierarchy of Roles

There are lots of titles in schools, and our professional identities are often literally defined by them. For example, we tend to introduce ourselves by sharing our role: "Nice to meet you. I'm Kilen, the multilingual specialist." We often even share our level of experience: "Hi, I'm Kesha, the new fourth-grade teacher." If in addition to describing our areas of responsibility, these roles serve to position us in relation to each other in spoken or unspoken ways, this may reveal some underlying beliefs. If people attach expectations to certain roles, notions of status may lead to expectations that need to be unpacked. If the experienced fourth-grade teacher and the multilingual specialist expect to have more of a voice in certain discussions or decision-making because of their role as the senior member or content expert, that can create issues that impact the quality of the discussions and decisions if the impact is that all voices are not invited to participate and valued.

Perceived Expertise

People's perceptions of the scope of their impact on the school or student outcomes can also create expectations of status. The specialist who sees every student in the school over the course of a week may feel more qualified to participate in decisions about hallway behavior expectations. The special education teacher who served on the district committee to redesign the identification process may feel entitled to provide feedback to the school's behavior data team when considering support plans designed for individual students in addition to targeted small-group supports. Or the teacher whose class has recently had consistently high scores on the state test for the last few years may expect to be consulted to share her insights. Tensions can emerge when opinions are shared in an area in which one person claims expertise.

Proximity to Work in the Professional Learning System

In the course of shifting the school's organization to focus on collaborative instructional decision-making, the principal and coaches are prioritizing the work in Grade-Level Team Meetings and Learning Labs. This priority drives their calendars, and therefore their availability, and can lead to a sense that the grade-level teams are at the center of organizational and practice shifts. While this is true in one sense, if seen in the context of the goal of working together to design the most effective experiences for students, it's just a function of the fact that teachers make the greatest number of decisions that affect students. It can also, however, create perceived importance or value. When the Instructional Leadership Team (ILT) members spend the majority of their time with a subset of adult staff, that subset can be perceived to have more status. Being thoughtful and intentional about messaging and giving people a window into the work happening in Grade-Level Team Meetings can address (but not fully eliminate) any resulting tension this creates.

As we strive to make more collaborative decisions and create communities across the school that support students in developing agency and independence, we strengthen those decisions by inviting more perspectives and developing a shared responsibility for enacting decisions. This necessarily changes the ways that adults interact, so understanding and anticipating how the adults will interact can prevent adult problems from developing and impacting the process. How we show up shapes the community *and* the community shapes how we show up, so it's important to recognize how status can create unspoken and unexpected expectations and behaviors. Anticipating shifts in status and how status may play out in working relationships can prevent or diminish distraction from the work.

HOW DO YOU MEASURE SUCCESS?

The principles shared in chapter 2 and the design of the professional learning system that we propose combine to reveal a set of underlying values and beliefs about what constitutes success. We suggest you start by examining your own values and beliefs. For example, in our work, we hold high standards for student learning and want students to engage in authentic and meaningful learning. We want students to be invested in and love school, to be affirmed and grow in their understanding of others. We want adults to deeply know the whole child as a learner and have the skills to recognize current skills and nudge growth such that every child makes more than a year's progress. Our starting point is where students are, not the distance they are from where they "should be." This is a critical distinction because we believe that "getting kids caught up" can happen without rushing them right past developing a love of learning in their community. Children need to develop a belief that ideas should make sense to them and they deserve to understand concepts and bring forth their questions. If you share a desire for the kind of change we have described throughout this book, you too will have to engage in looking beyond test scores, surveys, and staff longevity statistics as measures of success. Tests are part of our schooling system, so it's necessary and important to develop a realistic view of what testing does and doesn't reveal and some shared agreements about what value they do have. And not surprisingly, examining what we think scores mean and how we can and should use them in service of a shared vision for students can challenge adults.

Low test scores don't mean children are not learning, and high test scores don't mean children have strong subject matter skills and understandings. For example, in many communities, families are often moving because of economic opportunities and/or obstacles. So a class of fifth-graders may have only a small group of students who started kindergarten in that same school. This kind of mobility and prior school experience means that you have to examine which students are taking the state tests, how long they have been at the school, and how they are responding to the requirements of the testing context.

As a reader of this book, you are likely working in schools that don't have high test scores, which means you are under a lot of pressure to raise them. Despite decades of school improvement research, we have seen that when we chase test scores as a measure of success, we lose the focus on what matters. When we chase test scores, we try to implement strategies that will improve our scores, like focusing on the "bubble kids" (a term often used to identify children who are close to meeting standard on tests) instead of improving the quality of the learning experiences that students are having. How students perform in an unfamiliar, high-stakes environment over a few days in May should not be the primary indicator of the quality of their learning and thinking.

Assessment and feedback are essential for monitoring and informing our thinking about what is being learned, how, and by whom in order to shape our instructional decision-making. Classroom-level data that teachers and leaders use all year long should serve as the real measure of progress and success. An overemphasis on scores distracts from the question we should be pursuing: How are we continually attending to how children are developing their conceptions, skills, and identities as active thinkers who are invested in their own learning? There is no quick metric that responds to that question.

System priorities, new initiatives, and changes in political winds, leadership, or policy at a high level can all quickly and effectively undermine or outright kill nascent efforts to effect long-term adaptive change. Complex problems, such as inequitable student learning outcomes, have many underlying causes that must be addressed. This kind of change is not linear. Especially during the initial phases, monitoring progress can be tricky because positive change in one area can manifest as new challenges in another area. This is another reason why it's vital to have measures of progress, not just measures of success. Measuring progress toward adaptive change is hard to quantify and doesn't fit neatly into a school improvement plan list of accepted measures. So how do you know that you are improving and making progress toward your vision?

When your school functions as a learning organization focused on teachers' and students' learning, then the vision for high-quality teaching and learning is what everyone is oriented to and guided by. As the collective work takes hold and matures, we offer four important indicators that significant and worthwhile change is happening. First, members of the school learning community take ownership of and orient themselves to the vision. Second, educators and leaders in the school community become more interconnected and increasingly rely on each other for generating, experimenting, and evaluating the merits of new ideas and practices. Third, these shifts will be visible in the way people in the school talk with one another. Finally, more voices will be in conversation with one another, and they will better reflect the diverse perspectives in the school community.

Owning and Orienting to the Vision

Engaging in a shared purpose is a tangible experience. When people start to orient themselves toward and own the vision of the school as a workplace that embraces learning for teachers, leaders, and students, you can feel the eagerness and openness to the vulnerability and authenticity that come from everyone working in the same direction.

When you try to gauge whether adaptive change is trending in the right direction, reflect on:

- How are we enacting our commitment to the vision and principles?
- Do coaches and the principal know each teacher as a learner?
- Do teachers know each student as a learner?
- Are coaches and principals on the same page about expectations for instruction?
- Are they working together to share clear expectations and provide sufficient support for achieving the vision?
- Are students' experiences resulting in both personal and academic investment in their own learning and the community?
- Are teachers participating in Grade-Level Team Meetings with a clear sense that the focus of the discussions must be students and the actions we can take to meet them where they are?
- Do the adults in the school consider that rules, policies, and regulations shouldn't be blindly followed, but rather questioned to examine whether they serve the vision or are obstacles that need to be challenged and revised?

It's important to be watching and listening for the tipping point when everyone shifts from being concerned mostly about their own classrooms to instead being motivated by opportunities to share challenges and success that are affecting students.

Cultivating a Well-Connected Learning Community

When adults in the learning community are oriented toward a shared vision and motivated to strive to achieve it, the center of gravity shifts from individual concerns to collective ones. A tighter web of connectedness forms. Teachers will increasingly want to check in with coaches on a daily basis and will look forward to the next Grade-Level Team Meeting to sort something out. You'll know your context is shifting when teachers eagerly bring problems of practice to the group and principals hold themselves equally responsible for developing ideas. Observation and supervision will shift from comparing observed practice to best practices to, instead, observing how a teacher's practice is shifting in response to what they are learning and how students are responding. This has the powerful benefit of also positioning teachers, coaches, and principals on the same side of problems of practice, which allows teachers to see how principals sometimes can remove system barriers, and principals to see how teachers experiment with practices to better respond to learning outcomes. When we're all working from our individual roles to solve our problems of student learning, many more options emerge and our efforts enhance each other. Watch for the shift from *avoiding* individual risk or vulnerability to *seeking* collective experimentation toward solutions.

Shifting the Nature of the Dialogue

A natural outcome of adults orienting to the vision and developing stronger connections to one another is that the nature of the dialogue in the school shifts significantly. You'll notice that more and more conversations are about student sensemaking, student thinking, and student experiences. Detailed and specific conversations about subject matter learning and students' conceptions will happen across spaces in the learning system—Learning Labs, Grade-Level Team Meetings, and Classroom Visits. The informal conversations in the hallways, or by the mailboxes, between coaches and teachers will expand beyond greetings and logistics to sharing joyful classroom experiences, new surprises, and new challenges. You'll notice a significant shift in how children are talked about. The language of "high and low students" will diminish and won't be replaced by other euphemisms like "struggling students." Teachers, instead, will be much more specific and descriptive about what they are noticing their students are doing. They will see students' knowledge, skills, and behaviors as starting points to build from. Teachers will talk about their students in ways that convey that they know and appreciate the full child.

Expanding Whose Perspectives Define Success

Shifts in how people talk across the school are tangible indicators of progress, but whose perspectives are voiced and listened to are just as vital. Instead of looking at outside evaluations and metrics, the perspectives of educators, students, and families will matter most. Grade-level teams, together with coaches, will be assessing how well students are meeting unit goals by closely examining students' ideas and the characteristics of their work. Teachers will seek and value student voices and their reflections on their experiences, learning progress, and challenges. Students will report that they feel connected and belong to their classrooms and school communities. They will report that their teachers care about and listen to their ideas and experiences. The racial, cultural, and linguistic communities that the school serves will be present, active, and have influence within the school and on the committees and organizations that support the school. Family perspectives will be well known by teachers and school leaders. The design of and participation in school community events such as back-to-school events, open houses, and other school events will reflect the full racial, cultural, and linguistic diversity within the school community. Families will report that they have access to and regular communications with their children's teachers, and moreover, those communications will involve specific discussions of the characteristics and nature of students' work. Families' level of participation or engagement will not define their commitment to their children's success because the individual contextual and cultural dynamics that shape each family's involvement will be known and respected.

HOW SHOULD DATA BE USED (AND NOT USED)?

If you are using the principles described in this book to drive decisions about student and teacher learning, it will likely be necessary to both shift and expand how you use data. This will include expanding what you consider data. The power is in using data that drives reflection and action that is responsive to how well students are learning, as well as how well the full professional learning system is supporting teachers to build meaningful and joyful classroom communities.

For Student Learning

Teachers, coaches, and principals have to look at data as learning unfolds over the course of each unit of instruction in a way that allows teachers to shape and direct students' learning toward intended goals. For example, during Grade-Level Team Meetings, teachers continually work to clarify the big ideas and outcomes for each new unit. In addition, teachers are intentional about how they monitor and evaluate progress toward meeting those goals. For student data to be useful for teachers in the course of their actual teaching, they have to be able to identify what counts as progress in order to adjust their instructional decision-making along the way. If teachers are not looking at students' data as they are shaping it, then they might miss the most impactful use of data.

Student data has to be at a grain size that helps teachers in an ongoing way to make instructional decisions. Using data just to identify gaps in student learning leads to inequitable practices of labeling students as particular types of learners and sorting them into ability groups. This frequently leads to a focus on intervention strategies rather than on developing strategies and practices that better engage *all* learners. We can't "intervention" our way out of the inequitable outcomes that currently exist. Instead, we must use data in order to be students of our students and act on what we learn. When looking at daily student work or student performance on formative or summative assessments, the purpose is to characterize what students are doing and how they are approaching the task at hand. That helps teachers talk specifically about how students are making sense of the core concepts and skills within any unit of instruction. There will always be a range of student thinking. Monitoring and discussing student data help teachers figure out what ideas, strategies, or perspectives students have as starting points and what they can build from as they progress toward more sophisticated conceptual understandings. Data helps us when it's used to identify instructional decisions that will increase access and nudge students' developing understanding along.

The power of ongoing Grade-Level Team Meetings is that teachers are sharing their instructional decision-making as they work on common goals. Their reflections on the diversity of student work across their class-rooms help the group think about intentional next steps that might advance students' learning. If teachers are all aiming for the same clearly defined goal for each unit, noticing differences in what students are doing across classrooms can lead them to ask each other how some students are getting access to an idea and others not. This is how teachers collectively learn from each other in ways that can immediately benefit students. So, for example, if number lines are being used effectively in one second-grade classroom to work on subtraction but not in others, the grade-level team will notice that and discuss what's happening in that classroom that is giving students useful access to the number line as a tool to work out subtraction situations.

For Teacher Learning

Parallel to the mistaken belief that interventions will result in equitable outcomes, we must guard against using data to problematize or fix teach-ers. Using data that assists us to know and respond to teachers as learners is important. Evidence of how teachers are experiencing learning, how they demonstrate their investment in the school community and vision, and the nature of their working relationships with coaches and principals are important indicators and should be monitored and evaluated as evi-dence of progress. Working together in Learning Labs, Grade-Level Team Meetings, and classrooms will allow teachers to be in ongoing conversa-tions with the principal and coaches. Across these spaces, it will be impor-tant to listen for how teachers express their developing understanding of students' subject matter knowledge and the questions, insights, and chal-lenges they encounter as they create learning communities for the diverse learners they serve. The daily and weekly conversations teachers are hav-ing will be a natural source of data that reveals what's making sense to teachers and what supports teachers' need to make their classrooms thriv-ing learning communities. If the student work or descriptions of practice shared at Grade-Level Team Meetings reveal inconsistencies in how stu-dents are doing across classrooms, then it's important for both teachers and coaches to notice and ask questions about teachers' developing ideas and instructional decision-making. Using student learning data to identify and respond to teacher learning needs is a powerful data practice.

In a school community where teachers feel known and supported by coaches and the principal, teachers should be asking for support for subject matter coaching when they do not feel confident in their own understanding of the trajectory of students' developing ideas. It should not be a surprise, nor should it be shameful, for teachers to ask for and receive support for their instructional decision-making. Their questions and the coaches' and principal's familiarity with their current practice should enable school leaders to figure out how to use Learning Labs, Grade-Level Team Meetings, and Classroom Visits to work on questions, puzzles, and dilemmas *with* teachers. Depending on the nature of teachers' questions, coaches can make plans to probe more deeply into the teacher's developing knowledge and/or the use of subject matter content, curricular resources, or instructional routines. Adaptive goals require us to monitor adaptive change. Observational evidence of change in practice is an important predictor of future changes in student outcomes.

CONCLUSION

We believe that changing the school workplace so teachers learn alongside their students and with one another is paramount to creating better schools for children. In many respects, the changes will be welcome, and teachers and leaders will be invigorated by this new collaboration. But changing the status quo is far from easy. Our goal was to write a book that would support everyone—teachers, coaches, and principals—as they work toward a common vision. And the content of this chapter highlights the importance of this goal. We know that challenges and tensions will arise as adults negotiate their new roles and responsibilities in the effort to make student-centered and equitable school experiences a reality. In doing so, some practices and perspectives that we are used to, which have long gone unquestioned in schools, will have to be questioned and changed. The changes we are advocating for in this book go well beyond technical changes—they reorient us to principled ways of making school as much about teacher learning as it is about student learning. Everyone in the school needs to engage, respond, and adapt in order to create equitable structures and practices that reflect the principles. We all stand to benefit, but this means that everyone has to own the hard parts too. We believe that frank and thoughtful conversations will allow the adults across the school to navigate tensions as they arise and support them to see the progress that is unfolding.

IDEAS FOR GETTING STARTED

Teams *can* get better at getting better together, and you might as well start by practicing on a real problem that you are facing.

Acknowledge your current reality. Think about times at your school when tensions have arisen and consider:

- How quickly and willingly did people address the tensions?
- Are there unspoken rules or expectations that apply when the group faces a challenge?
- Are certain topics off-limits?
- Do people say what needs to be said in meetings rather than in the parking lot?

Identify ways to support each other in getting better. First, think individually, and then share your responses. The goal is to come to some agreement about how to engage in the future. The first draft doesn't have to be perfect. Get started, and then reflect and revise.

- What are the conditions or supports that help you when you're trying something new or engaging in a hard conversation?
- What are things others do that help you stay open and engaged?
- What makes it possible for you to ask for help?
- How can you tell when others value your perspective?
- What makes you feel safe to show up as your authentic self?

- How can people disagree with you in ways that still feel respectful?
- What shuts you down?

Practice working through a tension or problem. If there is not a problem that jumps out at you, we offer some questions here that may reveal underlying beliefs that you can grapple with collectively to examine how they align with your shared vision.

Think about how students are experiencing every part of their day. How do you assess the following:

- Are there consistent expectations of students across the school? Do they align with your vision of meaningful and joyful learning?
- Do you have a shared definition of what an engaged learner looks like at each developmental level?
- Do students experience different expectations in different spaces?
- Do you ask students how they feel about or experience different spaces across the school?
- Do you ask students how inclusive their community feels, and how authentic they can be?
- Where and how are teachers, principals, and coaches talking about students' experiences?
- What are the consistencies in how you approach socioemotional learning and the development of community for students across all the spaces they experience?
- What are the inconsistencies in how you approach socioemotional learning and the development of community across the school?
- What issues arise for students and adults because of those inconsistencies?

8

Working Together to Make Schools Work Better

Leadership is the sum of every big and little decision we each make. Organizing our schools to nurture teacher learning and create flourishing learning environments for each student challenges us to make different, more intentional and collaborative decisions. We close this book by examining how we must all shift in the effort to make decisions that better leverage resources and opportunities, such as funding, hiring, and operational flexibility, in service of our shared goals.

DON'T GET IT WRONG, *AND* GET BETTER AT GETTING IT RIGHT

Public education is a complex system with federal, state, and local requirements that define and constrain most aspects of the work we do at every level of the public school system. This complexity drives the need for specialized expertise. There are many examples of this. Someone in the system has to understand and manage the ever-changing and very complicated world of federal entitlement funding. It takes specialized skill to maintain and nurture the relationships and agreements with employee associations. Expertise and depth of knowledge are required to lead curriculum committees and adoption cycles. And assessment systems are so complex that a team is required to stay on top of the many layers of administration and reporting requirements. The real and understandable need to get these very complex things right results in silos of specialized knowledge, with guidance and management decisions flowing from many directions.

Certainly, we all want comprehensive program reviews, audits, and labor/management relations to go well. But at the school level, all the guidance and supervision can lead to the unintended conclusion that it's more important to avoid getting it wrong than it is to get better at getting it right. Certainly, we need to stay on the right side of ethical, financial, and policy requirements, but we also want to keep in sharp focus that all of this work, our collective expertise and efforts, are in service of children. Serving them better depends on us capably satisfying requirements and avoiding errors while vigilantly seeking to leverage every available resource and opportunity.

As we each enact our individual roles and responsibilities, it is incumbent upon us to identify limitations and expectations so that we maintain our integrity and the trust of our community. What we must recognize is that while this is a necessary function, it's an insufficient goal. It stops short of advancing the real goal of serving children better by developing practices that hold the promise of better outcomes. Once we've determined what we *can't* do, the efforts must proceed to the equally important responsibility of creatively identifying what we *can* do. This is what advances the work toward the goal of better serving students. This is how we sponsor innovation. Using their unique expertise and experience, each person in the system is responsible to leverage the resources and opportunities within their span of control. The people closest to the work with students need all the resources and flexibility they can get as they work to develop practices that will result in more equitable experiences and outcomes for students. But these efforts have to start somewhere. Based on our experience, we offer the six specific strategies described in this chapter as potent opportunities to align your actions to your vision.

Prioritize the Work of the People Closest to the Students

If we are to examine how decisions can better align with our vision, then examining the decisions that directly impact the people in classrooms and schools provides crucial perspective. Teachers are the most valuable resource we provide to students. Having teachers who are committed to and engaged in the vision is essential. The next critical component is the team of people around teachers who create the context and content that support her continuous growth.

Then, the conditions must exist for this teacher and team to work together to collectively and iteratively develop effective instructional practices and supportive, inclusive learning communities. So it takes the right teachers, the right teams, and the collective will and focus on the work of enacting the vision. *Role and responsibility definitions, hiring and retention practices*, and *funding* each significantly affect whether and how teachers are supported. And all of these are shaped by multiple influences originating at different levels of the system, often leaving schools with very little opportunity to innovate.

Align Roles and Responsibilities with the Vision

The responsibilities that we assign to people in their positions must allow them to enact their role in alignment with the shared vision. For simplicity, we will use our vision to illustrate what we mean. To work toward the goal of designing richer and more equitable experiences and outcomes for children, teachers must be willing and able to meet to work and learn together. Coaches must be free of responsibilities that prevent them from being in classrooms and planning and facilitating teacher learning, and principals must be able to devote the majority of their practice to sustaining the focus on teacher learning and collaboration. And there are so many reasons why this is not common. Most principals are required to perform duties or attend meetings that prevent them from devoting the time necessary to plan and participate in Grade-Level Team Meetings and full-day professional learning sessions. Coaches are often funded by state or federal entitlements that specify that they must deliver direct services to students a significant percentage of the time, or the local collective bargaining agreement defines their work as optional at the teacher's discretion, or they are loaded up with peripheral job requirements, such as acting as testing or intervention coordinator, that consume their time. And teachers often have contract protections that limit the amount of time that they can be required to meet with anyone during their planning time or outside negotiated work hours. These are examples that illustrate that even if you are willing to change the school workplace to support teacher learning, you may not be able to. The combination of how administrators are tasked with noninstructional responsibilities, how coaches are limited by funding or peripheral responsibilities, and how teachers' bargained autonomy can singly or in combination present barriers to the enactment of the roles that will support both teacher and student learning.

Shifting the common ways that principals, coaches, and teachers enact their roles requires everyone to hold a shared vision of what their roles should be instead, and act to advocate for the flexibility they need. And the right people must step up to the challenge of providing the necessary flexibility; this can happen only if those who have the necessary expertise about the constraints of their funding sources and those with the authority to examine what is being "required" and release them to try shifting their enactment get together and make it possible. When the initiative to shift the work starts with the people trying to do it better—the principals, coaches, and teachers—our experience has been that people outside the school are more open to hearing it. When those closest to the work advocate to those who define and protect their work, it can be a powerful driver of change. For example, we have seen how teachers' union leaders have creatively partnered with their own members, teachers, and coaches, who want to forgo bargained "protections" such as setting agendas at Grade-Level Team Meetings or using compensated time that must be voted on to work together on topics determined in collaboration with their principal. Because the people with authority were asked to participate in identifying ways around negotiated limits on teachers' time and workload, they had a firsthand view of the benefits to teachers and how teachers' interests were being better served by the shifts that the teachers were advocating for. This collaboration and resulting support had a secondary effect, in that it created positive pressure to provide the principal more flexibility to engage. If teachers were willing to commit to engaging in the learning system, then the principal had to have the capacity and flexibility to commit as well. This helped district leaders see how this aligned with their interests in principals acting as instructional leaders. This momentum supported ongoing district-level efforts to ensure that content coaches were not constrained by ever-changing funding source limitations, and further cemented district sponsorship of the developing vision that schools could be better organized to support teacher learning. These are examples of efforts to better align our responsibilities to the work of enacting our vision.

Work Toward Vision-Driven Hiring and Retention Practices

The processes that impact human talent selection and retention in schools are critical. For example, we are obligated to define "qualified," but that definition depends on your vision of the work. *Qualified for what?* The principles that we have elaborated drive a very specific definition of what "qualified" means as it relates to teachers, coaches, and principals. The job responsibilities are more nuanced than what can be captured in a list of qualifications in job postings when developing practice is the goal. This need to find people who will work toward a shared vision and grow in their practice poses challenges for our colleagues in human resources who bear responsibility for ensuring that hiring and evaluation practices are consistent across the system and in compliance with all prevailing code, policy and union agreements. In reality, the interests of "consistency in practice" and the processes defined in union agreements often have the most impact on the people trying to build the teams who want to do the work as we describe it. An interest in consistency, for example, can drive decisions about evaluation and contract-renewal timelines that don't align with the teacher growth patterns that we typically see over the course of a year when new teachers are engaged in a rich learning and collaboration system. Or seniority and displacement agreements result in a teacher having the contractual right to choose to transfer to a school where teams are actively participating in the learning and collaboration system when that teacher prefers to exercise her right to autonomy or does not share the vision that the school is working toward.

Consistency is important, agreements need to be honored and predictable, and transparent practices foster trust. As self-evident as these goals are, they do not exist in isolation; when their execution is shown to have a direct impact on who serves students and/or how students are being served, they can and should be examined for impact. Teachers will always be the most valuable resource we provide to students. And in a system designed to prioritize teacher learning, the coaches and principals are a close second. Each teacher, coach, and principal must share the vision, have the necessary will and skill to engage in the continual process of learning and developing better practices together, and be committed to creating classrooms and schools where students experience more equitable social and academic learning opportunities.

These educators absolutely exist, but how we successfully recruit, hire, and retain them doesn't always mesh with typical practices. For example, when a new teacher is hired into a school committed to the principles we have shared, it takes a period of time for her to both learn and adjust to them. As she is learning and approximating the new practices, the Instructional Leadership Team (ILT) and her grade-level team are supporting her growth along the trajectory. But in reality, even with high levels of support and collaboration, not every teacher finds this work to be a natural fit. Some prefer more freedom in curricular choices, some find the collective decision-making in professional learning communities confining, and still others value more traditional instructional or disciplinary practices. These preferences and beliefs are not consistent with our vision or practices, but that doesn't make such teachers bad. However, they do impact the collective culture.

Once a teacher is hired, whether she is willing to enact a school's vision—in other words, her fit with the school's practices and beliefs—is not a factor that allows schools to reevaluate a teacher's hiring. Currently, schools have no recourse that doesn't do harm to either the school or the teacher. Normally, in a case such as this, the principal would have only the evaluative process as a means to address this, and that is time-intensive for both parties and often creates friction. To honor both the teams who do want to continue to work collectively to enact the principles and the teacher who tried it but doesn't, for some reason, fit with it, it's possible to expand the options. Assuming that it is truly a mismatch in beliefs, and there are no actual performance issues, the system could choose to develop an alternative path forward that doesn't negatively affect this teacher's employment or her career trajectory and provides a much more efficient, respectful option that keeps students at the center of the decisions. Perhaps there is an option that could be triggered by the teacher to transfer to another school without any impact. The result would be that the system retains this teacher and the school has the opportunity to seek another teacher who is aligned with their vision and practices. Far less energy is diverted from the work of better serving students.

This example reveals what is possible when human resources and the teachers' union both lean in to learn about a school's problem of practice and contribute their expertise to reexamining the interests underlying past practices in consideration of the current impact on the people closest to the work. What could have been adversarial was instead mutually beneficial because when the people who had the positional knowledge and authority were called to act on behalf of the vision, they answered the call.

Align Funding to the Vision

In education, most money comes with strings, and there are many competing interests vying to influence how each dollar should be spent. But the reality is that if the right people aren't in the necessary positions with enough time to do the work together, nothing will change. There's no way around the fact that creating the coherent learning system teachers need in order to develop more engaging and equitable experiences for students requires committing to all of the interdependent parts of the learning system and the additional staffing it necessitates. Sometimes schools can fund all of the parts by themselves, but sometimes funding becomes a constraint that requires a commitment from the district. Substitutes who fill in for the teachers on teacher learning days must be paid. The budgets of schools without significant entitlement funding must be subsidized to ensure there are content-area coaches. And teachers can be assigned to only one of the grade-level teams that are the basis of the learning system. This last one is often the biggest challenge. Most districts allocate teacher staffing based on student enrollment, which leads to the creation of split grade-level classrooms, such as a second/third-grade split. In the teacher learning system that we advocate for, this would not be possible. And, just to address the impacts of the obvious and most common "solution," if you assigned the teacher to one grade-level team for professional learning and collaboration (let's say second grade), the students in third grade would not benefit from the same teacher learning and collaborative decisions as the rest of the third-graders. While there is a cost, with additional flexibility and collaboration, the school can also absorb some of the impact. For example, if student enrollment would normally dictate 2.5 second-grade classes and 3.5 third-grade classes, but the four kindergarten sections are small enough to be collapsed into three classes with only two students over the class-size target in each, this challenge could be met with the additional allocation of one teacher to this school and the agreement by that staff to use their allocated staffing to move a kindergarten teacher to second grade. This solution did require the funding of one additional teacher, but it also extended the flexibility and authority to the school to make a site-based decision about how to solve the second part of the problem. It's not perfect, but it's an example of how both the district staff and school staff can act to arrive at a middle ground to ensure that every teacher, and therefore every student, benefits equally from the learning system.

Find the Time

If you've been around education for a while, you've heard someone joke that bus schedules drive everything. Underlying this is the recognition (and frustration) that schedules, from arrival to dismissal, dictate when adults can meet because they are driven by when adults must be responsible for students. While this responsibility is paramount, it also creates significant constraints on every other adult responsibility. In addition, historically most collective bargaining agreements have created individual teacher conference, planning, and preparation time but have not extended to provide collaborative planning or learning time that is sufficient to enact the principles that we describe. And the planning time that exists is usually also negotiated to ensure that the teacher has discretion to determine how it is used. As a result, schedule limitations—bus schedules, recess supervision schedules, teacher planning schedules, and even break schedules—combined with limitations on who determines how time is spent essentially eliminate the flexibility needed to carve out the time for teacher learning and collaboration.

This brings us back to time and money. Learning and collaboration require spending time together. Designing learning and collaboration time so it's meaningful takes time. Being in classrooms together so we can learn from and with each other takes time. Implementing the learning system that is driven by the principles described throughout this book requires that we share the responsibility to find the time. Creating the conditions for adult learning requires that we find the time.

An example of working together to make it work: funding, flexibility, and advocacy

The following example illustrates that adaptive shifts in a system often require sustained effort and a combination of the strategies described in this chapter.

Context: The school has grant funding to cover the cost of substitutes for Learning Labs, and the school's budget has the capacity to fund both a literacy and a math coach. The teachers each have a self-directed conference and planning (C/P) time each day. Most weeks, students arrive late on one day in order to provide teachers with ninety minutes of contractually required collaborative planning time. The contractual agreement states that teachers determine who is on their collaborative team and the team sets the agenda. While the funding for the coaches is in place, the schedule provides no flexibility to allow time for them to meet with teams.

Outcome: Over the course of a year, this school figured out how to meet as grade-level teams twice each week using only existing resources.

The journey: First, they reconceived how they could use available stipend funds that were intended to compensate teachers for work done outside the school day to support their school improvement plan. Through whole-staff conversations facilitated by the principal, the teachers agreed that they wanted to use this funding as their compensation to meet weekly during the school day (C/P) to collaborate about one content area. Each team chose either math or literacy and met with that content coach and the principal to work on developing practices. Doing this required both the teachers' union and the district to agree that the compensation could be earned during the work day, when teachers are technically already being paid. The school argued that it was a trade because the planning that the teachers missed when they met one day a week still had to be done and now had to take place outside work hours. The union and district both agreed to this flexibility. This agreement supported teacher collaboration in one content area.

In the late fall, the principal engaged teams in self-assessing their grade-level team collaboration practices in both reading and math. Each grade-level team rated its own effectiveness significantly higher in the content area on which it worked together during its one coach-facilitated Grade-Level Team Meeting per week, and the teachers expressed the desire to extend their grade-level team work to both content areas. The principal suggested another option that required flexibility in the use of compensated time and teacher autonomy. Over the course of a year, the ninety minutes of delayed-start collaborative planning time already available each week were almost exactly equivalent to one teacher planning time (C/P) session each week. If teachers agreed to engage in a coach-facilitated Grade-Level Team Meeting each week (requiring them to forgo the autonomy of choosing their team and setting their agendas), then they could convert those delayed-start collaborative planning times into individual planning times. There was no loss of compensation, but it did require the teachers to allow coaches to take the lead in setting and facilitating the agenda of the second weekly content

Grade-Level Team Meeting. Because the teachers advocated to their own union to support this approach, and the principal advocated it to the district, both the union and the district once again gave them flexibility. After some work by the specialists, who teach the classes during teachers' planning time, and the principal to ensure that their planning schedule could support every team in having common planning twice each week, the pieces were in place. With that, they secured their second collaborative planning time each week.

In this example, we see how some additional money was necessary (substitutes for Learning Lab days), yet that many of the constraints were related to time or bargained agreements and could not be solved by money alone. Those shifts hinged more on flexibility. There were multiple factors constraining the learning system being fully implemented, but the will to address the constraints, some additional resources, and the flexibility to move beyond previous practice combined to effectively address the need for more collaborative time. And this was driven entirely by site-based advocacy to do it better in service of their own professional learning. This example also reminds us of the power of those closest to the work advocating it to those who define and protect their working conditions and expectations. It also underscores the need for intentional efforts to create lines of communication that support people in and out of school to share the work of identifying how the system can shift to support a school's efforts to develop better practices.

Provide Operational Flexibility

Time and money often pose challenges because they are resources that we typically do not have in sufficient amounts. But sometimes what we *do* have provides challenges. Developing instructional practices that orient students to each other, supporting them to grow ideas together and positioning them as sensemakers who construct conceptual understanding in the context of classroom communities where social emotional skills are taught and practiced, requires curriculum, assessment and instructional materials, resources, and timelines that align with this vision of instruction. Further, because we are organizing schools to work together on the iterative process of learning and developing practices based on the responses of their learners, typical district expectations and timelines may be out of sync or in opposition to developing better practices. Engaging in this work beyond a grade level or two will present a challenge that requires both the schools and the district to work together to pave a path forward.

Exploring and identifying that path forward require operational flexibility. In practice, this means that the district sponsors the work by opening the door to listening and acting when the school identifies barriers that can be addressed by making adjustments to district-determined expectations or processes. In very plain terms, it means that when the principal calls a director to explore how much flexibility there is in meeting an expectation, that director listens for the intent, identifies any objectionable impact that may result from the ideas being considered, and brings her expertise to bear in teasing apart what is really required by law, funding source, or policy to determine what is locally expected and can be adjusted. Identifying possible areas of flexibility calls on the principal to work to understand the essential aspects of an expectation, and on district staff to support the principal's effort to seek alternatives to avoid a problematic impact on students or teachers.

Creating operational flexibility requires examining decision-making authority, as well as spoken and unspoken norms. For example, in many districts, principals are expected to communicate with district staff through a supervisor, eliminating their opportunity to learn more about the expectations from the local expert or directly communicate their concerns. Or the unspoken rule of the district culture is that principals do not "push back." Similarly, if there is a cohort of content coaches across your district, they are likely led by a district director who facilitates district initiatives based on their authority to dictate the role that the coaches play in schools. This can create mixed messages and misaligned priorities at the school level if the team is attempting to innovate.

As a system that must respond to the continual onslaught of bulletins from state and federal agencies, meet the expectations of the School Board, stay compliant in meeting the commitments made to several unions, and manage thousands of employees, decisions do have to be made. Money does have to be budgeted. Plans do have to be made and implemented. Time does have to be scheduled in order for people to do the work. In the complexity of this, well-intentioned decisions can have unintended impacts. Operational flexibility is about creating a means of bringing the relevant people together to reflect and adjust.

An example of operational flexibility

In December, the Title I director reads in a state bulletin that the use of existing funds has been expanded to permit districts to fund positions that provide direct services to identified students; and she recalls that over the years, principals have advocated for more resources for interventions. After learning more about the exact conditions of this new possibility, she works with her team to build an intervention teacher position for several schools into next year's budget. She does all the necessary work to write the new job description and get the staffing allocations approved. In the spring, she is excited to announce this new resource to the principals of this subset of schools. After the meeting, one principal approaches the director with concerns about this new position. The principal wants to meet to explain her reluctance and explore the possibility of using the funding differently.

In a district sponsoring the work of enacting the principles that we have described, the Title I director would engage in this discussion to consider what operational flexibility is possible. She would hear the principal out as she explains that her school has adequate staffing to support students who need interventions outside the classroom, and that they are working on developing instructional practices that support students staying within the classroom community. The principal is concerned that having a person whose job requires her to pull students out will lead to pulling more students out of their classrooms, which is counter to the school's goals. Instead, she'd like to use that funding to hire another coach to support teachers in developing instructional skills related to social emotional learning. Providing the flexibility to do this will require time and effort from the director, who will need to explore whether the funding source will permit that, assist the principal in creating a new job description, and collaborate with the union on negotiated responsibilities for a new position. There will also need to be coordination with the human resources and business departments. The director's willingness to meet, learn about the impact of her decision, and explore a proposed alternative is an example of operational flexibility, in that she is engaging in reflecting and adjusting based on a school's feedback about a decision.

Operational flexibility is a strategy schools can use to address the unintended impacts of resources, expectations, and processes as they work to develop better practices. Again using our vision to illustrate this point, we provide the following questions to demonstrate how district-level decision-making can affect classroom practices in unintentional ways.

Curriculum

- Does the adopted curriculum dictate that teachers deliver scripted instruction?
- Does the instruction include opportunities for student discussion?
- Do lessons result in public records of student thinking and developing ideas?

Assessment

- Are there adequate formative assessments?
- Do any assessments produce lessons that students are assigned without teacher discretion?
- Is there an expectation that students are ability-grouped for intervention instruction based on assessment data?

Expectations

- Are schools expected to create school improvement plans that require them to identify how professional learning time and other resources will be used for the coming year?
- Are student disciplinary procedures and practices based on compliance or prescribed consequences?

When a need for operational flexibility is identified by the school, there must be a mutually understood path forward. Each decision, procedure, and expectation was made for a reason. Sometimes it's simple practicality, as in the case of an internal assessment deadline being set because there simply has to be an agreed upon date to close the portal that teachers use to upload data. In more complex cases, the people who understand all the perspectives on a decision must work together. It works best when the person with firsthand knowledge of the impacts in question communicates with the person who understands the external requirements and/or internal interests that shaped the decision. Ideally, if it's not the same district staff member, then the person with the authority to allow the requested flexibility should also participate in the problem solving.

SPONSORING CHANGE IS EVERYONE'S RESPONSIBILITY

Sponsorship requires action. It occurs when specific supports, resources, or protections are provided. But sponsoring *change* starts with committing to a vision. That vision is the shared understanding of the preferred future you are working toward. It is the north star that guides the choices you make to provide the necessary supports and address the constraints that will prevent you from realizing it. You must have both a shared vision and the commitment to sponsor the change needed to achieve it. This combination is what opens up opportunities to work together to be creative, stay determined, and find ways forward in service of the shared goal of better experiences and outcomes for students. Whether you're starting with one school in a large system, one grade-level team in a school, or a whole district, working together can result in schools where educators and students both accelerate in their growth. Working together toward a shared vision, the people in your system can carve out the space to develop fundamentally different organizing principles that better serve both teachers and students.

As you get started, we encourage you to lean into the commitment that there are things you'll need to start doing *and* things you'll need to stop doing, and this applies to everyone. *Everyone*—teachers, coaches, principals, paraprofessionals, district directors, union leaders, human resources staff, and superintendents—has an impact and the potential to contribute to the effort to organize our schools intentionally and explicitly to nurture teacher learning in service of creating flourishing learning environments for each student.

WHERE DO *YOU* START?

If, like us, you feel powerfully excited about working to create the schools that our teachers and students need and deserve; if you too believe that schools can and should be reorganized to intentionally prioritize teachers' learning and collaboration aimed at designing classroom learning communities that are joyful, inquiry-oriented spaces where students' thinking and identities are cultivated; if you can imagine yourself working in or supporting a school where every teacher actively participates in a team that is supported by instructional coaches and administrators who prioritized their teamwork as the core of their professional efforts, then we encourage you to turn back to chapter 2, where we share the principles that guide our vision. What are *your* guiding principles? Who will you start this work with? What will you commit to accomplishing this year?

We wrote this book for everyone because it will take everyone. We are all the leaders who can and should change the ways our schools function for teachers and for students. If we want something different, we are the ones who will have to create it. Together.

Notes

Chapter 1

1. Our work has focused on making elementary schools better places for teacher learning so they can be better places for student learning. Much of what we write may be relevant for high schools as well, but we will leave that for the reader to decide.

2. Throughout the book, quotations have been edited for clarity and confidentiality but not to change the intent or meaning of the speaker. For example, specific names have been removed. Conversational filler words, like "um," "ahh," and "you know," have been removed; repeated phrases have been edited, and missing referents have been added to clarify meaning for an outside audience.

3. Organizing schools for teacher learning has been a major focus of much research. We build on and draw on efforts to improve schools through a focus on teacher learning and have drawn inspiration from many scholars, including Megan Franke, Michael Fullan, Ron Gallimore, Claude Goldenberg, John Goodlad, Linda Darling Hammond, Ann Lieberman, Judith Warren Little, Virginia Richardson, James Spillane, and Ken Sirotnik.

4. By the end of the third year of our partnership, the percentage of fourth- and fifth-grade students who scored proficient on the state assessment in mathematics outperformed both the district and state averages, while third-grade students' passing rates approached the district and state averages. For example, from 2011 to 2014, passing rates for fifth graders grew from 20 percent to 79 percent. By 2015, there were no achievement differences among students as determined by race, language, or class. We know, of course, that it is possible to improve test performance and not improve teachers' and students' experiences and their sense of agency and empowerment, identity, and belonging. From our own research measures and analysis, analyses led by outside evaluators required by the grant, and informal observations, students and teachers were engaged in rich content conversations across the school. There was consistent and widespread use of shared instructional materials and practices, and teachers conveyed expectations that students were brilliant and capable of a high level of engagement and achievement.

5. Deborah L. Ball and David K. Cohen, "Developing Practice, Developing Practitioners: Toward a Practice-Based Theory of Professional Education," in *Teaching as the Learning Profession*, ed. Linda Darling-Hammond and Gary Sykes (San Francisco: Jossey-Bass, 1999), 3–32; Anthony S. Bryk et al., *Organizing Schools for Improvement: Lessons from Chicago* (Chicago: University of Chicago Press, 2010); Paul Cobb et al., *Systems for Instructional Improvement: Creating Coherence from the Classroom to the District Office* (Cambridge, MA: Harvard Education Press, 2018); Marilyn Cochran-Smith and Susan Lytle, "Relationships of Knowledge and Practice: Teacher Learning in Communities," *Review of Research in Education* 24, no. 1 (1999): 249–305, https://doi.org/10.2307/1167272; Muhammad Khalifa, *Culturally Responsive School Leadership* (Cambridge, MA: Harvard Education Press, 2018); Judith W. Little, "Organizing Schools for Teacher Learning," in *Teaching as the Learning Profession*, ed. Linda Darling-Hammond and Gary Sykes (San Francisco: Jossey-Bass, 1999), 233–262.

6. Dan Lortie, *Schoolteacher: A Sociological Study* (Chicago: University of Chicago Press, 1975).

7. We are primarily addressing grade-level classroom teachers. We know that specialists and classroom support staff interact with students in multiple ways throughout the day and contribute to the overall culture and climate of our learning communities. We have intentionally supported the practices of all educators in our buildings. We encourage readers who are undertaking the work described in this book to think carefully about how support staff and specialists are meaningfully included in collective learning.

8. Lynsey Gibbons et al., "Teacher Time Out: Educators Learning Together in and Through Practice," *Journal of Mathematics Educational Leadership* 18, no. 2 (2017): 28–46, https://doi.org/10.1016/j.tate.2021.103304; Lynsey Gibbons, Elham Kazemi, and Rebecca Lewis, "Developing Collective Capacity to Improve Mathematics Instruction: Coaching as a Lever for Schoolwide Improvement," *Journal of Mathematical Behavior* 46 (2017): 231–250, https://doi.org/10.1016/j.jmathb.2016.12.002.

9. Elham Kazemi, Alison F. Resnick, and Lynsey Gibbons, "Principal Leadership for Schoolwide Transformation of Elementary Mathematics Teaching: Why the Principal's Conception of Teacher Learning Matters," *American Educational Research Journal* 59, no. 6 (2022): 1051–1081, https://doi.org/10.3102/00028312221130706.

10. Elham Kazemi et al., "Supporting Teacher Learning About Argumentation Through Adaptive, School-Based Professional Development," *ZDM-Mathematics Education* 53, no. 2 (2021): 435–448, https://doi.org/10.1007/s11858-021-01242-5.

Chapter 2

1. The Principles for Teaching and Learning to Teach have developed over time and are based on collaborations with Magdalene Lampert, Megan Franke, Hala Ghousseini, and the research teams involved in the Learning in, from, and for Teaching project, as well as collaborations with Elizabeth Dutro. See, for example, Elizabeth Dutro and Ashley Cartun, "Cut to the Core Practices: Toward Visceral Disruptions of Binaries in Practice-Based Teacher Education," *Teaching and Teacher Education* 58, no. 2 (2016): 119–128, https://doi.org/0.1016/j.tate.2016.05.001; Magdalene Lampert et al., "Keeping It Complex: Using Rehearsals to Support Novice Teacher Learning of Ambitious Teaching in Elementary Mathematics," *Journal of Teacher Education* 64, no. 3 (2013): 226–243, https://doi.org/10.1177/0022487112473837.

2. Angela Valenzuela, *Subtractive Schooling: US-Mexican Youth and the Politics of Caring* (New York: SUNY Press, 1999).

3. We credit Leslie Herrenkohl for introducing us to the statement, "Teaching includes becoming a student of your students."

4. Gloria Ladson-Billings, *Culturally Relevant Pedagogy: Asking a Different Question* (New York: Teachers College Press, 2021).

5. According to Irby, "Black and Brown people's influential presence refers to the combined physical presence and deep integration of experiential knowledge and cultural practices into the fabric of the organization." Decoteau J. Irby, *Stuck Improving: Racial Equity and School Leadership* (Cambridge, MA: Harvard Education Press, 2021), 13.

6. Robin Wall Kimmerer, *Braiding Sweetgrass: Indigenous Wisdom, Scientific Knowledge, and the Teachings of Plants* (Minneapolis: Milkweed, 2015), 24.

7. Elham Kazemi and Allison Hintz, *Intentional Talk: How to Structure and Lead Productive Mathematical Discussions* (Portland, ME: Stenhouse, 2014).

8. We think instructional goals that are deeply understood by teachers are vital. We want teachers to understand what children need to know and be able to do. We think this understanding must include how children's ideas develop as they progress toward meeting disciplinary goals. We do not think that evidence of teachers having clear instructional goals can be reduced to writing a learning target on the board.

9. Mike Rose, *Possible Lives: The Promise of Public Education in America* (New York: Penguin, 1999).

10. We think about schools as being places where teachers continually learn to hone their judgment. Confer, as examples, the scholarship of Deborah Ball, Megan Bang, Paul Cobb, Elizabeth Dutro, Megan Franke, Kara Jackson, Gloria Ladson-Billings, Magdalene Lampert, Carol Lee, Abby Reisman, Mike Rose, and Mark Windschitl for examples of rich decision-making. We do not aim to teacher-proof instruction by mandating what teachers do.

11. This statement is based on Julia Cameron, *The Artist's Way: A Spiritual Path to Higher Creativity* (New York: Jeremy Tarcher/Putnam, 2002). The actual statement in the book is, "It is impossible to get better and look good at the same time."

12. Deborah L. Ball and Francesca M. Forzani, "Teaching Skillful Teaching," *Educational Leadership* 68, no. 4 (2010): 40–45.

13. See, for example, the scholarship of Megan Bang, Tom Carpenter, Elizabeth Dutro, Ann Dyson, Carol Lee, Ann Rosebery, and Beth Warren.

14. Broadly, this view of learning is a sociocultural perspective. See, for example, Barbara Rogoff, *Apprenticeship in Thinking: Cognitive Development in Social Context* (Oxford: Oxford University Press, 1990); Etienne Wenger, *Communities of Practice: Learning, Meaning, and Identity* (Cambridge, MA: Harvard University Press, 1998). Also consult R. Keith Sawyer, ed., *The Cambridge Handbook of the Learning Sciences*, 3rd ed. (Cambridge: Cambridge University Press, 2022); and Na'ilah Suad Nasir, Carol D. Lee, Roy Pea, and Maxine McKinney de Royston, eds., *Handbook of the Cultural Foundations of Learning* (New York: Routledge, 2020).

15. The initial version of this trajectory was developed early in the research-practice partnership during a collaborative meeting of the principals, coaches, and research team. We credit these thoughtful leaders for sharing their thoughts, experiences, and examples to support the development of a shared vision of how teacher growth progresses over time.

16. Leslie R. Herrenkohl and Véronique Mertl, *How Students Come to Be, Know, and Do: A Case for a Broad View of Learning* (New York: Cambridge University Press, 2010).

Chapter 3

1. Elham Kazemi et al., "Math Labs: Teachers, Teacher Educators, and School Leaders Learning Together with and from Their Own Students," *Journal of Mathematics Educational Leadership* 19, no. 1 (2018): 23–36.

2. Courtney Baker and Melinda Knapp, *Proactive Mathematics Coaching: Bridging Content, Context, and Practice* (Reston, VA: National Council of Teachers of Mathematics, 2023); https://www.teachersdg.org/services/#mathstudios; Aki Murata, "Introduction: Conceptual Overview of Lesson Study," in *Lesson Study Research and Practice in Mathematics Education*, ed. Lynn Hart, Alice Alston, and Aki Murata (Dordrecht, Netherlands: Springer, 2011), https://doi.org/10.1007/978-90-481-9941-9_1; Clea Fernandez and Makoto Yoshida, *Lesson Study: A Japanese Approach to Improving Instruction Through School-Based Teacher Development* (Mahwah, NJ: Erlbaum, 2004); Miriam G. Sherin and Sandra Y. Han, "Teacher Learning in the Context of a Video Club," *Teaching and Teacher Education* 20 (2004): 163–183, https://doi.org/10.1016/j.tate.2003.08.001.

3. Visit https://tedd.org/ to explore a set of resources for designing and facilitating professional development in multiple subject areas. You'll find video examples, descriptions, and planning templates.

4. Lynsey K. Gibbons, Elham Kazemi, Allison Hintz, and Elizabeth Hartmann, "Teacher Time Out: Educators Learning Together in and Through Practice," *Journal of Mathematics Educational Leadership* 18, no. 2 (2017): 28–46.

Chapter 4

1. Much of the content of this chapter is based on our research on principal leadership in our research-practice partnership (RPP). Consult the following publications: Elham Kazemi and Alison Fox Resnick, "Organising Schools for Teacher and Leader Learning," in *International Handbook of Mathematics Teacher Education: Participants in Mathematics Teacher Education*, 2nd ed., vol. 3, ed. Gwendolyn M. Lloyd and Olive Chapman (Leiden, Netherlands: Brill, 2020), 393–420; Elham Kazemi, Alison F. Resnick, and Lynsey Gibbons, "Principal Leadership for Schoolwide Transformation of Elementary Mathematics Teaching: Why the Principal's Conception of Teacher Learning Matters," *American Educational Research Journal* 59, no. 6 (2022): 1051–1081, https://doi.org/10.3102/00028312221130706; Alison F. Resnick, "Becoming an Instructional Leader for Elementary Mathematics: Transforming Principal Learning Through a Research-Practice Partnership," PhD diss., University of Washington, 2018, ProQuest (2084108093); Alison F. Resnick, "Professional Identity as an Analytic Lens for Principal Learning in Contexts of Transformation," *Educational Administration Quarterly* 59, no. 5 (2023): 1038–1072, https://doi.org/10.1177/0013161X231204883; Alison F. Resnick and Elham Kazemi, "Decomposition of Practice as an Activity for Research-Practice Partnerships," *AERA Open* 5, no. 3 (2019): 1–14, https://doi.org/10.1177/2332858419862273.

2. Cynthia E. Coburn, "Shaping Teacher Sensemaking: School Leaders and the Enactment of Reading Policy," *Educational Policy* 19, no. 3 (2005): 476–509, https://doi.org/10.1177/0895904805276143.

3. Michael Fullan, "Positive Pressure," in *Second International Handbook of Educational Change*, ed. Andy Hargreaves, Ann Lieberman, Michael Fullan, and David Hopkins

(Dordrecht, Netherlands: Springer, 2010), 119–130, https://doi.org/10.1007/978-90-48
1-2660-6_7.

4. Coburn, "Shaping Teacher Sensemaking."

5. Dan Lortie, *Schoolteacher: A Sociological Study* (Chicago: University of Chicago Press, 1975).

6. See chapter 8 in this book for a discussion of negotiating and reshaping district
expectations and process requirements.

Chapter 5

1. We recognize the value of mentoring and one-on-one coaching. For example, teachers
new to the profession benefit from a relationship with a coach or mentor who can help
them navigate all the expectations that new teachers face, such as supplies and materials,
fire drills, taking attendance, developing a well-managed and healthy classroom
community, and work-life balance. One-on-one coaching can help practitioners develop
a reflective practice. The new teachers we work with participate in this type of mentoring in addition to the coaching described in this chapter. While valuable, we believe
one-on-one coaching alone to be insufficient in the effort to affect how all teachers
are positioned and supported as a means of powerfully changing experiences for all
students.

2. Lynsey K. Gibbons, Elham Kazemi, and Rebecca M. Lewis, "Developing Collective
Capacity to Improve Mathematics Instruction: Coaching as a Lever for School-Wide
Improvement," *Journal of Mathematical Behavior* 46, no. 3 (2017): 231–250, https://doi.
org/10.1016/j.jmathb.2016.12.002.

3. To be clear, the type of coaching that we describe depends on close coordination
between the principal and the coach, which we address in chapter 6, as well as an
equally strong partnership between the teacher and the principal, which we have
described in chapter 4.

4. For more information, see a study that considers the impact of coaching when it is
framed as either intending to support individual change or systemic reform: Melinda
Mangin and KaiLonnie Dunsmore, "How the Framing of Instructional Coaching as a
Lever for Systemic or Individual Reform Influences the Enactment of Coaching,"
Educational Administration Quarterly 51, no. 2 (2015): 179–213, https://doi.
org/10.1177/0013161X14522814. Consult the following article for how facilitators of PD
create conditions for collaboration: Lynsey Gibbons, Rebecca Lewis, Hannah Nieman,
and Alison Fox Resnick, "Conceptualizing the Work of Facilitating Practice-Embedded
Teacher Learning," *Teaching and Teacher Education* 101 (2021): 103304, https://doi.org/
10.1016/j.tate.2021.103304.

5. These studies look at coaches working alongside elementary teachers. Jen Munson,
"Noticing Aloud: Uncovering Mathematics Teacher Noticing in the Moment," *Mathemat-
ics Teacher Educator* 8, no. 2 (2020): 25–36, https://doi.org/10.5951/mathteaceduc.8.2.fm;
Lynsey Gibbons and Ada Okun, "Examining a Coaching Routine to Support Teacher
Learning," *Investigations in Mathematics Learning* 15, no. 1 (2023): 11–28, https://doi.org/1
0.1080/19477503.2022.2139094.

6. A series of studies led by researchers at the University of Pittsburgh examined how
mathematics and literacy coaches supported teachers to deepen their knowledge about
teaching and change their instructional practices. While the studies examine one-on-
one coaching, they have implications for how coaches can facilitate interactions among

groups of teachers. Jennifer L. Russell et al., "Mathematics Coaching for Conceptual Understanding: Promising Evidence Regarding the Tennessee Math Coaching Model," *Educational Evaluation and Policy Analysis* 42, no. 3 (2020): 439–466, https://doi. org/10.3102/016237372094069; Mary Kay Stein et al., "Coach Learning to Help Teachers Learn to Enact Conceptually Rich, Student-Focused Mathematics Lessons," *Journal of Mathematics Teacher Education* 25, no. 1 (2022): 1–26, https://doi.org/0.1007/s10857-021-09492-6; Richard Correnti et al., "Effects of Online Content-Focused Coaching on Discussion Quality and Reading Achievement: Building Theory for How Coaching Develops Teachers' Adaptive Expertise," *Reading Research Quarterly* 56, no. 3 (2021): 519–558, https://doi.org/10.1002/rrq.317.

7. Kassia O. Wedekind and Christy H. Thompson, *Hands Down, Speak Out: Listening and Talking Across Literacy and Math K–8* (Portsmouth, ME: Stenhouse, 2020).

8. Susan Empson and Linda Levi, *Extending Children's Mathematics: Fractions and Decimals* (Portsmouth, NH: Heinemann, 2011), xiv.

9. Typically, students and teachers alike find fractions challenging. Often teachers themselves had negative experiences learning fractions and feel anxious and unqualified to teach the topic effectively. These past experiences can lead teachers to teach fractions procedurally. Available curricula are typically not grounded in research on children's thinking. Teaching fractions through a focus on procedures that need to be memorized rather than understood can reinforce the idea that mathematics doesn't make sense. In our work with fractions, we draw on resources that help teachers and students develop a strong conceptual understanding of fractions as quantities represented through area or linear models. We use these conceptions to develop strategies for adding, subtracting, multiplying, and dividing fractions that make sense. To do this, we have relied on Empson and Levi, *Extending Children's Mathematics.*

10. Clothesline math is an example of an instructional routine that can be used numerous times across different mathematical units of instruction. The clothesline is a flexible and interactive number line that can support students in learning about proportional reasoning, precision, equivalency between numbers, and magnitude of numbers. For example, see MPJ, "Clothesline Math," https://clotheslinemath.com.

Chapter 6

1. Julia Aguirre, Karen Mayfield-Ingram, and Danny B. Martin, *The Impact of Identity in K–8 Mathematics: Rethinking Equity-Based Practices* (Reston, VA: National Council of Teachers of Mathematics, 2024); Danny B. Martin, "In My Opinion: Does Race Matter?," *Teaching Children Mathematics* 16, no. 3 (2009): 134–139.

Chapter 7

1. Zaretta Hammond, *Culturally Responsive Teaching and the Brain: Promoting Authentic Engagement and Rigor Among Culturally and Linguistically Diverse Students* (Thousand Oaks, CA: Corwin, 2014).

Acknowledgments

Our work has been influenced by our current and past experiences in schools and by a wealth of scholarship on powerful teaching, student learning, leadership, coaching, and school transformation. We are indebted to all the people who have participated in and contributed to the journey that this book reflects. It will be impossible to name and acknowledge all of them, but we are filled with gratitude for each of them.

A federal school improvement grant initially brought us together. We thank Jane Chadsey and Phil Barber for introducing Elham Kazemi and Allison Hintz to Jessica Calabrese, which sparked the dreaming about what could be possible. The remarkable educators at Lakeridge Elementary School were the innovators and risk takers that provided the proof point for the ideas captured on these pages. This book is their legacy, and the foundation upon which many leaders, coaches, and principals have since built and advanced.

Since 2011, we have continued to learn more than this book can contain from the brilliant students and dedicated teachers, coaches, principals, assistant principals, paraeducators, and leaders in the Renton Innovation Zone. Their belief, creativity, intellectual engagement, and relentless effort to do better together for children laid the foundation of every step along this journey. They have shown us the possibilities that open up when teams of educators collaborate and innovate to transform student learning. In addition, district leaders provided critical sponsorship, and we especially thank Damien Pattenaude, Shannon Harvey, Art Jarvis, Vera Risdon, and Mary Alice Heuschel. Finally, the work could not have progressed as it has without collaboration with the Renton Education Association, and especially the support of Susan Ormbrek.

The idea to write a book began with a conversation with Jayne Fargnoli at Harvard Education Press, and we are grateful to her and Molly Cerrone for their encouragement, patience, and feedback throughout the writing process. We also thank Tracy Zager for helping us imagine a book that teachers, coaches, and leaders could read together. She pushed us to be more ambitious and take on a bigger challenge than we thought we could.

Our work as teacher educators was shaped by the Learning Teaching in, for, and from Practice research project; the research and professional development emerging from Cognitively Guided Instruction; and mathematics educators at the University of Washington, including Ruth Balf, Adrian Cunard, Allison Hintz, Kara Jackson, Megan Kelley-Petersen, Anita Lenges, Kendra Lomax, Emily Shahan, Gini Stimpson; and MERG (the Math Ed Research Group). The first Learning Labs, then called Math Labs, were designed and facilitated by Elham Kazemi in collaboration with Allison Hintz and Megan Kelley-Petersen in the Northshore School District. We thank Tom Stritikus for supporting our work as it was getting off the ground. Scholars who have developed ideas about creating systems and contexts for teacher learning have been vital to our thinking.

Several foundations funded various aspects of our work. Washington STEM, under grant number 2012 PORT01.02, supported our work with the Teaching Channel to develop beautiful video examples of teachers and students at work in mathematics discussions that we have continued to rely on for professional learning, which can be seen on the Teaching Channel and at Teacher Education by Design (tedd.org). Grant number 201500018, from the Spencer Foundation, provided resources to closely study the work of the principal and coach and grow our understanding of leadership for school transformation. Support for studying Learning Labs over the course of two years came from the James S. McDonnell

Foundation (grant number 220020523). The ideas expressed in our book are those of the authors and do not necessarily reflect the views of our funders.

Many people were gracious enough to read drafts and give us valuable feedback and suggestions: Candace Abrahamson, Carl Cohn, Robert Ettinger, Jany Finkielsztein, Megan Franke, Shannon Harvey, Heather Heon, Erika Klein, Stacy Lappin, Stephanie Latimer, Morva McDonald, Kelly Rudie, Laurie Wasson, and Kendall White. Matt Hagen took the beautiful pictures in this book.

Finally, we thank our partners and children for their support and for giving us the time we needed to meet and write so we could make this book a reality. Thank you for supporting our dream of sharing this work.

About the Authors

Elham Kazemi is a professor of mathematics education at the University of Washington. Her research has included the close study of classroom discourse and children's disciplinary identities, pedagogies of teacher education, and teacher educator and leadership practice. She collaborates with schools to build strong professional learning communities that make a difference for children's growth and development. Her work is informed by equity and justice-oriented research on children's mathematical thinking, classroom practice, and organizational learning. In addition to her academic publications, she consistently writes for practitioners, including two books called *Intentional Talk* (coauthored with Allison Hintz) and *Choral Counting and Counting Collections* (coedited with Megan Franke and Angela Turrou).

Jessica Calabrese is chief of school improvement for Renton School District and was the principal at Lakeridge Elementary, the school at which our research-practice partnership originated. During Jessica's five years as principal at Lakeridge Elementary, she led the development of professional learning and collaboration practices that resulted in the school's performance rising from the fifth percentile of schools in the state to exiting improvement status in four years and being recognized as a Distinguished School in 2015 and 2016. Lakeridge is considered one of the few successful turnaround schools in the federal School Improvement Grant

(SIG) program. She strongly believes in the power of the partnership between teachers and administrators to cultivate professional learning and collaboration structures that result in better instructional and social experiences for students and teachers. She continues to partner with mathematics education researchers at the University of Washington to study effective instructional leadership and teacher learning systems.

Teresa Lind was the mathematics coach at Lakeridge Elementary for seven years and the leader of the mathematics coaching network for the schools at the center of the research-practice partnership depicted in this book. In collaboration with the coauthors of this book, she designed and led opportunities for teachers including ongoing Learning Labs, weekly Grade-Level Team Meetings, and classroom coaching. Throughout the partnership, she continuously wove together these collaborative learning experiences with the supporting instructional practices that empowered children as sensemakers. Prior to this project, she served as a school-based instructional coach at another school for three years and taught kindergarten through fourth grade for twenty-one years. In addition, she was a contributing author of *Choral Counting and Counting Collections* (coedited by Megan Franke, Elham Kazemi, and Angela Turrou).

Becca Lewis is the current leader of the mathematics coaching network for the schools at the center of the research-practice partnership depicted in this book. She facilitates professional learning and collaboration experiences for the network's school-based math coaches, supporting them in their work to develop strong professional learning communities. She works alongside coaches to support teachers in creating classrooms where teachers and students are learning alongside one another. Previously, Becca also served as a school-based math coach, university-based teacher educator, researcher, classroom teacher, and consultant.

Alison Fox Resnick is a teacher and leader educator, learning systems designer, and researcher at the National Center for Research in Policy and

Practice at the School of Education at the University of Colorado Boulder. As a teacher at Lakeridge Elementary, she experienced school leadership that fostered empowering learning for both teachers and students. Her ongoing work seeks to uncover how powerful learning can be woven throughout educational transformation efforts. This work centers partnership with educational leaders to design and implement learning systems that support movement toward equitable classrooms, school systems, and research approaches. In puzzling through these local, collaborative efforts for change, she aims to develop insights that can be tangibly useful for supporting learning across contexts.

Lynsey K. Gibbons is an associate professor of mathematics education at the University of Delaware. She started in education as an elementary teacher and mathematics coach in Lexington, Kentucky. She received her MEd in educational leadership from the University of Kentucky and her PhD in mathematics education from Vanderbilt University. At the University of Delaware, she teaches future elementary teachers and instructional leaders. Her research seeks to explore teacher learning from an organizational and systems perspective, with special attention to professional learning routines, the roles of instructional leaders, and the role of coherent learning events that occur within the system. Across the United States, Lynsey has worked alongside district leaders, principals, and coaches to organize job-embedded professional learning for teachers. This work situates her to continually learn about students' mathematical thinking and teachers' and instructional leaders' lived experiences.

Index

adult community, shared goal of, 215–217
adult learning
    attending to status, 221–224
    creating context for, 163–165
    identifying goals, 130–131
    products of system, 217–221
    shared intentions, 209–235
    social emotional skill building, 215–217
    supporting, 108–109
advocacy, example of, 243–245
Asian American children, 2
assessing and reflecting, ILT
    bridging, 172–173
    development of practices, 165–169
    different perspectives, 169–172
    embracing learning to lead, 173–175
assets, collaboration, 45
assistant principals, 112–115
autonomy
    balancing with collaboration, 183–184
    teacher autonomy, 28–29

barrier of deficit thinking, confronting, 180–182
beliefs, decisions driven by, 20–21
biases, examining, 115–116
Black and Brown people's influential presence, 23
Black children, 2
Brown children, 2

C/P. See conference and planning
case study, ILT
    assess and reflect, 187–196
    intentionally coordinate, 199–205
    overview, 186–187
    plan and adjust, 197–199
challenges
    attending to status among adults, 221–224
    calibrating on, 105–106
    creating equitable experiences, 210–221
    data use, 229–233
    measuring success, 224–229
    overview, 209–210
change, sponsoring, 249–250
children, 1–4
    assistant principals and, 112–115
    becoming student for students, 22
    and coach-teacher partnership, 119–123, 125, 130, 134, 138, 146, 151
    creating schools we want for, 8–12
    dehumanizing, 23
    designing equitable instruction for, 23–24
    ideas and experiences of, 27
    and leading teacher learning and collaboration, 171, 177, 180–181, 186
    in Learning Labs. See Learning Labs
    measuring success in, 224–229
    and principal leadership for professional learning, 13–14
    as sensemakers, 22, 151
    in service of, 84, 236
    and sharing challenges, 209–219, 225, 228, 232

children (cont.)
    teacher autonomy, 28–29
    understanding teacher learning trajecto-
        ries, 29
    working together to make schools better,
        235–237
Classroom Visits
    and adult learning goals, 131–133
    principals learning and leading in, 105–107
    shifting nature of dialogue in, 228
    teachers learning and leading in, 107–109
classrooms
    assistant principal and, 112–115
    communities, 10, 19, 110, 113–114, 202, 218,
        219, 245
    discussions, 64, 108, 172, 192, 198, 202
    learning communities, 15, 52, 216, 250
    purpose of individual visits to, 65–67
    responsibilities in visiting, 69–70
    structure of visiting, 67–69
    teachers in, 49, 125, 195, 222, 262
coach-teacher partnership
    change from typical coaching model,
        120–124
    collaboration, 119–120
    creating partnership, 124–128
    creating responsive teacher learning goals
        and experiences, 128–133
    developing trust, 127–128
    nurturing relationships in, 125–126
    recognizing need for responsive learning
        experiences, 134–158
    roles and responsibilities, 125
coaches
    aligning roles and responsibilities with
        vision, 237–239
    change from typical model of, 120–124
    cherished perspective of, 129–130
    creating partnership with, 124–128
    developing trust with, 127–128
    foundational principles of learning
        together, 42
    hiring and retention practices, 239–241
    nurturing relationship with, 125–126
    partnership with teachers, 119–160
    as principal designers, 128–129
    responsibilities in Individual Classroom
        Visits, 69–70
    responsibilities in Grade-Level Team
        Meetings, 64–65
    responsibilities in Instructional Leadership
        Team Meetings, 72–73

responsibilities in Learning Labs, 60–61
role of, 129
starting point of, 16–17
typical weekly schedule of, 76
coaching
    change from typical model of, 120–124
    by invitation, 12–13
    as optional bonus, 12–13
    for professional learning, 12–13
    resources for, 160
collaboration, 31
    balancing with autonomy, 183–184
    coaching and, 119–124
    making more time for, 80
    supporting through spaces and practices,
        47–80
collaborative decisions, facilitating, 103
community, social emotional learning,
    112–115
competing demands, navigating, 184–185
concerns, 31
conference and planning (C/P), 243–245
conflict, embracing, 214–217
constraints, collaboration, 45
content, delivering, 31
coplanning, term, 4
COVID-19, 121

data, using, 229
    for student learning, 230–231
    for teacher learning, 231–232
decision-making
    engaging, 92–93
    engaging in, 101–102
    maintaining role as decision-maker,
        182–183
    making learning public to inform,
        104–105
deficit thinking, confronting barriers of,
    180–182
demands, competition between, 184–185
dialogue, shifting nature of, 228
dispositions
    balancing pressure and support, 87–89
    being a learner/leader, 85–86
    connecting decision back to "why," 86–87
    engaging as decision-maker, 92–93
    making practice public, 90–91
    taking risks through lens of inquiry, 91–92
    of teachers, 89–90
diverse learners, differentiating for, 31
dysregulation, 171, 212, 215

engagement, teacher-principal partnership
  Classroom Visits, 105–109
  evaluation spaces, 109–112
  Grade-Level Team Meetings, 102–105
  Learning Labs, 93–102
equitable experiences
  accepting responsibility, 213–215
  adults as products of system, 217–221
  creating, 210–211
  social emotion skill building, 215–217
equitable instruction
  designing, 23–24
equity, term, 4
evaluation spaces, 109–112
expectations
  letting go of, 111–112
  sharing in, 106
experiments, 40
expertise, perception of, 223

feedback, giving, 106–107
fifth grade, 5, 54, 57–58, 67, 69, 111, 131, 146,
    195–197, 251n4
first grade, 30, 50, 73, 97, 128, 171, 221
flexibility
  example of, 243–245
  providing, 245–247
formulaic answers, developing, 182–183
foundational principles, 19–20
  decision driven by beliefs, 20–21
  instructional decisions, 25–26
  new ways of working together, 37–39
  Principles for Learning to Teach, 26–34
  Principles for Teaching, 21–26
  Principles for the Adult Learning Context,
      34–37
fourth grade, 11, 30, 56, 65, 67, 69, 73, 128,
    132–133, 164, 180, 223
full engagement, 93–97
funding
  aligning with vision, 241–242
  example of, 243–245

gatekeeping, 185
getting started, trying, 31
grade-level meeting, term, 4
Grade-Level Team Meeting, 28, 42, 188,
    190–191, 198, 200–205, 227–228
  and adult learning goals, 131–133
  aligning roles and responsibilities with
      vision, 237–239
  assessments in, 181–182

attending to status among adults, 221–224
and change from typical coaching model,
    121–124
and Classroom Visit structure, 67–68
crafting professional learning system,
    73–78
data use in, 230–232
navigating competing demands in,
    184–185
principals learning and leading in, 102–103
privacy of practice in, 179–184
as professional learning system, 48
purpose of, 61–62
shifting nature of dialogue in, 228
structure of, 62–63
teacher, coach, and principal responsibili-
    ties in, 64–65
teachers learning and leading in, 104–105
underpinning, 65
growth trajectory, 29–34

Hands Down Conversations, 131
hiring and retention practices, 239–241
human talent, selecting, 239–241

ideas for getting started
  addressing tensions, 233–234
  coach-teacher partnership, 158–160
  foundational principles of learning
      together, 39–45
  Instructional Leadership Team (ILT),
      206–208
  partnerships, 115–117
  professional learning system, 78–80
ideas/experiences, centralizing, 27
ILT. See Instructional Leadership Team
in-relationship, 213–214, 216–217
Indigenous children, 2
Individual Classroom Visits
  crafting professional learning system,
      73–78
  as professional learning system, 48
  purpose of, 65–67
  structure of, 67–69
  teacher, coach, and principal responsibili-
      ties in, 69–70
Informal Hallway Conversations
  crafting professional learning system,
      73–78
  as professional learning system, 48
  purpose of, 70
  structure of, 71

inquiry, taking risks through lens of, 91–92
instruction, ensuring equitable access to, 183–184
instructional coaching, term, 4
instructional decisions, 25–26, 168
Instructional Leadership Team (ILT), 18, 49
   case study, 186–205
   coach and principal responsibilities, 72–73
   context for adult learning, 163–165
   definition, 163
   leadership practices, 165–179
   overview, 161–162
   preparation for, 164, 166
   as professional learning system, 49
   and proximity to work, 223–224
   purpose of, 71, 163
   structure of, 71–72
   sustaining vision in daily practice, 179–186
   See also ILT meetings, 114, 130, 240
internalized beliefs, principles for teaching, 31
inviting others in, 107–108
Irby, Decoteau, 23

kindergarten, 15, 50, 85, 97–98, 122–123, 132, 225, 242, 262

Ladson-Billings, Gloria, 22–23
lead learner, 174
leadership practices, ILT
   assessing and reflecting, 165–175
   intentionally coordinating, 177–179
   planning and adjusting, 175–177
   protecting, 174–175
learner stance, 36
learning spaces in action, case study
   January 15, Grade-Level Team Meeting, 152–158
   January 7 Learning Lab, 138–146
   January 8 conversation, 146–147
   January 9 Classroom Visits, 147–152
   overview, 134–136
   planning for January 7 Learning Lab, 136–138
learning community, cultivating, 227–228
Learning Labs
   and adult learning goals, 131–133
   crafting professional learning system, 73–78
   first phase, 55
   fourth phase, 59–60
   full engagement in, 93–97
   informing plans, 99–100

positioning students as sensemakers, 97–99
principals learning and leading in, 93–100
as professional learning system, 48
purpose of, 52–54
second phase, 55–56
shifting nature of dialogue in, 228
structure of, 54–60
teacher, coach, and principal responsibilities in, 60–61
teachers learning and leading in, 100–102
third phase, 56–59
learning to teach. See Principles for Learning to Teach
learning, being, 101
little celebrations, 31
looks like/sounds like, 40

Mathematician, 25, 31, 168–169, 182, 218
messaging, importance of, 178–179
messiness
   embracing, 31
   learning being, 36
motions, going through, 31

new ways of working together, 37–39
normalization, partnerships, 112
norms, developing, 117

operational flexibility
   affecting classroom practices, 248–249
   example of, 247–248
   providing, 245–247

paralysis, 87
partnerships
   coaches and teachers, 119–160
   principals and teachers, 81–117
PD. See professional development
perspectives, expanding, 229
planning
   adjusting and, 175–177
   informing, 99–100
PLCs. See professional learning communities
possible lives, 24
practice
   challenging privacy of, 179–180
   making public, 90–91
pressure
   balancing with support, 87–89
   in process of coordinating, 179

principal-teacher partnership
  assistant principals, 112–115
  engaging in, 93–112
  normalization of, 112
  overarching dispositions, 84–85
  principal dispositions, 85–89
  sharing work, 82–84
  working together, 81–82
principals
  aligning roles and responsibilities with
      vision, 237–239
  assistant principals and, 112–115
  being student of students, 102–103
  calibrating on progress and challenges,
      105–106
  disposition of, 85–89
  and evaluation spaces, 109–112
  facilitating collaborative decisions, 103
  foundational principles of learning
      together, 41–42
  full engagement with, 93–97
  giving feedback, 106–107
  hiring and retention practices, 239–241
  informing plans, 99–100
  leadership for professional learning, 13–14
  learning and leading in Classroom Visits,
      105–107
  learning and leading in Grade-Level Team
      Meetings, 102–103
  learning and leading in Learning Labs,
      93–102
  positioning students as sensemakers, 97–99
  relationship with teachers, 81–117
  responsibilities in Grade-Level Team
      Meetings, 64–65
  responsibilities in Individual Classroom
      Visits, 69–70
  responsibilities in Instructional Leadership
      Team Meetings, 72–73
  responsibilities in Learning Labs, 60–61
  sharing in expectation, 106
  on sharing work, 82
  starting point of, 17–18
  typical weekly schedule of, 77
Principles for Learning to Teach, 174
  centralizing student ideas/experiences, 27
  continual process, 27
  internalized beliefs, 31
  making teaching public, 27–28
  sustaining learning experiences, 28
  teaching as something that can be learned, 26
  understanding trajectories, 29–34

Principles for Teaching
  children as sensemakers, 22
  designing equitable instruction, 23–24
  equitable instruction, 24
  overview, 21
  school environment, 24
  teachers becoming students, 22
Principles for the Adult Learning Context,
      34–37, 128
  connected and coherent learning, 35
  embedding learning in work, 36–37
  evolving visions, 35–36
  learner stance, 36
  messy learning, 36
privacy, challenging, 179–180
problems of practice, 9–10
professional development (PD), 5–6
  teachers experiencing, 10
professional learning
  coaching for, 12–13
  principal leadership, 13–14
  term, 4
professional learning communities (PLCs),
      48, 240
professional learning norms, leveraging/
      strengthening, 43–44
professional learning system
  crafting coherent system, 73–78
  defining, 47–48
  examples of, 48–49
  ideas for getting started, 78–80
  proximity to work in, 223–224
  purpose, structure, and responsibilities,
      51–73
  shifting nature of dialogue in, 228
  teachers' views, 49–51
progress, calibrating on, 105–106
public education, making better
  example of working together, 243–245
  finding time, 242–245
  funding, 241–242
  getting better at getting it right, 235–236
  hiring and retention practices, 239–241
  operational flexibility, 245–247
  prioritizing work of people closest to
      students, 237
  role and responsibility definitions,
      237–239
  sponsoring change, 249–250
purposeful talk, 31

qualified, term, 239

Reader, 25, 168–169, 182, 218
relationship, nurturing, 125–126
research-practice partnership (RPP), 2–3
resiliency window, 213–214, 217
responsibilities
   accepting, 213–215
   defining, 237–239
restorative discipline, 212–213
roles
   defining, 237–239
   hierarchy of, 223
RPP. *See* research-practice partnership

school environment, responding to, 24
School of Distinction, 3
schools
   assistant principals in, 112–115
   changing roles in, 12–15
   creating, 8–11
   creating experience of, 29
   designating as "egg crates," 90
   hiring and retention practices in, 239–241
   measuring success in, 224–226
   starting point of, 15–18
Scientist, 25, 168–169, 182, 218
second grade, 6, 50, 68, 121–123, 126,
   192–193, 242
self-reflection, 41
self-regulation, 212–214, 216–217
sensemaking
   children as sensemakers, 22
   fostering, 177–179
   positioning students as sensemakers,
     97–99
   test scores and, 180–182
shared purpose, experience of engaging
   in, 227
social emotion skill building, 215–217
social emotional learning community, role of
   assistant principal in, 112–115
spaces and practices, professional learning
   system
   examples, 48–49
   overview, 47–48
   purpose, structure, and responsibilities,
     51–73
   teachers' views, 49–51
started but stuck, 31
status, attending to
   hierarchy of roles, 223
   overview, 221–222

perceived expertise, 223
proximity to work, 223–224
student learning
   foundational principles, 19–45
   professional learning spaces and practices,
     47–80
   teaching for, 14–15
student ownership, 31
student thinking, instruction based on, 31
students
   adults as products of system shaping,
     217–221
   assistant principals and, 112–115
   being student of, 102–103
   bringing into learning, 105
   centralizing ideas/experiences of, 27
   creating equitable experiences for, 210–221
   and data use, 230–231
   getting students to do things, 31
   measuring success in, 224–229
   positioning as sensemakers, 97–99
   and shifting nature of dialogue, 228
   teachers becoming, 22
   and test scores, 180–182
success, measuring
   cultivating learning community, 227–228
   expanding perspectives, 229
   overview, 224–226
   owing and orienting to vision, 227
   shifting nature of dialogue, 228
support
   balancing with pressure, 87–89
   in process of coordinating, 179

teacher learning
   decision driven by beliefs about, 20–21
   foundational principles, 19–45
   professional learning spaces and practices,
     47–80
Teacher Time Outs, 58–59, 95
teachers
   aligning roles and responsibilities with
     vision, 237–239
   assistant principals and, 112–115
   autonomy of, 28–29
   becoming students, 22
   being learners, 101
   bringing students into learning, 105
   and data use, 231–232
   doing better for, 1–18
   engaging in decision-making, 101–102

and evaluation spaces, 109–112
focus on learning by, 184–185
full engagement with, 93–97
hiring and retention practices, 239–241
instructional decisions and, 25–26
inviting others in, 107–108
learning and leading in Classroom Visits, 107–109
learning and leading in Grade-Level Team Meetings, 104–105
learning and leading in Learning Labs, 100–102
leverage of, 23–24
maintaining role as decision-maker, 182–183
making learning public to inform decision-making, 104–105
making more time for collaboration, 80
monthly collaboration and professional learning time, 75
partnership with coaches, 119–160
problems of practice faced by, 9–10
relationship with principals, 81–117
responding to school environment, 24
responsibilities in Grade-Level Team Meetings, 64–65
responsibilities in Individual Classroom Visits, 69–70
responsibilities in Learning Labs, 60–61
on sharing work, 83
and shifting nature of dialogue, 228
starting point of, 16
for student learning, 14–15
supporting adult learning, 108–109

talking about being, 6–8
and trajectories, 29–34
views on professional learning systems, 49–51
tensions, emergence of
attending to status among adults, 221–224
creating equitable experiences for children, 210–221
data use, 229–233
measuring success, 224–229
test scores
deficit thinking driven by, 180–182
and measuring success, 224–226
Thinker, 25, 168, 194, 218, 226
third grade, 7, 51, 62–63, 110, 129, 146
time, finding, 117
trajectories, understanding, 29–34
trauma-informed, 212–215
trust, developing, 127–128

video of instruction, 40–41
vision, 11
aligning funding to, 241–242
aligning roles and responsibilities with, 237–239
and hiring and retention practices, 239–241
owning and orienting, 227
term, 19–20

weekly schedule, 76–77, 79
window of tolerance, 213
work, proximity to, 223
working together, example of, 243–245
Writer, 25, 168